About The Author

John Baechtel is a former editor of both Hot Rod and Car Craft Magazines. He has also produced the Pontiac Motorsports newsletter and high performance tech manuals, authored numerous high performance books and more than 1100 magazine articles. John is a land speed record enthusiast and he currently holds the C/Gas Coupe speed record at Bonneville, running more than 221 mph in his '91 Pontiac Firebird. He presently does the production work on Cartech's SA Design automotive books out of his Mira Loma, California facility. This facility is also very active in producing magazine articles and technical literature for various aftermarket manufacturers. It is equipped with a SuperFlow engine dyno and numerous aftermarket manufacturers use it for testing and developing new components. Several race teams also use John's facility because they are able to keep their testing and engine building secrets private from their competitors. John and his wife Laura have one son, Andrew, and John has two grandchildren through his eldest daughter Tammy. His hobbies include reading, golf, photography and surfing the net.

Credits

No one person ever writes these books. They are almost always a collaborative effort on the part of many people whose contributions vary greatly. When it comes time to thank them for their input, there is never enough room to adequately thank everyone for all their contributions, both large and small. The following people have either directly or indirectly influenced or contributed to this book. Some of them may not even know it because their input came years earlier during a conversation or a troubleshooting session on the dyno, but all those small tidbits of information eventually gel into something that the reader can hopefully put to good use. The hardest part is figuring out where to start and how to make certain you don't leave anyone out.

My old friend Chuck Jenckes helped me with a lot of my early fuel injection knowledge, and his influence abounds within this book. Mike Doyle was always available to answer EFI questions, as was Bill Howell, John Callies, John Erickson, Louie Hammel, Mark Sanchez, Ron Zimmer, Jim McFarland, Harold Bettes, Marlan Davis, Jeff Smith, John Meany, John Lingenfelter, Jim Feuling, Rick Voegelin at High Performance Communications and countless unnamed writers who put together the GM service manuals which GM graciously permitted us to pick through and reproduce for this book. As always, the people at GM provided first rate assistance. Special thanks go to Tom Hoxie, Kay Ward, Jeff Tate, Jack Underwood and Gene Reamer for assistance with photos and licensing. Thanks also to Scott Killeen at the Petersen Publishing Photo Lab, and to Barbara Killeen for copy editing.

To those whom I somehow forgot to mention, my thanks and sincerest apologies. In this business, many of our contacts are infrequent and irregular, but the knowledge we gain from each other lingers long afterward. And it is this vital exchange of information that sustains our daily efforts. It is my sincerest hope that the readers of this book can extract the useful information that will help them build and enjoy their projects.

By JOHN BAECHTEL

All text, photographs, drawings, and other artwork (hereafter referred to as information) contained in this publication is sold without any warranty as to its usability or performance. In all cases, original manufacturer's recommendations, procedures, and instructions supersede and take precedence over descriptions herein. Specific component design and mechanical procedures—and the qualifications of individual readers—are beyond the control of the publisher, therefore the publisher disclaims all liability, either expressed or implied, for use of the information in this publication. All risk for its use is entirely assumed by the purchaser/user. In no event will Cartech, Inc. or the author be liable for any indirect, special, or consequential damages, including but not limited to personal injury or any other damages, arising out of the use or misuse of any information in this publication.

This book is an independent publication, and the authors and/or publisher thereof are not in any way associated with, and are not authorized to act on behalf of any of the manufacturers included in this book. Chevrolet®, Chevy®, Chrysler®, Ford®, Mopar®, Pontiac®, Oldsmobile®, GMC Trucks® and General Motors® are registered trademarks. The publisher reserves the right to revise this publication or change its content from time to time without obligation to notify any persons of such revisions or changes.

Chevy TPI
Fuel Injection Swapper's Guide
By JOHN BAECHTEL

Copyright © 1997 by John Baechtel. All rights reserved. All text and photographs in this publication are the property of John Baechtel, unless otherwise noted or credited. Cover photography used by permission of GM Media Archives. Selected sidebar photography picked up from other Cartech®, Inc. It is unlawful to reproduce—or copy in any way—resell, or redistribute this information without the expressed written permission of the author.

EDITED BY
BARBARA KILLEEN

PRODUCTION BY
JOHN BAECHTEL

OVERSEAS DISTRIBUTION BY:

BROOKLANDS BOOKS LTD.
P.O. BOX 146, Cobham, Surrey, KT11 1LG, England
Telephone 01932 865051 · FAX 01932 868803

BROOKLANDS BOOKS LTD.
3/37-39 Green Street, Banksmeadow, NSW 2019, Australia
Telephone 2 9695 7055 · Fax 2 9695 7355

CARTECH®, INC., 39966 Grand Avenue, North Branch, MN 55056
(651) 277-1200 or (800) 551-4754
www.cartechbooks.com

CONTENTS

- INTRODUCTION 4
  - ELECTRONIC CARBURETORS 4
  - ELECTRONIC FUEL INJECTION 5
  - ELECTROMECHANICAL FUEL INJECTION 5
  - MODERN ELECTRONIC FUEL INJECTION 5
  - PORT FUEL INJECTION 7
  - TPI APPLICATIONS AND FEATURES 7
  - TPI RETRO-FIT PROS AND CONS 8
  - TPI REFERENCE DEFINITIONS 9
  - TUNED PORT FUEL INJECTION 10

- HOW TPI WORKS 12
  - ECMs & ENGINE MANAGEMENT 12
  - ECM USAGE GUIDE 13
  - UNDERSTANDING EFI ELECTRONICS 18
  - STATIC ELECTRICITY 18
  - TPI MANIFOLD AND PLENUM ID 20

- MASS FLOW VERSUS SPEED DENSITY 22
  - MASS FLOW FUEL INJECTION 23
  - TPI/MAF DETAILS 24
  - SPEED DENSITY FUEL INJECTION 24
  - N ALPHA FUEL INJECTION 25

- CLOSED LOOP OPERATION 26
  - STOICHIOMETRIC AIR/FUEL RATIO 27
  - OXYGEN SENSORS 27
  - FUEL INTEGRATOR AND BLOCK LEARN MEMORY .. 28
  - CLOSED LOOP OPERATING CONDITIONS 29

- TUNED PORT SENSOR GUIDE 30
  - COOLANT TEMP SENSOR 30
  - MAP SENSORS 31
  - MAT SENSOR 32
  - MASS AIR FLOW SENSORS 32
  - OXYGEN SENSOR 32
  - THROTTLE POSITION SENSOR 34
  - VEHICLE SPEED SENSOR 35
  - KNOCK SENSOR 35
  - REVOLUTIONS PER MINUTE 35
  - PARK/NEUTRAL POSITION SWITCH 36
  - SYSTEM VOLTAGE 36
  - OXYGEN SENSOR CONTAMINATION 37

- INJECTOR SELECTION AND TUNING 38
  - DETERMINING INJECTOR SIZE 39
  - FUEL PRESSURE VS FUEL FLOW 39
  - INJECTOR COMPATIBILITY 39
  - CALCULATING INJECTOR SIZE 40
  - BALANCING INJECTOR FLOW 41
  - MSD INJECTORS 41
  - DUTY CYCLE 41
  - WHEN YOU NEED LARGER INJECTORS 42
  - INJECTOR SELECTION SOFTWARE 43
  - FUEL INJECTION FORMULAS 43
  - OEM INJECTOR IDENTIFICATION 43
  - TPI FUEL RAIL SELECTION GUIDE 44

- TROUBLESHOOTING GUIDE 48
  - TROUBLE CODES 49
  - NONSCAN DIAGNOSTIC CIRCUIT CHECK 50
  - NO SERVICE ENGINE LIGHT 51
  - NO ALDL DATA OR CODE 12 52
  - ENGINE CRANKS BUT WON'T RUN 55
  - FUEL PUMP RELAY CIRCUIT 59
  - FUEL SYSTEM DIAGNOSIS 61
  - COLD START VALVE CIRCUIT TEST 65
  - CODE 13, OXYGEN SENSOR 67
  - DTC 14, COOLANT TEMP SENSOR 69
  - CODE 15, COOLANT TEMP SENSOR LOW 71
  - THROTTEL POSITION SENSOR, HIGH 73
  - THROTTLE POSITION SENSOR, LOW 75
  - MANIFOLD AIR TEMPERATURE, LOW 77
  - VEHICLE SPEED SENSOR 79
  - MANIFOLD AIR TEMPERATURE, HIGH 81
  - CODE 32, EGR CIRCUIT 83
  - CODE 33, MASS AIR FLOW SENSOR, HIGH ... 85
  - CODE 33, MASS AIR FLOW SENSOR, HI.LOW VAC. .. 87
  - CODE 34, MASS AIR FLOW SENSOR, LOW 89
  - CODE 34, MAP SENSOR, LOW-HIGH VACUUM .. 91
  - CODE 36, MASS AIR FLOW BURNOFF CIRCUIT .. 93
  - COD E 41, CYLINDER SELECT ERROR 95
  - CODE 42, ELECTRONIC SPARK TIMING 96
  - CODE 43, ELECTRONIC SPARK CONTROL 98
  - CODE 44, OXYGEN SENSOR, LEAN 102
  - CODE 45, OXYGEN SENSOR, RICH 104
  - CODE 46, VEHICLE ANTI-THEFT SYSTEM 106
  - CODE 51, MEM-CAL ERROR 107
  - CODE 52, CALPAK ERROR 107
  - CODE 53, SYSTEM OVER VOLTAGE 107
  - CODE 54, FUEL PUMP CIRCUIT 108
  - ECM PINOUTS 110
  - CHART C-2C, IDLE AIR CONTROL 113

- MODIFYING TPI SYSTEMS 114
  - CALIBRATION 114
  - FACTORY CALIBRATION 115
  - MODIFYING TPI SYSTEMS 116
  - CALIBRATION REQUIREMENTS 116
  - FUEL CALIBRATION 116
  - OTHER MIXTURE CONSIDERATIONS 117
  - AFTERMARKET ECMS 117
  - CAMSHAFT RECOMMENDATIONS 119
  - USING NITROUS OXIDE WITH TPI 120
  - TPI EXHAUST SYSTEMS 121

- TPI BUYERS GUIDE 122

- TPI SOURCES 128

ON THE COVER

Our cover photo is courtesy of the GM Media Archives, GM Corporation. It is used with permission of GM/GMMA, copyright 1985. It is a color cutaway view of the tuned port induction system on a 1985 Corvette engine.

CHEVY TPI Fuel Injection Swapper's Guide
Introduction

Electronic engine management systems are the heart of today's fuel-efficient, low-emissions automobile engines. Emissions standards first enacted in 1980 made it virtually impossible for automakers to continue fueling their vehicles with basic carburetors. Although carburetors were certainly capable of meeting all contemporary power requirements, they lacked the precise metering necessary to meet new emissions and fuel economy requirements. Electronic engine management offered the most practical and cost-efficient means of maintaining existing performance levels while meeting increasingly strict emission standards.

ELECTRONIC CARBURETORS

Electronically controlled carburetors were the first major step in our wholesale conversion to fuel-injected automobiles. The carburetor is a basic fuel metering device designed to mix fuel and incoming air in the proper proportions to support efficient combustion. It creates a pressure differential between normal atmospheric pressure (14.7 psi) and the carburetor throat by accelerating incoming air through a venturi. Fuel flows from the float bowl through a metering jet and into the venturi. The float bowl is vented to atmospheric pressure while

Electronic carburetors such as this Rochester Quadrajet from a mid-eighties Monte Carlo SS predated tuned port fuel injection systems. These carburetors performed well, but they couldn't provide the precise mixture control required to control emissions across a broad range of driving conditions.

air in the venturi is at something less than atmospheric pressure. This pressure difference allows atmospheric pressure to push fuel into the venturi at a rate determined by air flow and the size of the metering jet. As air flow increases so does the pressure differential between the venturi and atmospheric, causing a proportional increase in fuel flow.

The advent of stricter new emissions standards forced manufacturers to seek a more accurate way of controlling air/fuel ratios. The most expedient solution was to attach the carburetor's metering rod to a computer-controlled electronic solenoid, creating the first electronic carburetor. The Mixture Control Solenoid (MCS) oscillates at 10 cycles per second to control fuel flow to the main jet. An exhaust gas oxygen sensor (O_2 sensor) provides air/fuel ratio feedback to the computer, which makes the appropriate adjustments to the MCS.

Electronic carburetors were a logical first step toward computerized fuel systems, but on-board computers could only make limited adjustments to the mixture because primary fuel flow was still controlled by jetting. It was faster for OEMs to add mixture control solenoids to existing carburetors than to engineer complete electronic fuel-injection systems from scratch. This approach was rudimentary and expedient, but next generation Throttle Body Injection (TBI) systems have fewer parts and cost less while outperforming earlier electronic carburetors.

ELECTRONIC FUEL INJECTION

Fuel injection addresses the same concerns by providing the engine with the proper amount of fuel under an almost infinite number of driving conditions.

Tuned Port Injected Camaros were the top-of-the-line performance sedans of the late eighties. They performed well in every respect and were second only to the Corvette in all out performance.

Mechanical fuel injection is not a recent invention—it has been used on diesel engines since the early 1900s. Chevrolet utilized Rochester mechanical fuel-injection to coax 283 BHP from the 283-cubic-inch '57 small block Corvette engine. Variations of this fuel injection system served on small block Corvette engines until 1965, and derivatives of the same type of system are still sold today by Bosch.

ELECTRO-MECHANICAL FUEL INJECTION

Bosch became the world's leading supplier of fuel-injection systems by selling hundreds of thousands of CIS mechanical fuel-injection systems throughout Europe and America in the seventies. The CIS system is similar to the Rochester FI system used on the '57 Corvette. A high-pressure electric pump provides fuel first to a bypass-type pressure regulator and then to a metering and distribution block. A mechanical air sensor adjusts a valve in the metering block based on air flow. This valve controls fuel flow to eight mechanical injectors located one to each port. The injectors require high fuel pressure and they operate continuously. If you can appreciate Corvette's early Rochester fuel injection, you easily can appreciate today's modern electronic systems.

Bosch introduced an electronic modification to this basic mechanical system in 1977 to help address forthcoming 1980 emissions laws. This modification took advantage of the then new O_2 sensor. A computer-controlled solenoid located between the fuel supply and a bypass, metered fuel based on readings from the O_2 sensor. This controlled air/fuel ratio to near optimum settings for emissions. This system was used on most European cars that came to America. It is far superior to carburetors under almost all conditions, yet its mechanical aspects limited its performance when compared to the purely electronic port injection systems offered today.

MODERN ELECTRONIC FUEL INJECTION

Electronic fuel injection combines the tremendous power of the computer with the mechanical advantages of fuel injection. A computer processes only one instruction at a time; however, it can process up to eight million instructions per second. With that kind of processing power, a computer can make the air/fuel ratio near perfect under almost any conditions. That's why we now have cars that outperform most traditional musclecars, while meeting current emissions levels and delivering exceptional fuel economy.

Modern performance cars are built with two types of electronic fuel injection: throttle-body injection and port injection. Throttle-body injection represents the stepping-stone technology between electronic carburetors and sophisticated port fuel injection. The primary difference is that fuel is introduced via pressurized injection rather than by atmospheric pressure. The throttle body is a single or dual-throat air valve mounted in the same location as a conventional carburetor, while the injectors (usually two) are mounted above the carburetor-like throttle plates. Throttle-body injection is still a wet-flow system because fuel is injected into the air valve throats above the manifold plenum chamber instead of directly into the port. This means that a throttle-body injection system can still experience any mixture distribution problems inherent in the existing intake manifold. The pintle- and seat-style injectors are fed by an electric fuel pump with a bypass regulator maintaining a constant fuel pressure between 9 and 13 psi.

Fuel flow is controlled by varying the pulse width or duty cycle of the injectors. Pulse width is the time in milliseconds that the injector is open, while duty cycle is the injector's overall percentage of open time. A 70% duty cycle means that the injector is open 70% of the time. TBI injection uses the Speed Density method of calibration. The computer calculates engine air flow by measuring rpm (speed) and manifold vacuum (load), and referring to a preprogrammed table to determine air flow. A significant degree of computation is required because the computer must also compensate for the density (pressure and temperature) of the incoming air to correctly calculate the amount of fuel required; hence the name Speed Density. The computer also utilizes the O_2 sensor's interpretation of the engine's rich/lean condition to back up its air flow calculations before determining the necessary injector pulse width.

At idle, the TBI's throttle plates must be open slightly since the fuel is sprayed on top of them. This can cause less-than-ideal fuel distribution, so an Idle Air Control (IAC) motor is used to control an air bleed to the manifold, thus regulating idle speed.

TBI systems are a compromise between carburetors and state-of-the-art port fuel injection systems. TBI is simple and reliable with very few parts, but fuel distribution is often poor. Performance modifications such as intake manifolds, headers, and camshafts can often confuse the computer's calculations. This makes the selection of performance equipment for TBI systems more critical because of the effect they can have on the computer. The major sensors for a throttle-body fuel-injection system include:

1. Manifold Absolute Pressure— MAP (vacuum)
2. Manifold Absolute Temperature— MAT (air temperature)
3. Throttle Position Sensor— TPS (% open)
4. Coolant Temperature— CT (water temperature)
5. Exhaust Gas Oxygen— EGO (O_2 sensor)
6. Battery Voltage (volts)

Chevy tuned port fuel injection systems offered nineties-style looks and performance in the mid-eighties. There are thousands of them around now, and with a little effort, you can count on them to deliver exceptional fuel economy, tire shredding torque, and good, strong mid-range performance.

PORT FUEL INJECTION

Port fuel injection, as the name implies, injects fuel directly into each port just upstream of the intake valve. This type of injection uses at least one injector per cylinder. One of the main advantages is that fuel can be introduced very near the valve, leaving most of the intake manifold dry. This in itself allows near-perfect cylinder-to-cylinder fuel distribution. A dry-flow intake manifold is much easier to design since fuel distribution is not a problem. Port injection also promotes superior fuel atomization and subsequently more efficient combustion because fuel is injected at high pressure through a small hole directly into the high-speed air flow.

Port fuel injection uses two different types of air flow calibration: speed density and mass flow. It is further characterized by two types of injection: batch or group fire and sequential fire. Speed density calculates air flow based on input from the same sensors already listed for TBI injection. Mass flow fuel injection actually measures air flow instead of calculating it. This allows the fuel injection to compensate for moderate engine content changes (i.e., cam change, different cylinder heads, etc.) whereas a speed density system cannot because its fuel map hasn't been programmed to understand or acknowledge fuel requirements that exceed its range.

Mass flow sensors include:

1. Mass Air Sensor—MAF (air flow)
2. Manifold Absolute Temperature—MAT (air temperature)
3. Throttle Position Sensor—TPS (% open)
4. Coolant Temperature—CT (water temperature)

Tuned Port Induction Applications & Features

1985 TPI
- Mass Air Flow System
- ECM #1226870 (Prom and Calpack design)
- Cold Start Injector
- Bosch MAF power and burn-off relay
- Cast iron cylinder heads (all 5.0L engines)
- Conventional electronic HEI distributor with coil in cap

1986 TPI
- Mass Air Flow System
- ECM #1227165 (Mem-cal design)
- Cold Start Injector
- GM conventional MAF power and burn-off relays
- Aluminum heads on Corvette 350s in mid-'86

1987 TPI
- Mass Air Flow System
- ECM #1227165 (Mem-cal design)
- Cold Start Injector
- GM conventional MAF power and burn-off relays
- Roller lifters incorporated
- Two center intake manifold bolts on cast iron head engines drilled at a steeper angle
- Camaros/Trans Ams switch to remote coils and smaller diameter distributors
- Pontiac Formulas retain conventional HEI with coil in cap

1988 TPI
- Mass Air Flow System
- ECM #1227165 (Mem-cal design)
- Cold Start Injector
- GM conventional MAF power and burn-off relays
- Roller lifters
- Two center intake manifold bolts on cast iron head engines drilled at a steeper angle
- Camaros and Trans Ams retain remote coils and smaller diameter distributors
- Pontiac Formulas retain conventional HEI with coil in cap
- Corvettes and Trans Ams equipped with GM Vehicle Anti-Theft System (VATS) mem-cals

1989 TPI
- Mass Air Flow System
- ECM #1227165 (Mem-cal design)
- Cold Start Injector eliminated
- Cold start fuel included in Mem-cal calibration
- GM conventional MAF power and burn-off relays
- Roller lifters
- Two center intake manifold bolts on cast iron head engines drilled at a steeper angle
- Camaros and Trans Ams retain remote coils and smaller diameter distributors
- All TPI mem-cals programmed for GM Vehicle Anti-Theft System (VATS)

1990-92 TPI
- Speed Density fuel metering calibration
- ECM #1227730 (Mem-cal three-connector design)
- Corvettes equipped with underhood ECMs
- Cold-start fuel included in Mem-cal calibration
- Roller lifters
- Two center intake manifold bolts on cast iron head engines drilled at a steeper angle
- Camaros and Trans Ams retain remote coils and smaller diameter distributors
- All TPI & TBI mem-cals programmed for GM Vehicle Anti-Theft System (VATs)
- All V8s can be run with the Camaro ECM

5. Exhaust Gas Oxygen—EGO (O_2 sensor)
6. Battery Voltage (volts)

Port fuel injection can be either sequential or group (batch) fire. Sequential injection means that the injection of fuel is timed to coincide with the valve opening, while group fire triggers a bank of injectors with each ignition cycle. Sequential injection is the current state-of-the-art in electronic fuel management. Sequential injection is found on top performance cars such as the Mustang 5.0L V8 and the Buick Grand National. Grand Nationals use only mass flow calculation while the Mustang uses either mass flow or speed density depending on the year.

Tuned port injection systems on 5.0L and 5.7L Camaros and Firebirds use port fuel injection, but it is the group fire variety, not sequential. Tuned Port systems also use mass flow or speed density calculations depending on the model year (see chapter 2). GM cars started out with mass flow systems in 1985 and converted to speed density in 1989, while Ford used speed density in '86, '87, and '88 49-state cars.

Ford switched to mass flow on 1988 California cars and all '89-'92 cars. Ford also offered mass flow conversion kits for speed density-equipped cars (M-9000-A51 for manual cars and M-9000-B50 for automatics). Mass flow air measurement is more accurate and more expensive. It reduces the calculations required and reacts faster to changes in air flow while speed density is cheaper but less precise. TBI injection systems are used on base V8 engines in the Camaro and Firebird and on GM trucks. TBI systems are all speed density systems.

TPI Retrofit Pros and Cons

Advantages
- Clean, high tech appearance
- Superior low speed and mid-range power
- Increased fuel economy
- Improved cold starting and idle quality
- Reduced emissions at idle and part throttle
- Reduced risk of engine fire
- Replacement sensors readily available
- Unlimited hop-up potential
- More precise altitude compensation
- More precise adjustment for atmospheric conditions

Disadvantages
- Expensive compared to conventional carburetion
- Sophisticated electronics are potentially intimidating
- Requires more careful thought and attention to detail to ensure a successful installation
- Some replacement sensors are still expensive

Ranking these systems in order of precision, value, and cost pretty much follows the same course. The most accurate and costly system is sequential mass flow, followed by sequential speed density, then group fire mass flow, group fire speed density, and group fire speed density on a throttle body.

To avoid confusion, keep in mind that all of these systems (including port fuel injection) actually use a throttle body to regulate air flow. Port fuel systems use the throttle body strictly as an air valve while throttle-body injection systems

Tuned port injection systems are ideal for building high torque engines that will still run strong on the top end. The long runners promote torque, and larger modified runners with more volume deliver good high-speed performance.

Quick-change filters and shielded air ducts kept road debris and moisture far away from the delicate mass air sensor.

Tuned port system incorporated a sleek looking center feed, dual inlet air duct with twin air filters to ensure free breathing.

must also flow fuel through the throttle body butterflies. Port fuel systems are dry; throttle-body systems are wet.

With this basic look at electronic fuel injection evolution, we now can progress to a discussion about the technical differences between injectors, calibration requirements, sensor operations, and more to help you gain a

Clean intake air is ducted from the grill area, while cooling air for the radiator is deflected to the radiator by a small chin spoiler under the nose of the car.

TUNED PORT Fuel Injection Tips & Tricks

tuned port injection Reference Definitions

AC	Air Conditioning
AIR	Air Injection Reaction System
ALCL	Assembly Line Connector Link
ALDL	Assembly Line Diagnostic Link
AT	Automatic Transmission
CCC	Computer Command Center
CCP	Controlled Cannister Purge
CONN	Connector
CTS	Coolant Temperature Sensor
ECM	Electronic Control Module
EGR	Exhaust Gas Recirculation
EOS	Exhaust Oxygen Sensor
ESC	Electronic Spark Control
EST	Electronic Spark Timing
GND	Ground
HEI	High Energy Ignition
IAC	Idle Air Control
MAF	Mass Air Flow
MAP	Manifold Absolute Pressure
MAT	Manifold Air Temperature
MEM-CAL	Memory Calibrator
OD	Overdrive

5.0L sequentially injected Mustangs are the Camaro and Firebird's chief competitor. Mustang's injected 302-cubic-inch powerplants have utilized both mass air flow and speed density engine management strategies to gain the best combination of power, fuel efficiency, and emissions quality.

complete understanding of basic electronic fuel injection before we examine it as it applies specifically to GM tuned port injection systems.

TUNED PORT FUEL INJECTION

Chevrolet's unique tuned port injection system (TPI) was first offered on the 1985 215 HP 305-cubic-inch IROC Camaro. It was designed to deliver a dramatic boost in low speed torque and throttle response while providing superior fuel economy under both street and highway driving conditions. Tuned-length intake runners with individual fuel injectors were optimized for maximum torque in the 2000-4000 rpm range. Stock TPI equipped cars exhibit an abundance of torque and sharp throttle response, even from a dead idle. The 1985 system replaced the electronically controlled Quadrajet carburetor used on some high-performance third-generation Camaros from 1982 through 1986. Tuned port injection was used on both 305 and 350 cubic inch engines through the 1992 model year while a less sophisticated throttle body induction system (TBI) was incorporated on standard models in 1987. TBI differed from TPI in that it used a more conventional intake manifold arrangement with a centrally located throttle body containing two injectors to feed all eight cylinders.

The layout of a TPI system is elegantly simple. Long tuned length runners route intake air to each port via a criss-cross style cast aluminum intake manifold. The individual intake runners are fed by a common centrally located plenum that is throttled by a twin blade throttle body assembly located on the front of the plenum casting. The 1985 Camaro system is less sophisticated than later models because its electronic control module (ECM) has limited self-diagnostic capabilities. All 1985 to 1989 TPI systems use the mass air flow meter method to directly measure intake air flow. On 1990 through 1992 models, a speed density system was adopted to calculate intake air flow based on sensor information regarding engine speed and

Cutaway view shows the long, but relatively unobstructed path incoming air must follow to reach the valve in a tuned port injection setup. The long individual runners and common plenum are what give the L98 engine its powerful low-end torque and mid-range grunt.

Tuned port injection was abandoned in 1992. Later model Camaros and Firebirds such as this 1995 Trans Am are equipped with newer LT1 powerplants and most recently with LT-4 based engines. These engines deliver more power than the original tunedpPort injection engines, but most of them don't really feel as strong on the low end. A good TPI-equipped car can still beat these things across an intersection, and it will run right with them up high with only a few modifications.

load. The accompanying chart (page 7) illustrates the primary differences in TPI systems from 1985 to 1992. Although seemingly complex and intimidating, TPI Systems are surprisingly simple. Their high tech appearance and sophisticated performance have made them increasingly popular for retro-fit installations on all types of street rods, street machines, off-road vehicles, tow vehicles, daily drivers, and just about anything with small block Chevy V8 power.

Today's LT1 based systems deliver more power out of the box, but the TPI led the technological charge into the fuel-injection age, and nothing can beat the low-speed and mid-range torque it produces. When appropriately modified, TPI systems will run with any LT1-based system. It's all a matter of where you want the power and torque to fall in the engine's most frequently used rpm range.

Top view of L98 Corvette engine with tuned port injection system shows the unique layout of the individual runners from the common plenum.

Post TPI LT1 engines are rated at 285 HP in F-bodies and 300 HP in Corvettes. They use a central plenum with short, direct runners. Don't give up your TPI engine for one of these powerplants. The aftermarket is loaded with hop-up equipment that will make your TPI-equipped engine equal or better than any LT1 or LT4.

Chevy TPI Swapper's Guide

CHEVY TPI Fuel Injection Swapper's Guide

How TPI Works

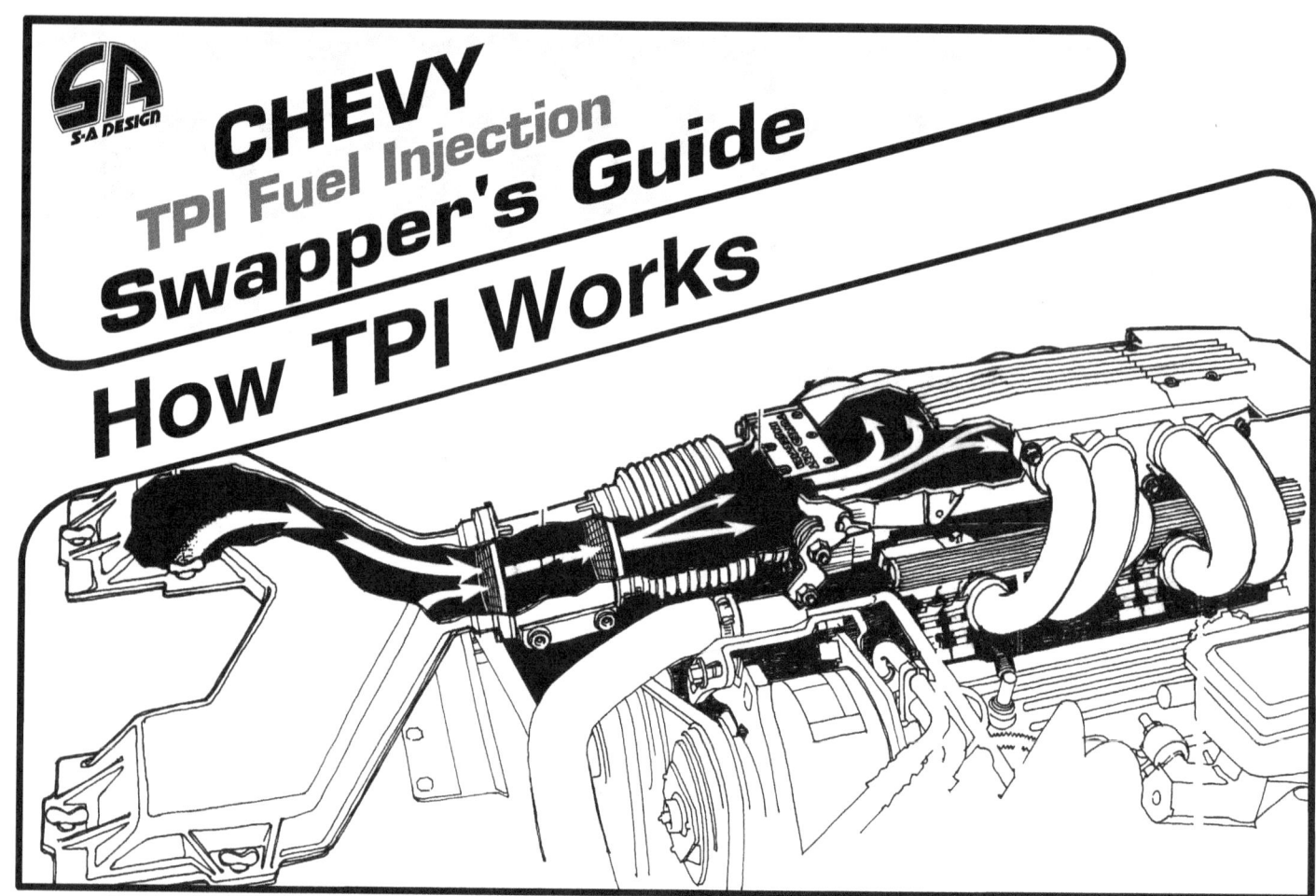

Tuned port injection is surprisingly simple once you understand the basics. In subsequent chapters we will look at the various components in detail, including ECMs, sensors, and all the attending hardware. Here we will briefly examine the basic concept of tuned port injection and how it works.

When you make the jump from carburetors to fuel injection, you're still utilizing many of the same functions. Carburetors are required to provide appropriate fuel metering for a broad range of engine operating requirements, including engine startup enrichment, cold-running enrichment, idle speed and air/fuel ratio control, cruise air/fuel ratio control, moderate load enrichment, and acceleration enrichment. To perform these functions, the carburetor provides choke operation, an idle circuit, main circuit, power valve, and accelerator pump circuit.

Fuel injection tackles the same tasks with different tools. Cold startup is handled by either a cold start injector or main injector enrichment based on coolant temperature sensor input. Cold running enrichment is maintained by coolant sensor input while idle speed and air/fuel ratio is controlled by an idle air control valve and the mass air flow (MAF) sensor or a manifold absolute pressure (MAP) sensor. Cruise air/fuel ratio is controlled by the MAP or MAF and the oxygen sensor with the oxygen sensor having priority over fuel management decisions. Load enrichment is handled by the throttle position switch (TPS) and either the MAP or MAF. Acceleration enrichment is controlled by the TPS and the fuel pressure regulator.

Once incoming air flows past the air filters it can be handled in two ways depending on the year of the engine and the type of engine management being used. Mass air flow-equipped engines actually measure the air flow into the engine and calculate the appropriate fuel and spark settings to accommodate current conditions. Speed density-equipped systems only know engine speed and load—they calculate air flow based on known values or a map of the engine's performance characteristics.

ECMs AND ENGINE MANAGEMENT STRATEGIES

An on-board computer or ECM (Electronic Control Module), monitors an array of sensors which tell it the vehicle's current state of operation. These sen-

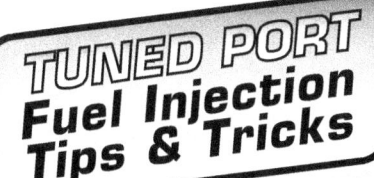

ECM USAGE GUIDE

YEAR	VEHICLE	ENGINE	ECM #
1985	F, Y	5.0L, 5.7L	1226870
1986-89	F, Y	5.0L, 5.7L	1227727
1990-	F	5.0L, 5.7L	1227730
1990-	Y	5.7L	1227727

Y = Corvette   F = Camaro/Firebird

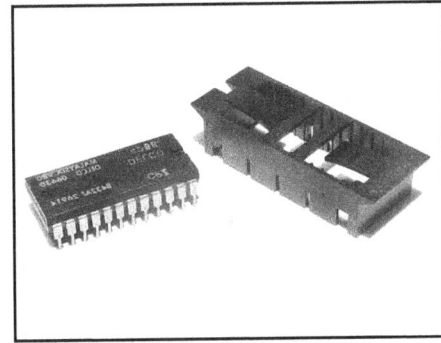

Early ECMs used a removable 24 pin PROM or chip containing specific calibration information on the vehicle and engine combination. A separate chip or CALPAC contained a reduced set of instructions that served as a backup or "limp home" mode in the event of an ECM failure.

sors tell the computer how fast the vehicle is moving, how much load is placed on the engine, and a host of engine operating parameters. These parameters include engine speed, coolant temperature, inlet air flow, inlet air temperature, air fuel ratio, manifold pressure, engine knock information, throttle position, transmission gear, and AC and power steering load.

Based on these inputs, the computer makes appropriate decisions regarding timing, fuel delivery, idle speed, air pump operation, radiator cooling fan operation, and torque converter clutch operation. Most of the monitoring and sensing functions utilize a five volt reference signal while the controlling devices operate at 12 volts.

ECMs used in tuned port injection cars changed over the life of the TPI system and they are not interchangable. The original mass air flow style ECM #1226870 used the mass air flow sensor and control module to directly measure dynamic engine air flow. In 1986 the control module was incorporated as an integral unit and the ECM was changed to # 1227727.

Through 1988 all TPI systems used a cold-start injector or "9th injector" for cold-start enrichment. This was dropped in 1989 and cold-start enrichment was controlled through the primary injectors. The MAF sensor was dropped in 1990 and engine management was switched over to Speed Density control. This eliminated actual measurement of incoming air flow in favor of air flow

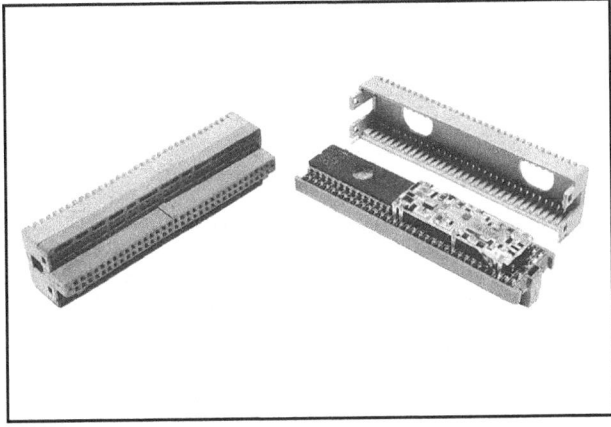

1988 and later PROMs and CALPACs were combined on a single 66-pin PROM holder that made PROMs less susceptible to installation damage and static electricity.

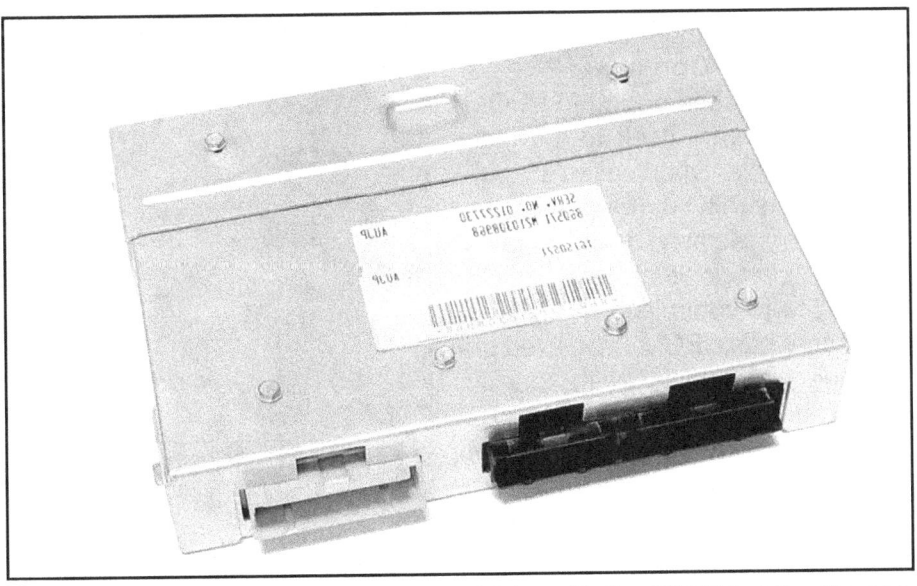

The basic ECM is used on a variety of vehicles with the PROM holding the specific calibration data for any given vehicle. ECMs use microprocessors to monitor and activate various EFI functions. The RAM (Random Access Memory) is volatile. It holds temporary information that is lost if power is removed. ROM, or Read Only Memory, handles the basic computer functions of the ECM while the PROM (Programmable Read Only Memory) provides the specific calibration. Once the ECM makes a decision, it uses driver circuit transistors to turn individual component actuators on or off.

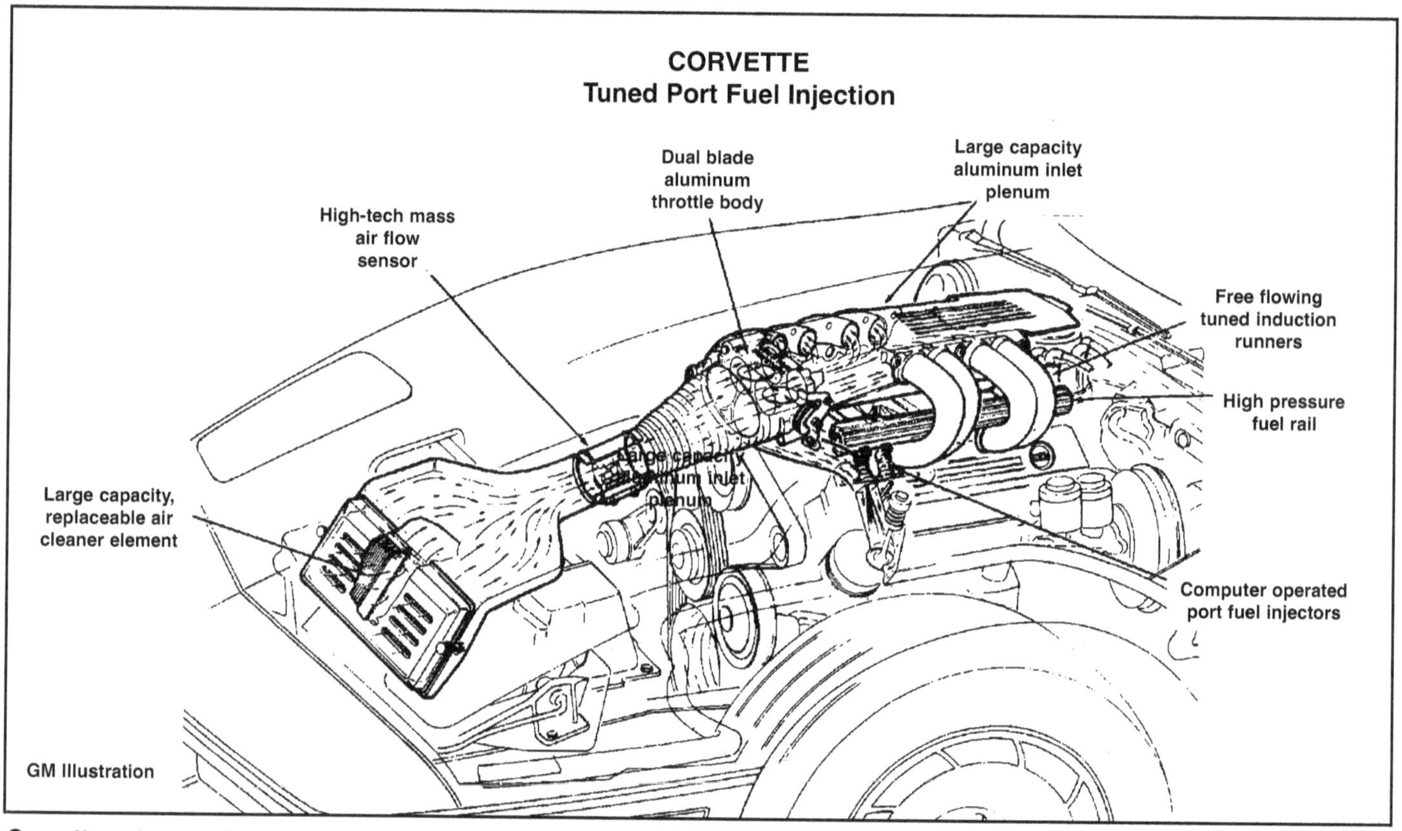

CORVETTE
Tuned Port Fuel Injection

Corvette cutaway shows the primary TPI components in place. The air cleaner mounted ahead of the radiator ducts cooler, denser air to the engine through a high-flow filter assembly. A mass air flow sensor provides highly accurate air flow measurement, while dual blade throttle body and large common plenum offer high-volume air supply. Tuned length individual inlet runners offer high volumetric efficiency while computer operated solenoid fuel injectors at each port deliver high-level fuel metering accuracy for optimum power and economy.

estimates based on engine speed and manifold absolute pressure (MAP) to determine fueling requirements. This system used a new ECM #1227730 for Camaros and Firebirds, and #1227727 for Corvettes.

The ECM uses a plug-in PROM chip to calibrate itself to the individual vehicle. Often called a "calibrator," the PROM (Programmable Read Only Memory) chip contains information specific to the vehicle the ECM is controlling. It enables the same basic ECM to be used on a variety of vehicles with specific calibrations for each one. As PROM requirements grew, GM had to increase their storage capacity from the original 32K in 1985 to 128K on 1986-89 PROMs and 256K on 1990 and later units.

PROMs typically contain specific information that helps the ECM make the correct fuel and spark decisions for best overall performance. PROM's usually will contain specific emissions control data, rear axle and transmission ratio data, and VATS (Vehicle Anti-Theft System). Implemented in 1987 the VATS system tells the computer not to start the car

Side view shows the compact nature of tuned port injection systems, even though it features a large plenum chamber and long individual runners. You can almost envision the low hood lines this system was designed to fit.

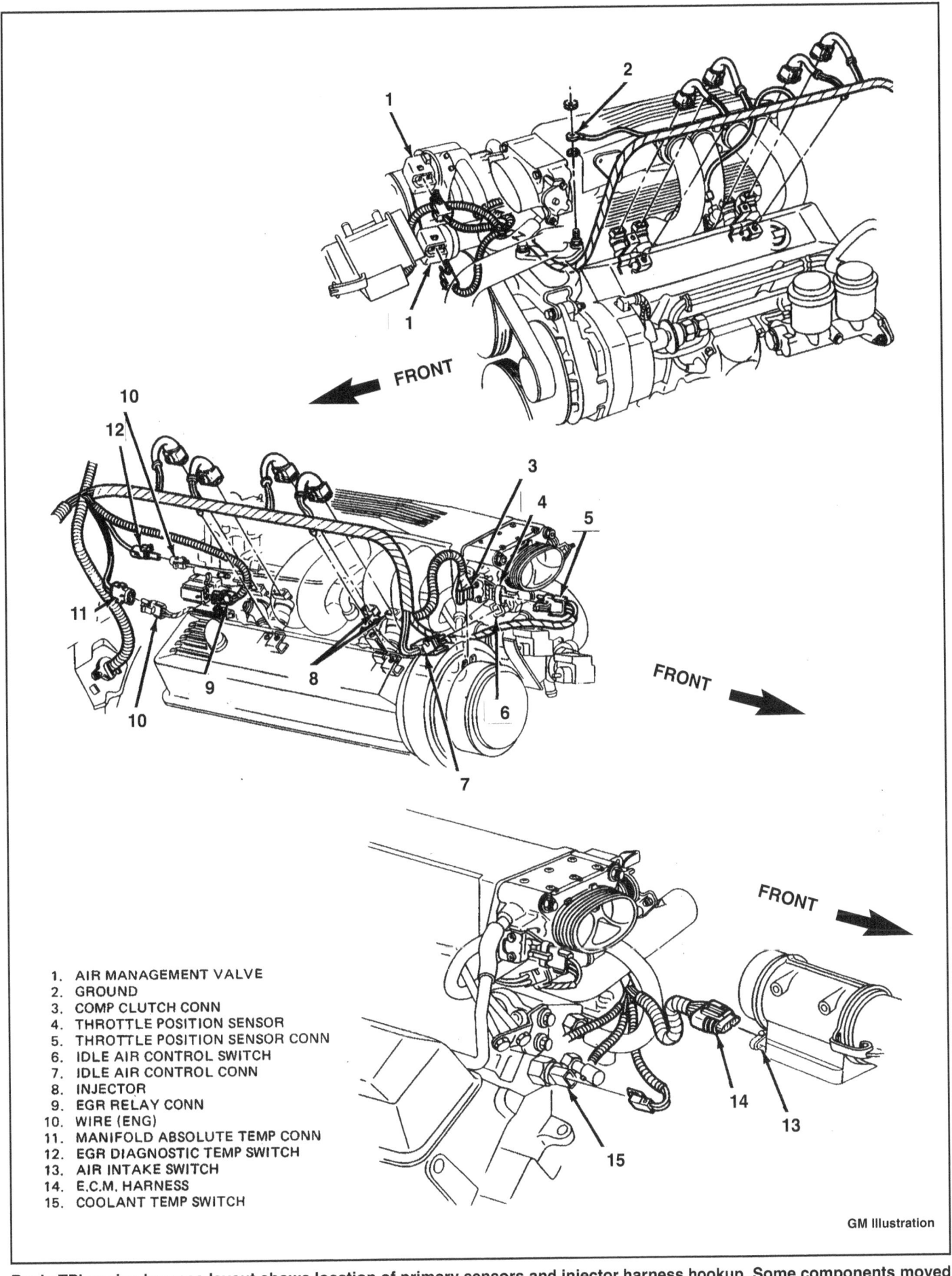

Basic TPI engine harness layout shows location of primary sensors and injector harness hookup. Some components moved around slightly over the years, but the same basic layout prevails throughout the TPI years.

GM Illustration

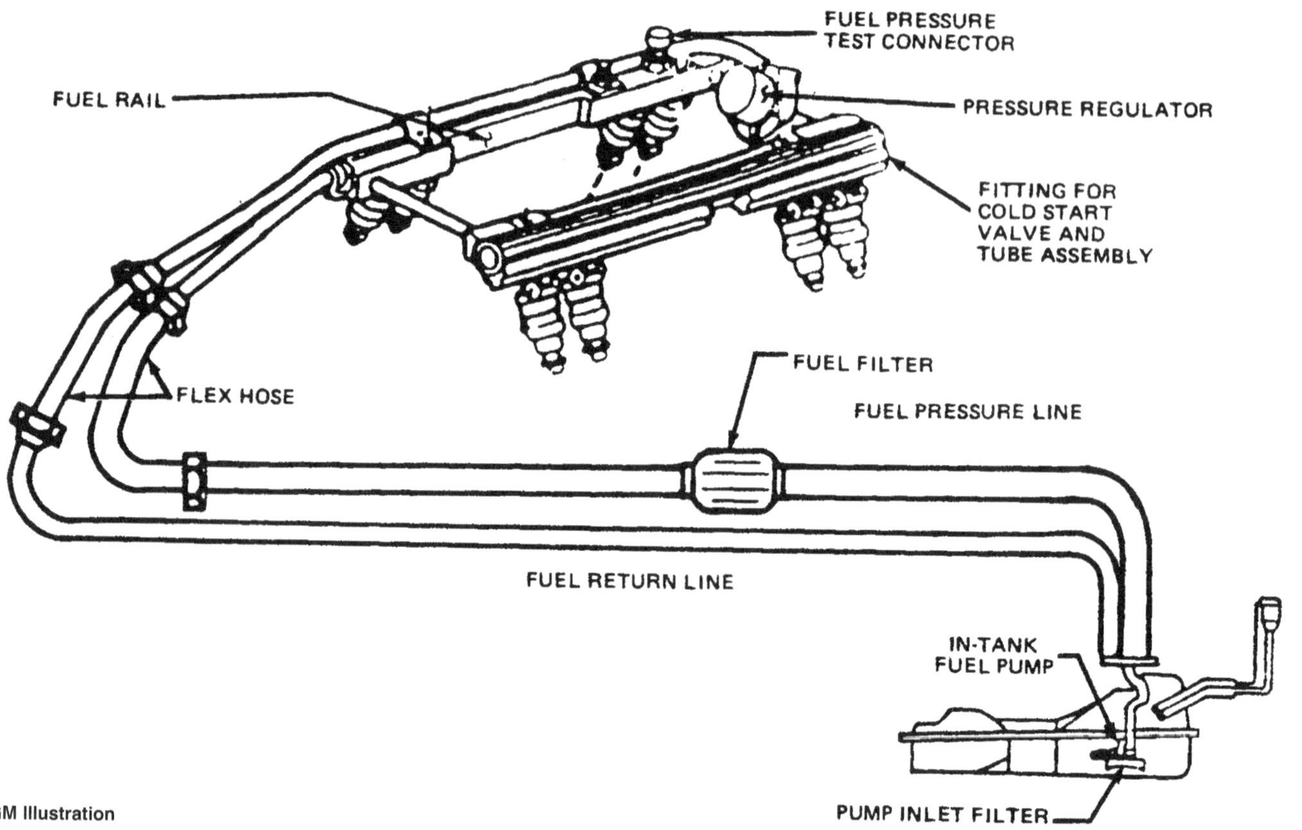

Fuel system layout illustrates the major fuel components from the fuel tank to the injectors. The fuel "pressure" line supplies fuel to the fuel rail where pressure is regulated to approximately 43 psi. When each bank of injectors is energized, atomized, high-pressure fuel is sprayed down the port toward the back of the intake valves. Excess fuel that the pressure regulator bleeds off to maintain the correct fuel pressure is returned to the fuel tank via the fuel return line. The fuel pressure regulator is referenced to intake manifold pressure so it will increase fuel pressure when the engine is under load.

GM Illustration

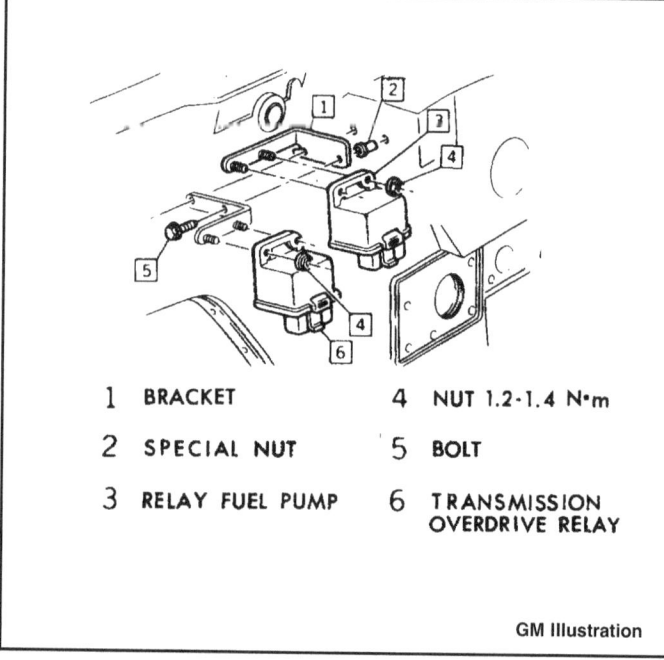

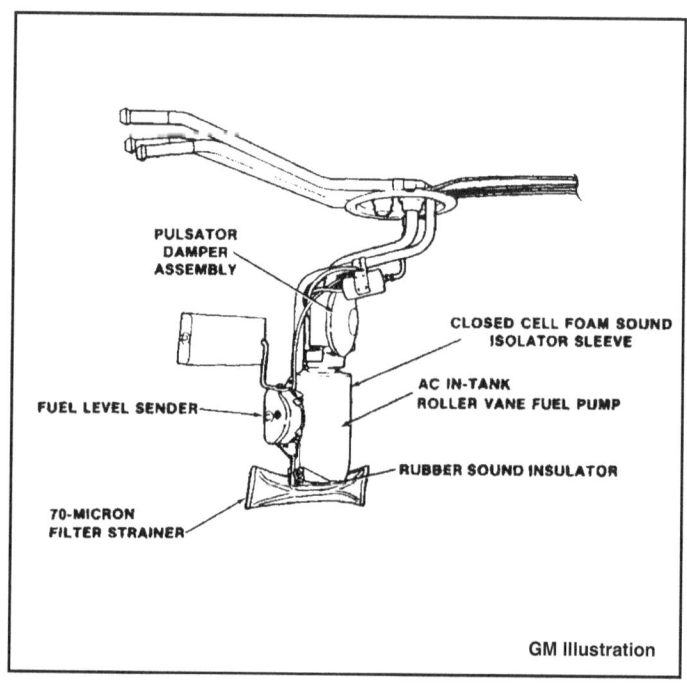

Fuel pump operation is controlled by a fuel pump relay. When the ignition switch is turned to "Run", the fuel pump relay activates the fuel pump for 1.5 to 2.0 seconds to prime the injectors. If the ECM does not receive a distributor reference pulse indicating engine cranking, it will turn the pump back off. It will reactivate the pump once it receives distributor reference pulses indicating an attempt to start the engine.

GM Illustration

The high-volume, roller vane, electric fuel pump is attached to the fuel sending unit inside the fuel tank. The pump is self-cooling via the fuel passing through it, and it is fitted with a large "sock" filter to prevent ingestion of any large dirt particles or other contamination. A check valve in the fuel pump prevents fuel in the pressure line from draining back through the pump to the tank. A high-capacity inline fuel filter also is installed between the pump and the injector fuel rail.

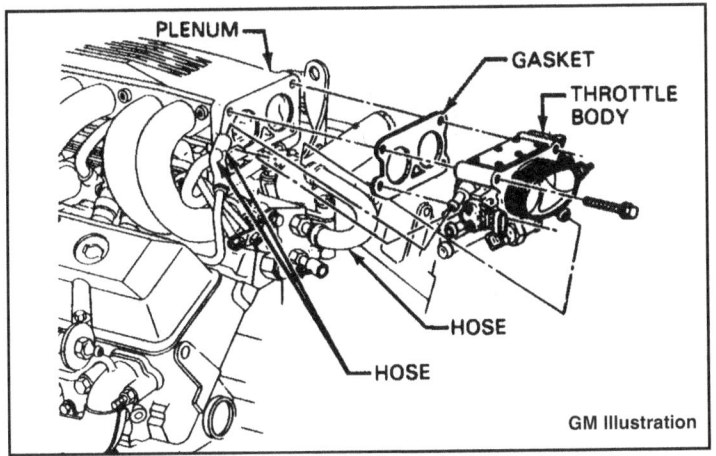

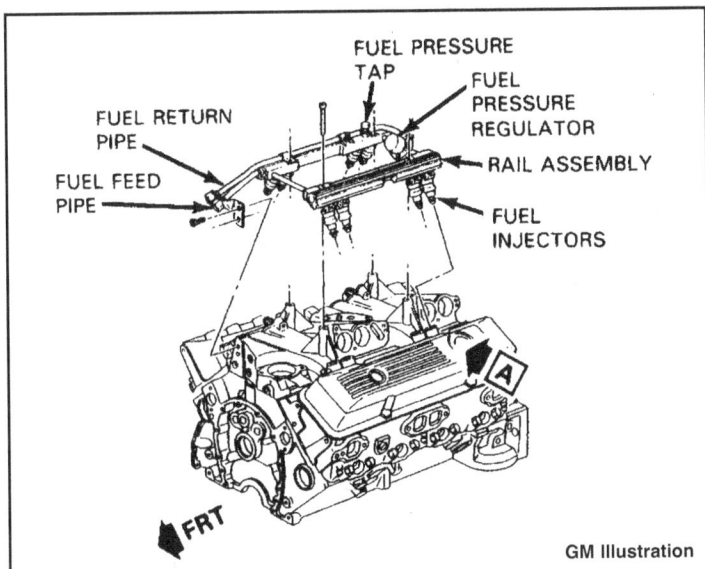

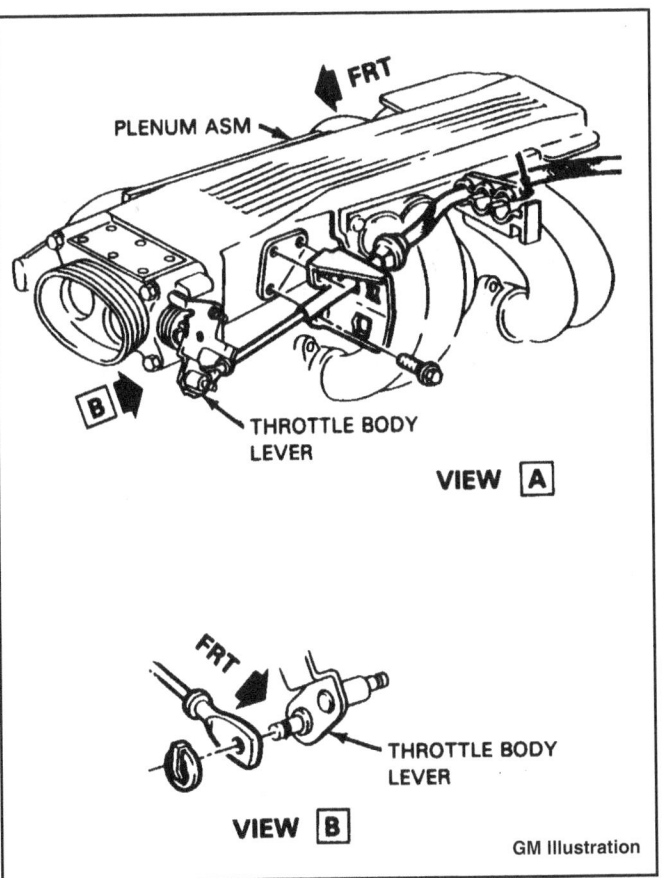

TPI illustrations show position and relationships between primary components. Minor variations occur, but most tuned port systems incorporate the components shown here. Later speed density units will not have the MAF unit. Depending on the year, different systems will incorporate different engine management strategies as detailed in subsequent chapters.

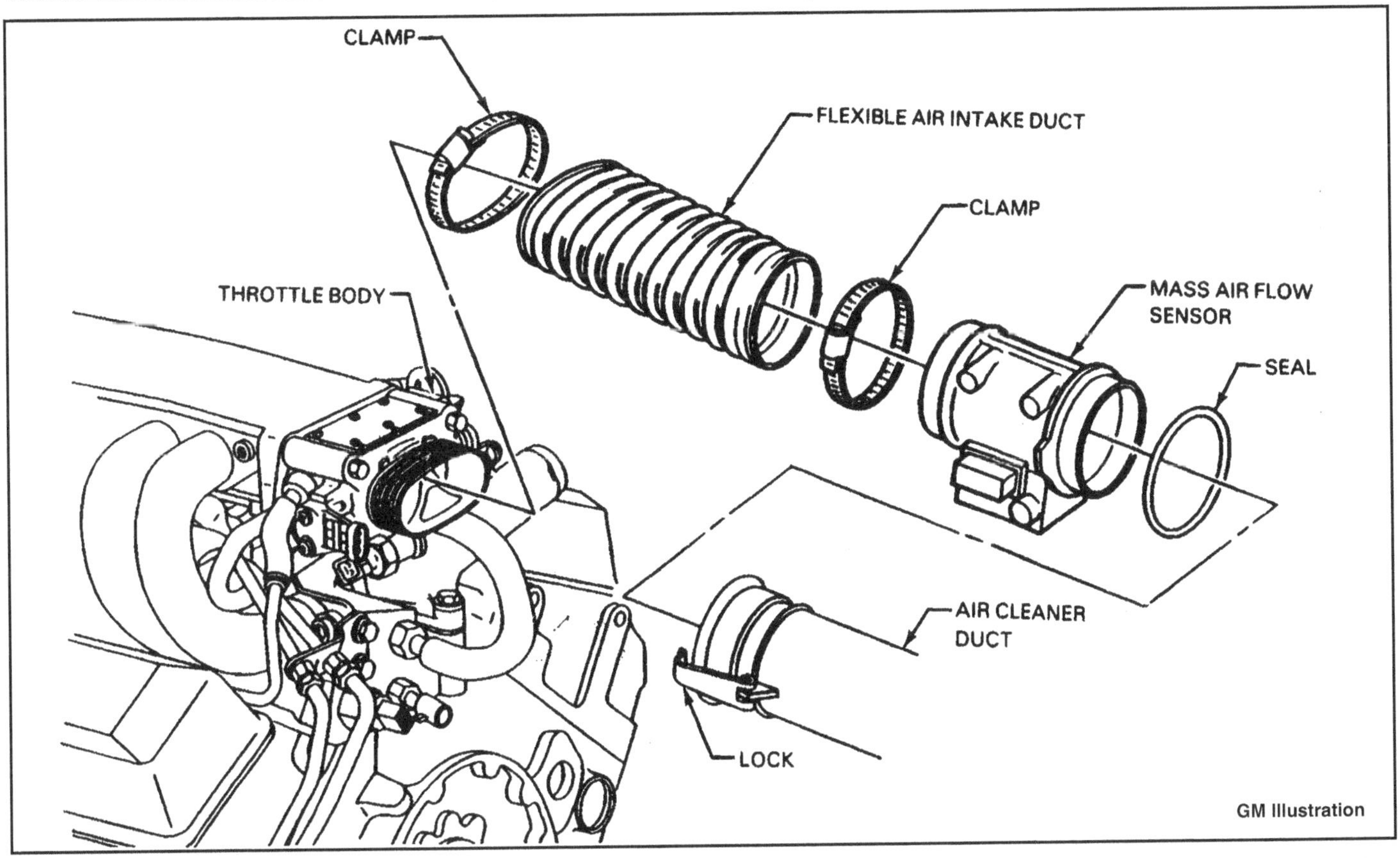

Chevy TPI Swapper's Guide 17

unless the correctly encoded key is in the ignition switch. This feature has cause more than a few no-starts when enthusiasts are changing chips.

UNDERSTANDING BASIC EFI ELECTRONICS

Electronic fuel injection systems operate on the same basic electrical principles that operate most of the conveniences in our lives. Voltage and changes in voltage are fundamental to the operation of electronic fuel injeciton systems. Voltage is a measurement of electrical pressure, while amperage is the flow rate of electricity at any selected point in a circuit. Voltage is created in a car's battery when the chemical reaction of submerging two dissimilar metallics in a solution of sulfuric acid and water (electrolyte) converts chemical energy to electrical energy. Oxygen sensors also operate on this principle. These sensors contain a zirconium dioxide ceramic element that becomes conductive for oxygen ions at temperatures above 600 degrees.

Voltage is also produced in the alternator where AC voltage is induced into the stator winding and converted to DC voltage with a diode rectifier bridge. This process applies an output voltage of 13.5 to 14.9 volts to the battery.

Most circuits in an electronic fuel injection system have low current flow with high resistance in the ciurcuit. A current-limiting resistor inside the ECM protects many of these circuits from excessive current flow. Many circuits carry current measured in milliamps, which is very small indeed. Most of these are monitoring circuits, but there are also driver, or actuator, circuits that have less resistance and higher current flow that is necessary to generate magnetic fields strong enough to operate the solenoids and relays that control the engine. Resistance is measured in ohms as related in Ohm's Law. Ohm's law specifies the relationship between voltage, amperage, and resistance. If the source voltage remains constant, a change in resistance (more ohms) will cause current flow to decrease. If the resistance is changed to less ohms, current flow will increase. If you remove too much or all resistance the current flow will probably destroy the circuit.

While Ohm's Law is fundamental to automotive circuitry, it is really Kirchoff's Law that enables ECMs to gather data and make decisions regarding engine management. Kirchoff's Law states that the sum of voltage drops in a series circuit is equal to the source voltage, and the algebraic sum of current flowing toward a point is zero. As a voltage drop occurs at each source of resistance, the ECM can read the change and evaluate it as data.

Automotive voltage changes are measures as waveforms. They come in two forms: sine waves and square waves. These waveforms can only be seen on an oscilloscope. Sine waves are are smooth forms where voltage builds slowly and falls off slowly. They can be either AC or DC, butr are typically associated with AC voltage as produced in an alternator and ignition pick-up coil.

Square waves are on/off pulses where voltage does not build slowly and then decrease; rather it is measured as either high or low. Square waves are used to either monitor or control a device. mass air flow sensors and Hall effect sensors use square waves. The ECM uses square waves to control the opening and closing of injectors and the switching of the ignition coil. Square waves have four primary characteristics that affect the way they operate.

AMPLITUDE

Amplitude is the least important characteristic. It is simply the amount of voltage change that occurs as the current in a circuit is switched on and off.

FREQUENCY

Frequency is the number of on/off cycles that occur within a given time period. Frequency is measured in Hertz which are measurements per second. For example , if you have 10 ons and 10 offs in one second, you have a frequency of 10 Hertz (Hz).

TUNED PORT Fuel Injection Tips & Tricks

STATIC ELECTRICITY

Static electricity can ruin your whole day, not to mention your ECM. The ECM is designed as a low-voltage component. It can only handle 17 volts, but jolts of static electricity can range from 1000 to 5000 volts. When you are handling the ECM, PROM chips, and, or other electronic devices, take care not to let static electricity destroy them. Always discharge static electricity by touching a separate metal object prior to handling an electronic component. You can also purchase a static strap from Radio Shack or other electronic supply stores. This strap allows you to ground yourself while handling electronic components.

DUTY CYCLE

Duty cycle is the relationship of current on and off time measured as a percentage. If current is flowing eighty percent of a given time period, the device is said to have an eighty percent duty cycle.

PULSE WIDTH

Pulse width is the amount of time that an actuator is energized. In a tuned port injection system, pulse width is used to control injector on- time, which is measured in milliseconds.

TYPES OF DEVICES

Within the TPI system there are various components that allow the system to function. A quick review of these units will help you understand their function and purpose in monitoring and controlling a TPI system.

RESISTORS

Resistors are electronic devices designed to limit current flow in a circuit. A voltage drop is produced wherever a resistor is applied. Depending on the applications, the resistor might be used to limit current flow or provide a voltage drop. Resistors are used to limit current flow to the sensors and actuators and to protect the ECM from damage.

The ECM uses carbon-type resistors in low current flow ECM circuits. The ECM's output or driver circuits have resistors in series with the output to keep the driver circuit from overloading if the circuit is accidently grounded or shorted to voltage. One of the primary uses of resistors is their function as circuit safeguards.

THERMISTORS

Thermistors are special resistors that change their resistance value according to changes in temperature. As temperature rises, the resistance of a thermistor decreases. This makes them useful for measuring temperatures in the engine coolant and the intake air charge. The mass air flow MAF sensor also uses thermistor measured air temperature to assist in its calculation of inlet air flow.

DIODE

A diode is sort of a one-way electronic check valve that allows current to flow in one direction but not the other. In EFI applications diodes are used to protect the ECM from high voltage spikes occuring when the air conditioning compressor switch is turned off.

STRAIN GAUGE

MAP sensors utilize the strain gauge to measure changes in pressure. The strain gauge contains a thin, flexible silicone chip that forms a diaphragm conected to stretch resistors at the corners. As pressure changes, the resistors are stretched and their resistance values change. Using a five volt reference, the MAP sensor strain gauge sends pressure change data to the ECM as a variable voltage signal based on the amount of resistance change in the stretch resistors.

POTENTIOMETER

A potentiometer is a resistor with a moving metal contact that changes resistance with the position of the contact. The throttle position sensor is a potentiometer. The TPS potentiometer has three connectors; one is a five volt reference , one is grounded through the ECM, and the third is referenced to the ECM to determine the position of the throttle based on the variable voltage signal being sent to the ECM.

ROM
READ ONLY MEMORY

ROM is the core program of the ECM. It contains non-volatile memory, which means that its programming and memory are maintained when power is removed. ROM contains basic instructions that tell the ECM to do something specific whenever it sees a specific input.

RAM
RANDOM ACCESS MEMORY

RAM is the portion of the computer used to store temporary information or to perform math. Current information is always moving through RAM, and a portion of RAM is used to store information about the engine's air/fuel usage and any problems that the ECM has detected in the sensors and driver circuits.

PROM
PROGRAMMABLE READ ONLY MEMORY

The PROM contains the specific calibration that allows the same ECM to be used on different types of cars. The PROM is non-volatile, although it can be wiped out by static electricity. It tells the ECM specific information about the car, including vehicle size, weight, engine size, final-drive ratio, transmissions type, rolling resistance, camshaft type, wind resistance, and emission calibrations. This information is used to help the ROM make intelligent decisions about the operation of the vehicle.

TUNED PORT INTAKE MANIFOLD AND PLENUM IDENTIFICATION

Tuned Port Fuel Injection Tips & Tricks

Tuned Port systems varied slightly over the years that they were produced. Depending on your application and the original source of your TPI setup, it is important that you get a "matched" set of components. The primary differences involve the cold start injector, sensor compatibility, and intake manifold bolt angles.

As seen in the photos on the right, the two center intake manifold to cylinder head attaching bolts have different angles depending on the year of the intake. TPI engines built through 1986 with cast iron cylinder heads used the manifold shown on the left (casting number 14081005). It is configured with central EGR heat riser passages and standard intake manifold bolt angles as used on all pre-'87 small blocks.

Corvette aluminum heads have no exhaust heat riser provisions so the intake base has a relocated EGR flange at the rear near the distributor (B). The EGR valve is still centrally mounted, but the exhaust gas is routed through this rear flange and a separate external tube connected to the exhaust manifold.

The center manifold bolt angles retain the standard angles. This manifold (casting # 18436572) was used only on '86 Corvettes where both cast iron and aluminum cylinder heads were offered in the same year.

All 1987 and later Vette engines used aluminum heads exclusively so their intake bases don't have the (A) EGR flange as found on the earlier intakes. 1987 and later cast iron heads have revised center intake bolt angles as shown by the drill bits inserted through the bolt holes on these manifold bases. The manifold base on the right (casting # 18483572) shows the steeper center bolt angles.

When constructing a TPI system, use the left-hand manifold base with pre-'86 cylinder heads that have exhaust heat provisions. Use the center ('86 Vette) manifold base with any head except '87 and later production heads (blocking off the appropriate EGR passage). Use the 1987 and later intake base with heads that lack exhaust heat passages. Use the intake on the right for all '87 and up production cast iron cylinder heads.

Intake plenums also differ. All plenums have an EGR passage (1) while '85-'88 plenums also have a cold start passage (2) that mates with the cold start injector used in those applications. The 1989 manifolds eliminated the cold-start passage (center) and 1990 to 1992 plenums with speed density fuel management used a MAP boss shown at (3).

The photo at the right shows (IAC) idle air control passage use on '85 to '88 TPI systems (arrow). An early throttle body cannot be used on a later model plenum without the IAC passage; a late throttle body can be used on earlier plenums if desired. One other way to identify the later plenum unit is by the cast fins on the top. Early plenums with the IAC passage have fins that extend farther forward than the later plenums.

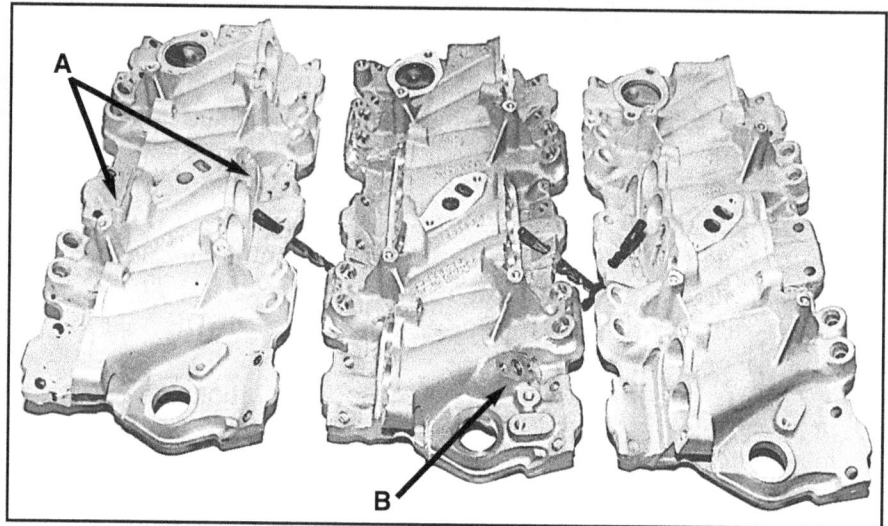

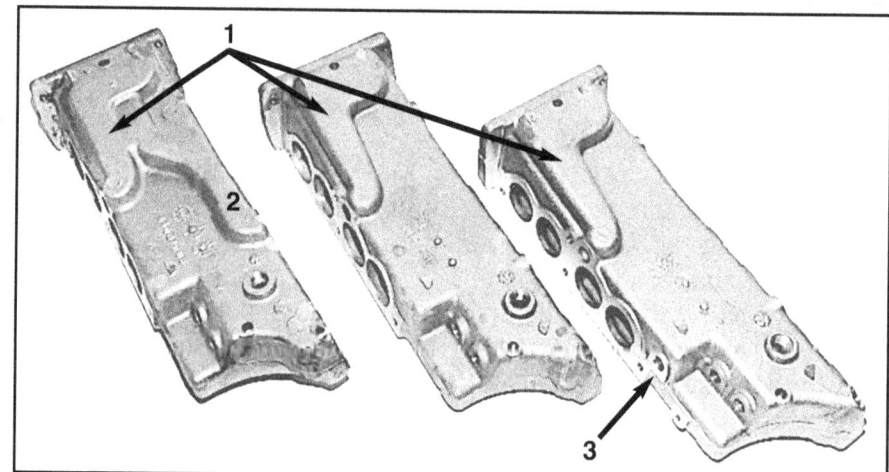

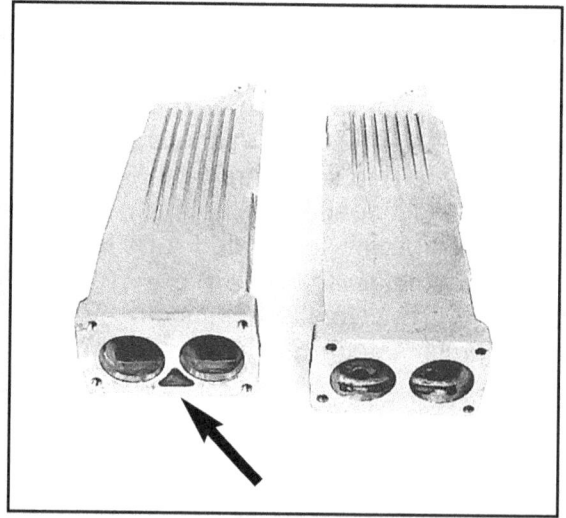

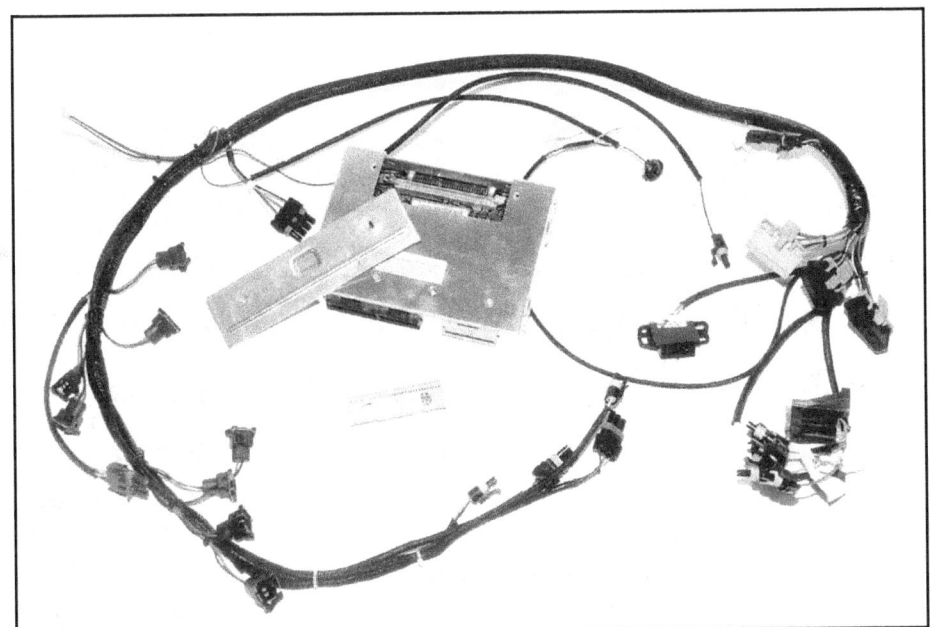

This in-line connector must be disconnected prior to setting the ignition time or the ECM will always default to the original factory specified initial timing. On factory wiring harnesses this connector is located near the heater/air conditioning core box on the firewall.

The difficulty of getting a reliable factory wiring harness from a used vehicle has been circumvented by the availability of high-quality aftermarket harnesses like this one from Howell Engine Developments. These harnesses are capable of running all factory accessories and either MAF or speed density management.

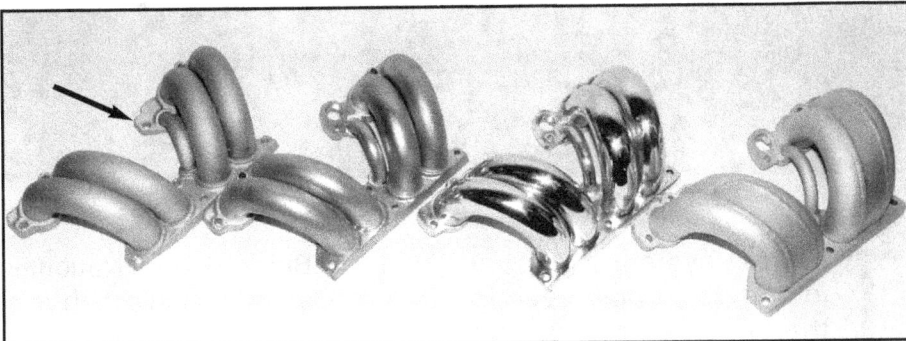

Enlarging TPI intake runners is a popular and effective modification. The first runner to the left is missing the cold start injector hole (arrow) indicating a 1989 or later engine. The other runners are for earlier engines. The polished runners from Arizona Speed and Marine flow 275 cfm as opposed to 170 cfm from the stocker. Siamesed runners like the one on the right offer maximum performance but may sacrifice some torque on the low end.

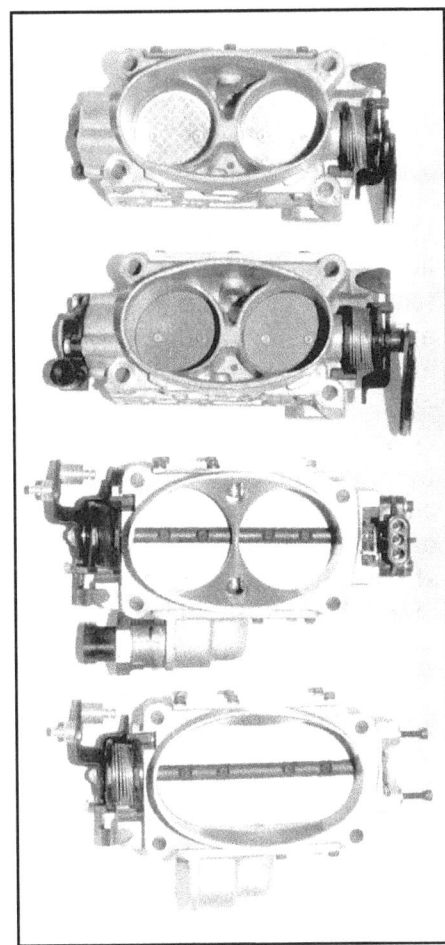

Top to bottom: A stock 48mm throttle body flows about 630 cfm and is good up to about 325 HP. Arizona Speed & Marine offers the 750 cfm 52mm unit good through 400 HP, a 1000 cfm unit for up to 470 HP, and a 1300 cfm single-blade unit normally reserved for big block applications.

OEM injectors for TPI systems have been supplied by Bosch, Lucas, and AC Rochester. If your engine came with aluminum heads you can be sure it has 350-sized injectors. To verify this, note the manufacturer's ID, part number and GM part number stamped on the injector.

Chevy TPI Swapper's Guide

CHEVY TPI Fuel Injection Swapper's Guide
Mass Flow vs Speed Density

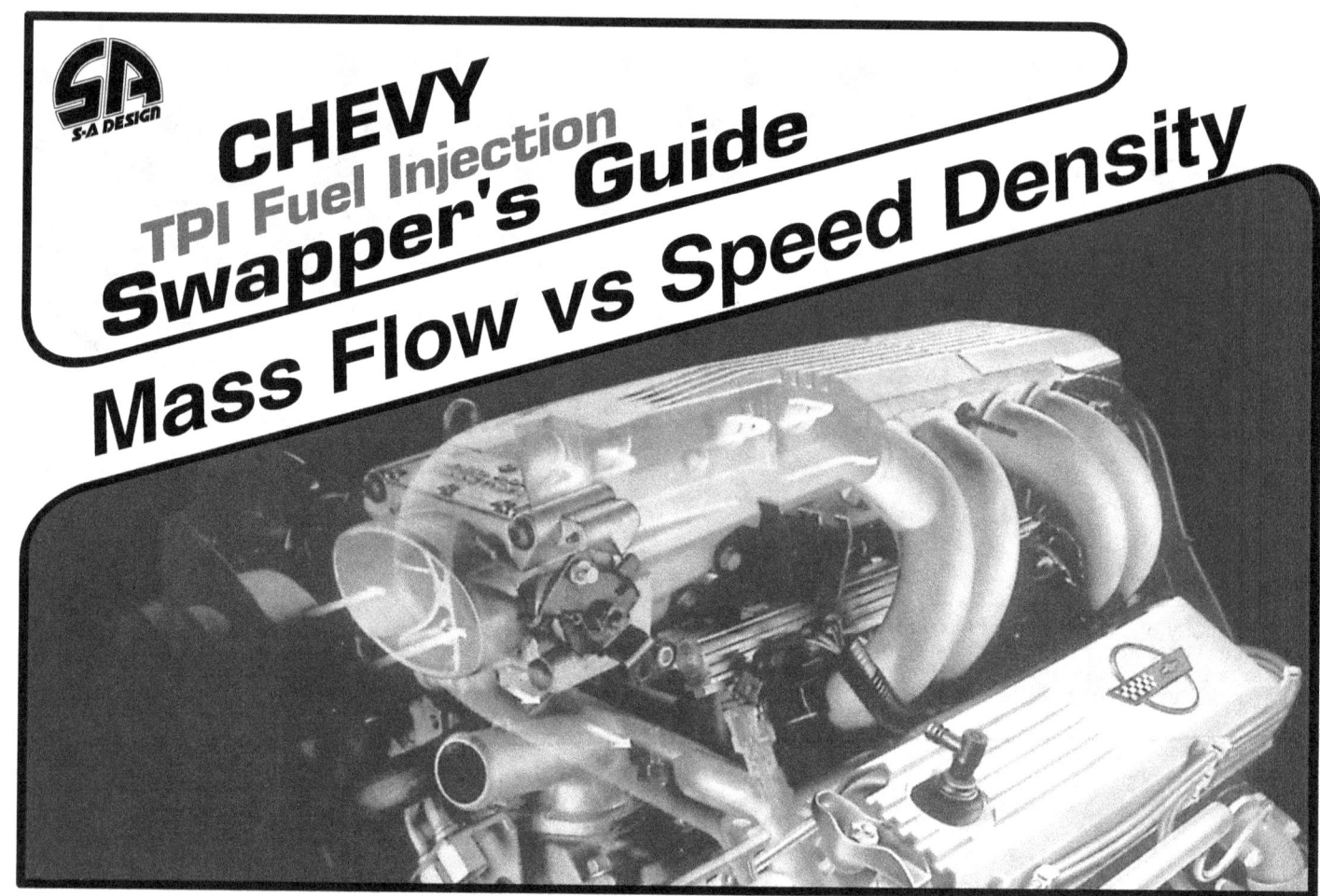

The fuel system's primary job is to supply fuel to the engine across its total operating range from idle to wide-open throttle. The goal is to maintain the correct air/fuel ratio under all operating conditions. To meter the proper amount of fuel consistently, the fuel system must be able to sense or estimate the amount of air the engine is consuming. The method by which air flow is measured or estimated characterizes the different types of fuel injection. The two most prevalent EFI systems today are mass flow and speed density.

Mass flow fuel injection utilizes a sensor placed in front of the throttle to measure the mass of air inducted into the engine. This type of system is used on GM tuned port V8s through 1988, Mustang 5.0L V8s since 1989, and on Buick Grand Nationals. Speed Density fuel injection uses the speed of the engine and the density of the air, along with a manifold vacuum sensor to calculate engine air flow. Speed Density is used on GM tuned port cars from 1989 to present, and it was used on 5.0L Mustangs from 1986 to 1988. Most aftermarket EFI systems also use Speed Density. Another system, the N Alpha system, is the most basic, using only the speed of the engine (N) and the throttle angle (alpha: the Greek letter engineers use to denote an angle) to calculate the appropriate amount of fuel. Before looking at the different fuel systems, it helps to review some important basics about spark ignition engines. The work that an engine does and the speed at which it operates are controlled by restricting air flow with the throttle. In a spark ignition engine the fuel metering system is required to maintain an appropriate air/fuel ratio (approximately 15:1) no matter what the air flow. If the throttle is almost closed, only a small amount of air will enter the engine and an even smaller quantity of fuel will be added to it. On the induction stroke, the pressure in the intake manifold and the cylinder will be far below atmospheric.

The amount of heat created by the combustion of this mixture will be a tiny fraction of what would have occurred if the throttle were open. The resulting engine speed will be low, and if the engine is not driving the car at this time it is idling.

If the throttle is gradually opened with the car in gear, engine speed will increase until engine torque balances the load of driving the car. The speed of the engine is controlled by the throttle position (air flow) and by the load placed on it (assuming the fuel system maintains a constant air/fuel ratio). A particular engine speed can be maintained by increasing throttle opening as the load increases (going uphill), and by decreasing throttle position as load decreases (going downhill). Air flow is a measure of the load placed on the engine, hence the fuel system must know how much air the engine is breathing so it can maintain the correct air/fuel ratio for optimum efficiency.

MASS FLOW FUEL INJECTION

Mass flow fuel injection systems use a Mass Air flow sensor (MAF) to measure the mass of the air being inducted into the engine. Intake air is ducted past the MAS which measures total air flow in one of several different ways depending on the type of MAF. The most prevalent type is the hot wire sensor pioneered by Bosch. The hot wire sensor routes air flow past a heated wire (hot wire). This wire is part of an electronic circuit that measures electrical current in milliamps. Current flowing through the wire heats it to a temperature that is always above the inlet air temperature by a fixed amount.

Air flowing across the wire draws away some of the heat, so an increase in current flow is required for it to maintain its fixed temperature. When air flow is low (idle) little current is required to heat the wire to temperature. At high air flow (wide-open throttle) it takes a lot of current to heat the wire because heat is being removed from it more quickly. The current necessary to heat the wire is proportional to the mass of air flowing across the wire. A temperature sensor in the MAS provides a correction for intake air temperature so that the output signal is not affected by it. A circuit in the MAS converts the current reading into a voltage signal for the Electronic Control Module (ECM) that converts it to grams per second. The output of this sensor is not linear with respect to air flow; it is sensitive to low air flow and less sensitive at high air flows. Idle speed air flow is typically about 4 to 7 grams per second, increasing with rpm. The hot wire is made of platinum and is sensitive to contaminants or deposits, therefore, it is superheated after engine shutdown to burn off any contaminants or deposits.

Mass flow fuel systems measure the mass of the air directly, so there is no need for the ECM to correct for air density. Other inputs to the ECM include a throttle position sensor and an O_2 sensor for closed loop air/fuel ratio control. Once the ECM knows the amount of air entering the engine, it looks at the other sensors to determine the engine's current state of operation (idle, acceleration, cruise, deceleration); then it

The Mass Air Flow or MAF sensor is the preferred way of determining engine loading because it actually measures the amount of incoming air. This makes it tolerant of engine modifications such as camshaft and cylinder head changes. Up to a point, the MAF simply measures the increase in air flow brought about by these changes.

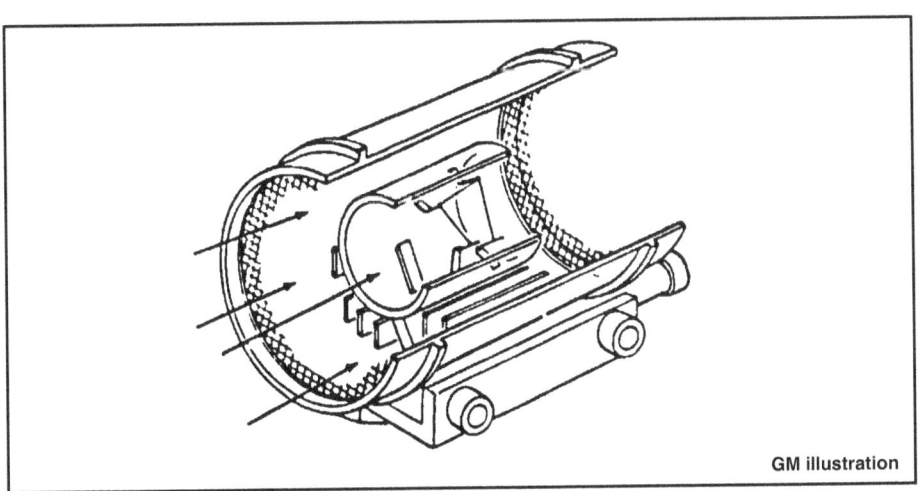

MAF sensors use an exposed hot wire to measure air flow through the unit. Air flow changes cause voltage change as the ECM attempts to maintain the calibrated wire temperature. The ECM interprets voltage changes as specific air flow changes.

refers to an electronic table or map to find the appropriate air/fuel ratio and select the fuel injector pulse width required to match the input signals. Finally, the ECM energizes the fuel injector for the appropriate number of milliseconds to inject the fuel. On a GM tuned port car, the sensor readings and subsequent calculations are made at a rate of 160 calculations per second to ensure high accuracy.

A mass flow fuel system adapts easily to changes in the engine as well as hardware because air flow is measured directly. In other words, a mass flow system is self-compensating for most reasonable changes to the engine and is extremely accurate under low-speed part-throttle operation. The downside is that the sensors are expensive and sometimes unreliable. Many MAFs also provide a considerable restriction to air flow in high horsepower engines, limiting their power (between 300 HP and 350 HP). The mass flow system found on many high-performance GM cars (Corvette, Camaro, Firebird, Grand National) simply cannot read high air flow values, thus the combination of air flow restriction and the loss of the self-tuning feature causes many people who want to build very high horsepower (in excess of of 325 HP) engines to change to speed density fuel systems. The Accel Power Process is designed specifically to support this change, allowing a complete conversion on GM cars.

TPI/MAF DETAILS

As used in 1985-89 TPI engines, the mass air flow system supplies the ECM with information about the amount of air passing through it. If the ECM sees large amounts of air flow, it indicates acceleration, wide open throttle or high power demand, while small amounts of air indicate low power demand, deceleration, or idle.

The MAF used in 1985-89 TPI systems is a Bosch hot wire type where current supplied to the sensing wire attempts to maintain a calibrated wire temperature. The current will vary with temperature and the ECM interprets this as either an increase or decrease in air flow. The ECM supplies a current-limiting five volt reference source on the MAF signal line. The MAF will pull the voltage low, to about .4 volt with low air flow and as high as five volts with high air flow. Accuracy is maintained by a MAF burnoff circuit that briefly heats the sensing wire to about 1000 degrees after engine shutdown to burn off contaminants.

SPEED DENSITY FUEL INJECTION

As previously discussed, it is critical for the ECM to know how much air is being consumed by the engine. A speed density system calculates the air flow of the engine since it has no sensor to measure it directly. If you simplify the engine as an air pump, theoretically, it will move half of its displacement in air for every rotation of the crankshaft (half because it is a four-stroke engine). Thus the engine becomes an air meter. Engines, however, rarely flow the theoretical air flow due to restrictions in the inlet, the cylinder head, and the exhaust.

The volumetric efficiency (VE) of an engine is defined as the ratio of the actual mass air flow to the theoretical mass air flow. If an engine flows its theoretical air flow, then the VE would be 100%. At wide-open throttle, high-performance engines can approach a VE value of 100%, and racing engines can exceed 100% because of more efficient inlet and exhaust tuning. All engines will have very low VE values at part throttle (except for engines equipped with a turbocharger or supercharger where the inlet manifold is often pressurized under part-throttle conditions). The volumetric efficiency of an engine changes for every throttle position and engine speed. A large table or map of these values can be generated on an engine dynamometer by measuring the actual air flow at all the speed load points and calculating the VEs. This procedure is called mapping an engine.

Speed density systems use this map of engine volumetric efficiency to calculate the air flow of the engine under any operating condition. These systems measure engine vacuum via a manifold absolute pressure (MAP) sensor. This sensor reads absolute pressure in KPA (Kilopascals) and supplies a voltage to the ECM proportional to manifold vacuum. All of the VE maps are referenced by manifold vacuum and rpm; the computer reads engine speed (RPM) and manifold vacuum (KPA) and looks in the reference table to find the volumetric efficiency at this speed load point. Once the computer finds the VE value, it computes the air flow directly. As most racers know, air density changes with temperature, therefore the computer must then correct the calculated air flow value based on a sensor reading of the air temperature in the manifold.

The computer's calculations are all based on the map of VEs. Production variations and wear and tear are not compensated for when a test engine is mapped. If the intake or exhaust manifolds were changed, this seriously would affect the volumetric efficiency of the engine and throw the computer's calculations into error. A racing engine would be remapped to incorporate any changes, but this is obviously not feasible for car manufacturers. Production cars compensate for wear and production variation through the closed-loop control provided by the exhaust gas oxygen (EGO) sensor. This sensor supports calculation of the air/fuel ratio based on the oxygen content of the exhaust. The ECM looks at the air/fuel ratio from the EGO sensor (also known as the O_2 sensor) and corrects fuel delivery for any errors. This works fine when the engine is in closed loop control mode (all part-throttle driving conditions), but when the engine is at wide-open throttle (WOT) it is not under closed-loop control and correction factors are not very accurate. Obviously the ECM is doing a lot of number crunching with a speed density system.

N ALPHA FUEL INJECTION

N Alpha fuel systems are a very simple design for engines that operate primarily at WOT and are thus used extensively in racing. N Alpha uses only the speed of the engine (N) and the throttle angle (alpha) to calculate the required amount of fuel delivery. These are simple speed density systems that use throttle angle to approximate load instead of a MAP sensor, This approach is logical for racing engines with aggressive camshaft profiles that generate weak manifold vacuum signals and spend very little time at part-throttle, N Alpha systems are just as accurate as speed density systems at WOT, but have much less accuracy at part-throttle due to the reduced size of the engine map,

Speed density systems typically have thousands of VE points that require weeks to fully map on an engine dynamometer, This process is obviously costly and time consuming, not something that is likely to work on racing engines. N Alpha systems have only a few map points so they are much easier to map. They generally do not have a closed-loop mode for air/fuel correction, which means that their part-throttle calibration is crude at best when compared to speed density systems, This also makes them incompatible with current catalytic converters. Any significant change to the engine requires remapping, but the reduced map makes it feasible for racing applications.

JUST THE FACTS

mass flow systems rely on the accurate measurement of air entering the engine. They are self-tuning for most reasonable engine changes and provide extremely accurate air/fuel ratio control under low-load part-throttle conditions. The factory MAF will become a restriction to air flow for high-horsepower applications and may limit them to approximately 325 horsepower. Serious modifications may require a large aftermarket sensor or conversion to speed density control using OEM or aftermarket components.

Speed density systems calculate air flow based on a preprogrammed map of values that relate engine speed and manifold vacuum to engine air flow. These systems rely on a closed-loop correction from the O_2 sensor to compensate for changes in the engine's condition; however, major changes to the engine still require reprogramming of the computer. Speed density systems have no inherent restriction to air flow, so theoretically they have the ability to handle an unlimited amount of horsepower with the appropriate programming.

Modifying a speed density-controlled engine without custom programming can be a problem if the modifications are aggressive. Speed density systems are especially sensitive to camshaft changes since manifold vacuum is a key element in the computer's calculations. Camshafts that are advertised as computer compatible are your best bet. Many aftermarket manufacturers have computers or hardware that will allow the adjustment of the fuel system to handle significant changes to the engine.

N Alpha fuel injection is a simplified speed density system used primarily for racing. It is much easier to calibrate, but has no closed-loop correction feature. This is a race-only system that can handle any engine configuration, but requires constant calibration work.

No one type of fuel injection system is best; each has its strengths and weaknesses. The key is to select the type of system that meets the specific requirements of your particular application. If you own a car with a factory-equipped system, aftermarket companies offer products to allow you to optimize your fuel system without complete replacement.

And now that you know a little more about the differences in EFI systems, you can make more intelligent decisions about the modifications you choose to make to your EFI-equipped engine.

CHEVY TPI Fuel Injection Swapper's Guide
Closed Loop Operation

All new cars sold in America have a closed-loop fuel system. What is a closed-loop system, and why do all new cars have it?

A closed-loop system is also called a feedback system. A perfect example of feedback control is the thermostat that controls the heater in your house. The thermostat measures the temperature in the room directly and turns the heater on if the set temperature (set point) is above the room temperature. If the room temperature is above the set point, the heater is turned off. The thermostat measures room temperature and feeds it back to the controller, closing the loop so the controller can turn the heat on or off. This is closed-loop control of temperature.

An open-loop heater would be like the one found in most cars. You turn it on and it heats, and it keeps heating until you turn it off. Unless the car is equipped with a climate control system, there is no thermostat to measure temperature and no set point to be controlled. An open-loop system has no feedback and output is unregulated.

Closed-loop control of air/fuel ratio is based on the oxygen content of the exhaust gas as

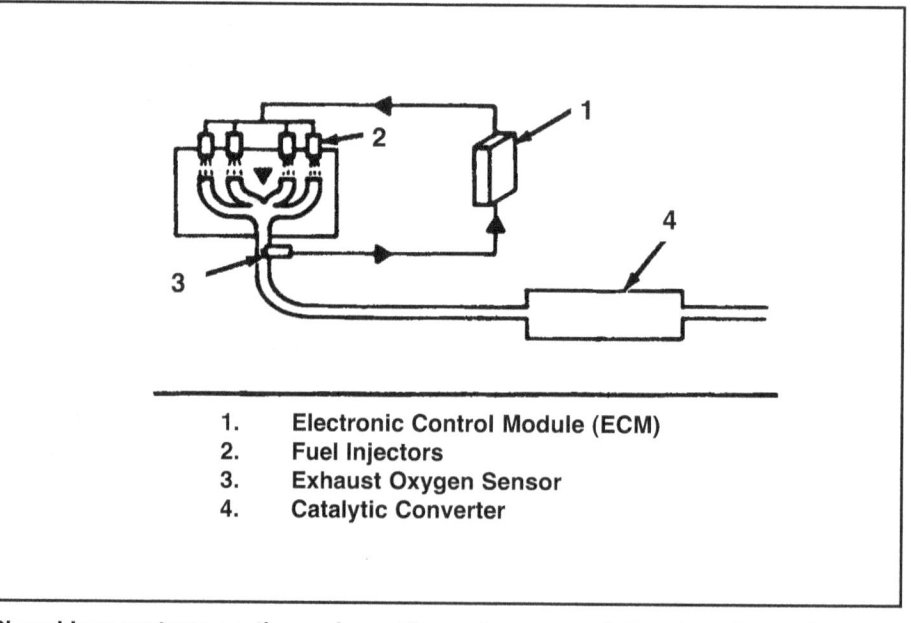

1. Electronic Control Module (ECM)
2. Fuel Injectors
3. Exhaust Oxygen Sensor
4. Catalytic Converter

Closed-loop systems continuously monitor and compensate for changing engine operating conditions. The primary control in a closed loop system is the oxygen sensor.

measured by the exhaust gas oxygen sensor (O_2 sensor). The oxygen content of the exhaust gas is proportional to the engine's current operating air/fuel ratio. An electronic control module (ECM) reads the output signal from the O_2 sensor and adjusts the mixture so that the air/fuel ratio matches a predetermined value (the set point). When this happens, the loop is closed, as in the thermostat example.

An open-loop system has no feedback and relies solely on jetting or calibration for air/fuel ratio control. In this regard, a typical Holley four-barrel carburetor may be considered a full-time open-loop system, and all modern EFI systems and feedback carburetor systems also operate in open-loop mode when running at full throttle. The carburetor only has jetting to control air/fuel ratio, while an electronically controlled system defaults to a preset calibration (power enrichment) when it goes open-loop.

A closed-loop system can compensate for changes in production variations, weather conditions, altitude, normal wear and tear, and engine hardware changes. Open-loop systems could require rejetting or recalibration under some or all of these circumstances.

WHY CLOSED-LOOP FUEL SYSTEMS ARE NECESSARY

Closed-loop control of air/fuel ratio was developed to help reduce exhaust emissions while increasing fuel economy and improving driveability. Bosch introduced closed-loop control in 1976. New three-way catalytic converters were developed to provide less back pressure than the restrictive designs of the mid-Seventies. The new catalysts would operate only in a narrow window of engine air/fuel ratios. The open-loop (set and forget) fuel systems of the day could not supply adequate air/fuel ratio control for proper operation of these new catalysts.

When Bosch introduced the 02 sensor with closed-loop control, the new threeway catalysts were successfully used. In 1977, Volvo was the first company to mass-produce cars with closed-loop control. Closed-loop operation provides much better performance as well as improved fuel economy and emissions.

Not surprisingly, closed-loop control was quickly adopted by all major auto makers. In the mid- to late-seventies, cars were not much fun to drive because they barely ran. The introduction of the 02 sensor and closed-loop control launched a renaissance in performance that started in the early Eighties and brought us to the outstanding performance cars we enjoy today.

WHAT IS A STOICHIOMETRIC AIR/FUEL RATIO?

A stoichiometric air/fuel ratio is a theoretical or chemically correct air/fuel ratio. In perfect stoichiometric combustion, there is just enough air and just enough fuel to burn completely with no by-products. Because an engine can never be perfectly efficient, even a stoichiometric reaction can have byproducts. Every fuel has a stoichiometric air/fuel ratio. For gasoline, this ratio is approximately 14.7:1, which means that for every 14.7 pounds of air inducted, one pound of fuel is inducted. This air/fuel ratio isn't optimal for all conditions, such as power production or fuel economy, just for minimizing combustion by products or emission. Best power production is usually slightly richer than 14.7:1 and best fuel economy is usually slightly leaner.

THE OXYGEN SENSOR

The oxygen sensor is the heart of a closed-loop fuel system. An O_2 sensor consists of a ceramic body that is closed at one end (it looks like a thimble). The inside and outside surfaces of the ceramic body are coated with a thin layer of platinum (the same material used in catalytic converters). The platinum surfaces serve as electrodes. The outside surface is exposed to the exhaust and the inside surface is exposed to ambient air, which serves as a reference point. At approximately 300°C the ceramic material conducts O_2, which activates the sensor. A difference in oxygen concentration between the exhaust gas and the ambient air results in a voltage differential between the two surfaces. This voltage then serves as a measure of the oxygen concentration in the exhaust gas since the oxygen content of ambient air is relatively constant.

As stated earlier, the oxygen content is proportional to the air/fuel ratio. A rich mixture is defined as one deficient in oxygen and a lean mixture as one with excess oxygen. The O_2 sensor outputs 1.0 volt when the mixture is rich and 0.1 volt when the mixture is lean. The ideal or stoichiometric ratio causes an output of 0.5 volt.

The response of an oxygen sensor is affected by temperature, and until the sensor is fully warmed up it will not operate. In order to make the sensor active in the shortest possible time, and to stabilize temperature related to performance, sensors with an internal heating element

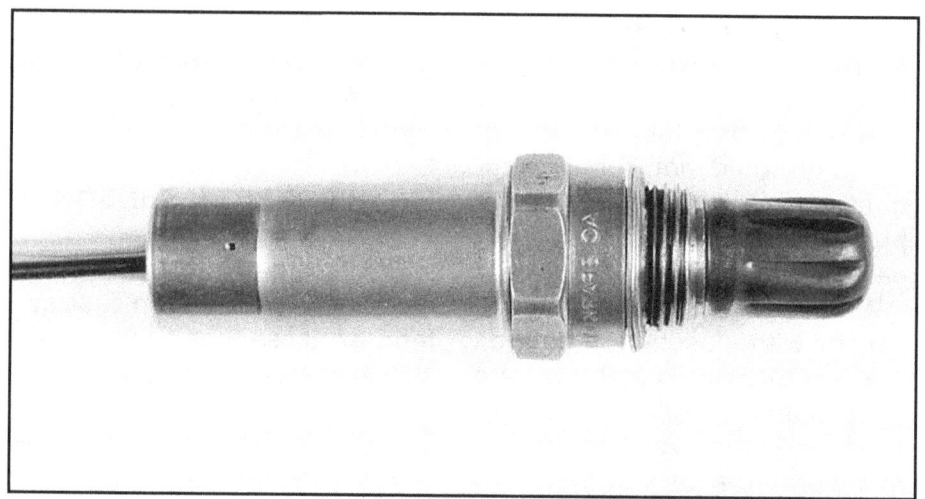

Oxygen sensor (02 sensor) runs the show in a closed loop system. It should be placed within 12 inches of the exhaust port to measure oxygen content and send a signal that the ECM converts to air fuel ratio.

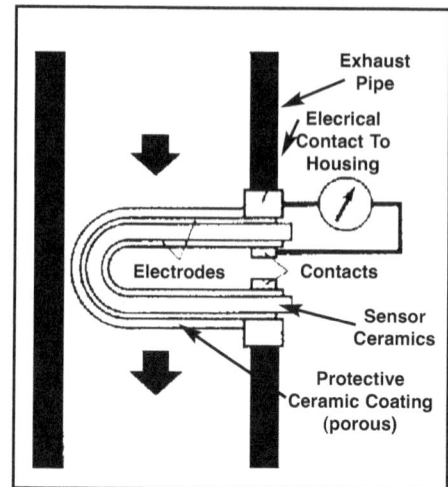

The oxygen content between the exhaust side and the ambient side of the sensor generates voltage between the electrodes—thus generating an air fuel ratio reading based on voltage.

were created. These heated oxygen sensors are more expensive, but they offer an extended performance range.

It is important to note that an oxygen sensor's voltage output is not linear with respect to air/fuel ratio. The voltage stays low until the air/fuel ratio is near stoichiometric, then it rises rapidly to 1.0 volt. The sensor "switches" from low to high or high to low when the engine goes from lean to rich or rich to lean. The switch point is 0.5 volt, thus the sensor is only accurate at or near stoichiometry.

CLOSED-LOOP OPERATION

Once warmed up, the oxygen sensor transmits a voltage signal to the ECM which then signals the fuel management system (injection or electronic carburetor) to adjust the fuel mixture, richer or leaner as required. The ECM tries to correct the air/fuel ratio to the point where the oxygen sensor switches constantly from high to low to high. If the sensor's voltage is low, the ECM adds more fuel; if the sensor's voltage is high, it supplies less fuel.

FUEL INTEGRATOR AND BLOCK LEARN MEMORY

The corrections that the ECM makes to the air/fuel ratio must be smooth and steady, not abrupt, or drivability will suffer. For this reason, the ECM corrects the air/fuel ratio based on the oxygen sensor's output using a fuel integrator factor.

The fuel integrator is a "fudge factor" for the ECM based on a moving average with respect to time. Fuel integrators are usually an additive correction. In other words, the fuel integrator value at any given instant is the num-

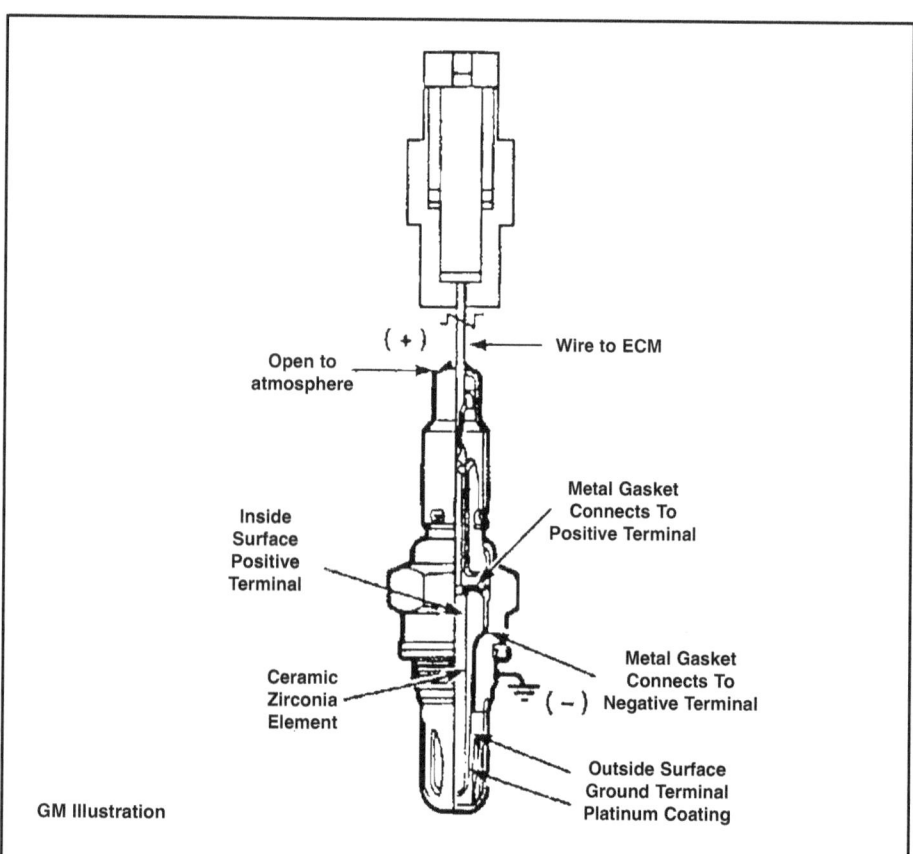

Oxygen sensor cutaway shows the outside and inside surfaces where a low voltage differential is generated by the oxygen content of the exhaust gases. The Oxygen sensor must reach 600 degrees F before it becomes a semiconductor.

ber that, when added to the current value, will make it correct.

The fuel integrator must be programmed to take into account the amount of time it takes for the fuel to be added to the engine, combusted, and to reach the oxygen sensor. This transport time varies with engine speed and load. During idle, the transport time may be very long. But under wide-open-throttle conditions the time is very short. For this reason, the air/fuel ratio is never perfect; however, it can be held in a narrow window near stoichiometry.

The fuel integrator is the instantaneous correction. A more powerful and longer term correction based on the oxygen sensor is the block learn memory (BLM). The BLM correction provides a means for the ECM to adapt for engine-to-engine variations as well as changes in the engine's operating characteristics. Block learn values are usually separated into tables. The tables have columns of rpm values and rows of load (map or air flow) values. This way the fuel system can be made richer in some areas and leaner in others, if necessary. The BLM is a multiplicative correction, so it can have a much more significant impact than the fuel integrator. BLM tables are saved even when the engine is off, as long as battery voltage is not disconnected from the ECM.

BLM values are usually incremented by a fixed amount based on the oxygen sensor output. If the output indicates lean, the BLM value for the appropriate cell will be increased by a fixed amount. If the O_2 sensor indicates rich, the BLM value will be made leaner by a fixed amount.

In summary, the fuel integrator is an additive correction that occurs continuously. The BLM correction is a multiplier and is saved in a table. Typically, the BLM correction will be made first, then the fuel integrator correction.

Final Value = (Initial value x BLM) + Fuel Integrator

The integrator memory register contains a number between 0 and 255. The short term or immediate neutral value is 128. While the ECM monitors oxygen sensor output, it continuously adjusts the short term fuel trim value. Corrections to the long term fuel trim are made by the block learn matrix, which arranges cells according to rpm and MAP. Each cell in the block learn is a memory register just like the integrator values.

As the ECM monitors operation over time, it switches from cell to cell to determine what "Block Learn Number" to use in calculating the base injector pulse width. It also continues to monitor the integrator. If the integrator changes far enough from 128, the block learn value will be corrected to force the integrator back to 128. The ECM will continue to do this until it determines that the integrator is balanced at 128. When the engine operates at wide open throttle or near wide open throttle, the ECM temporarily "locks" the integrator at 128 so the "closed loop" factor and the block lean will not attempt to correct for the temporary rich condition.

Integrator and block learn values also have limits that, once exceeded, will cause a trouble code to set, and the "Check Engine" light to be switched on.

WHEN DOES AN ENGINE OPERATE UNDER CLOSED-LOOP CONTROL?

Closed-loop corrections only take place after the vehicle is warmed up (1-1/2 to 2 minutes of operation) and only at part-throttle. Current passenger car technology does not allow for closed-loop corrections at wide-open throttle. Wide-open-throttle closed-loop control does not occur because today's sensors are only accurate at or near 14.7:1 air/fuel ratio. A new universal exhaust gas oxygen (UEGO) sensor has been developed that can read air/fuel ratio from very rich (9:1) to very lean (18:1) accurately and quickly. These sensors are expensive (up to $900), but will allow closed-loop control at wide-open throttle. Think about that for a moment; a fuel system that can constantly adjust itself for best power! When these sensors are reduced in cost and broadly applied in the not-too-distant future, another milestone in superior vehicle performance will have been reached—total real-time control of air/fuel ratio for optimized power and efficiency under all operating conditions.

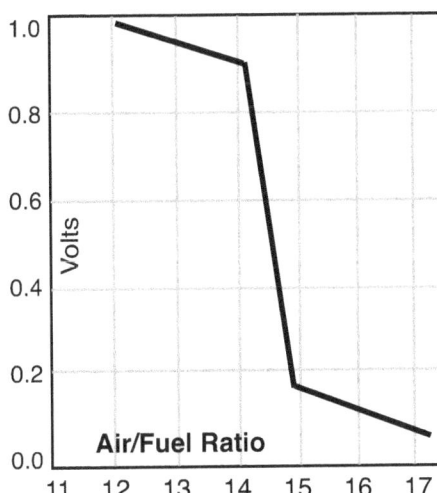

O_2 sensor is very accurate near 14.7:1 and less accurate approaching rich or lean conditions.

CHEVY TPI Fuel Injection Swapper's Guide
Tuned Port Sensor Guide

An EFI system's sensors continually measure the engine's operating parameters and report the data to the computer in a language that it can understand. The sensors' functions are critical to the optimum performance of an EFI system because all the computer's decisions are based on the sensors' output. To work comfortably and successfully with any EFI system, it is important to understand how the sensors work and how their performance impacts the operation of the fuel system.

COOLANT TEMPERATURE SENSOR

The coolant temperature sensor (CTS) is a resistance-type temperature measuring device called a thermistor. A thermistor is simply a resistor that changes resistance based on temperature. This sensor is placed in contact with the engine coolant so that the Electronic Control Module (ECM) knows the engine's operating temperature at all times. Low coolant temperatures produce a high resistance, while high temperatures cause low resistance.

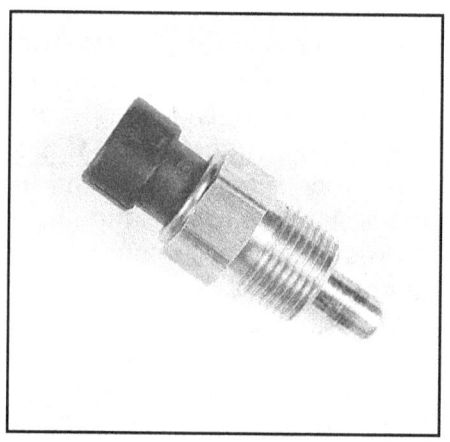

Coolant Temperature Sensor or CTS, monitors engine temperature, usually at the cylinder head. The ECM uses its input to calculate fuel and spark.

Resistance values range from 100,000 ohms at 40° F to 70 ohms at 255° F.

The ECM supplies a voltage (usually five volts) to the CTS and then reads the voltage output from the sensor. The output voltage will vary with a change in the sensor's resistance according to Ohm's Law:

$E = IR$
Where:
E = Voltage
I = Current
R = Resistance

The ECM uses the coolant sensor in most of its functions. The coolant sensor tells the ECM when to add extra fuel. For example, when the engine is cold, extra fuel is needed to aid starting and simulate the choke. Temperature also affects how much fuel is added under load

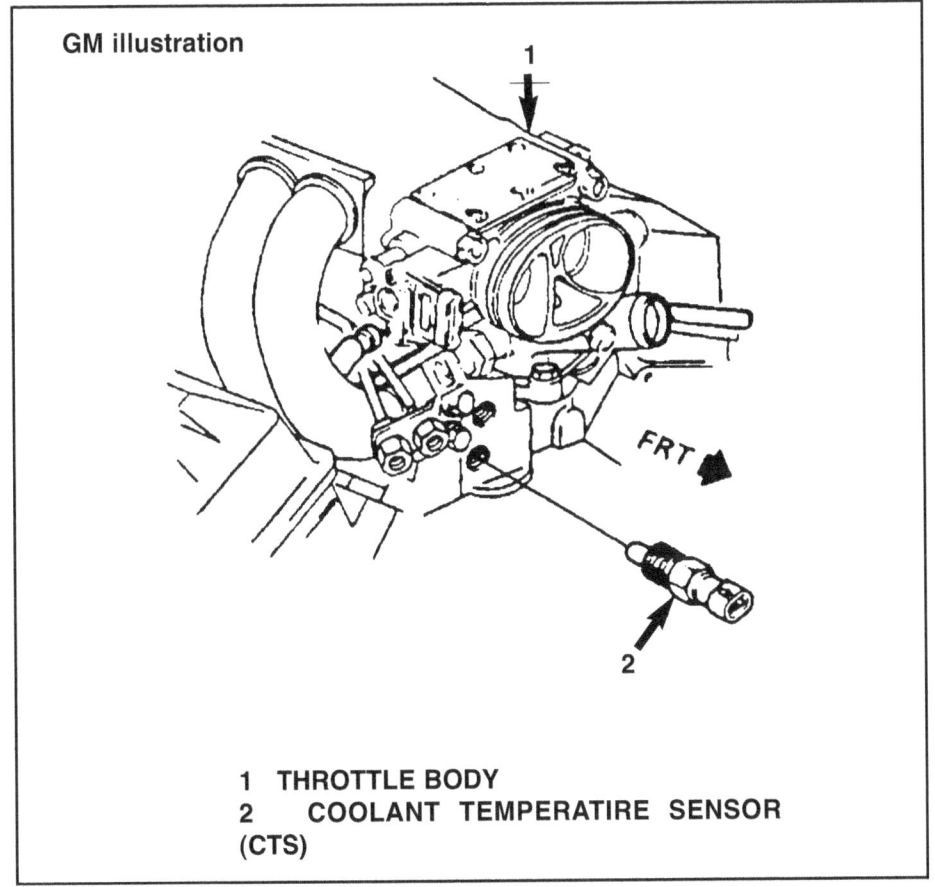

1 THROTTLE BODY
2 COOLANT TEMPERATIRE SENSOR (CTS)

MANIFOLD ABSOLUTE PRESSURE (MAP) SENSOR

MAP sensors are found on cars using the speed density method of calibration. In the absense of actual air flow measurement with a MAF sensor, the computer must rely on a MAP sensor for information about engine loading. The MAP sensor is a pressure transducer that measures changes in intake manifold pressure as a result of engine speed and load. The MAP sensor converts Manifold Absolute Pressure readings to a voltage between zero and five volts. High vacuum conditions (idle) produce a sensor voltage near 0, and low-vacuum wide-open-throttle (WOT) conditions produce a sensor output near five volts.

The MAP sensor reads a percentage of the barometric pressure; that's why it reads high at wide-open throttle and low at idle. A vacuum gauge reads high at idle and low at WOT. A vacuum gauge reads the difference between the barometric pressure and the pressure in the manifold, which is called differential pressure. The engine has its greatest pressure difference between the manifold and atmosphere when the throttle plates are closed. and the least when the throttle is open.

An Absolute Pressure gauge is like a barometer: it would read zero only in an absolute vacuum and the pressure reading is referenced to this point. The MAP sensor also reads the barometric pressure under certain conditions. This allows the computer to correct for different altitudes and radical changes in weather. The ECM supplies a five volt reference to the MAP sensor. The MAP sensor has a bridge circuit that changes its

with power enrichment (power valve). There are temperature corrections for spark advance, open-loop air/fuel ratio, and idle speed. In addition, the coolant temperature sensor tells the ECM when to operate the EGR valve and the carbon canister purge solenoid, when to go closed-loop, and when to turn on the cooling fans.

If a failure occurs in the coolant sensor circuit, a Code 14 or Code 15 will be set in the computers diagnostic memory. (See Trouble Code chapter for specific information on reading and diagnosing trouble codes).

The manifold absolute pressure sensor (MAP) is one of two primary sensors used on speed density controlled engines, the other being the oxygen sensor. The MAP sensor provides the computer with a voltage differential indicating the degree of engine loading.

Chevy TPI Swapper's Guide **31**

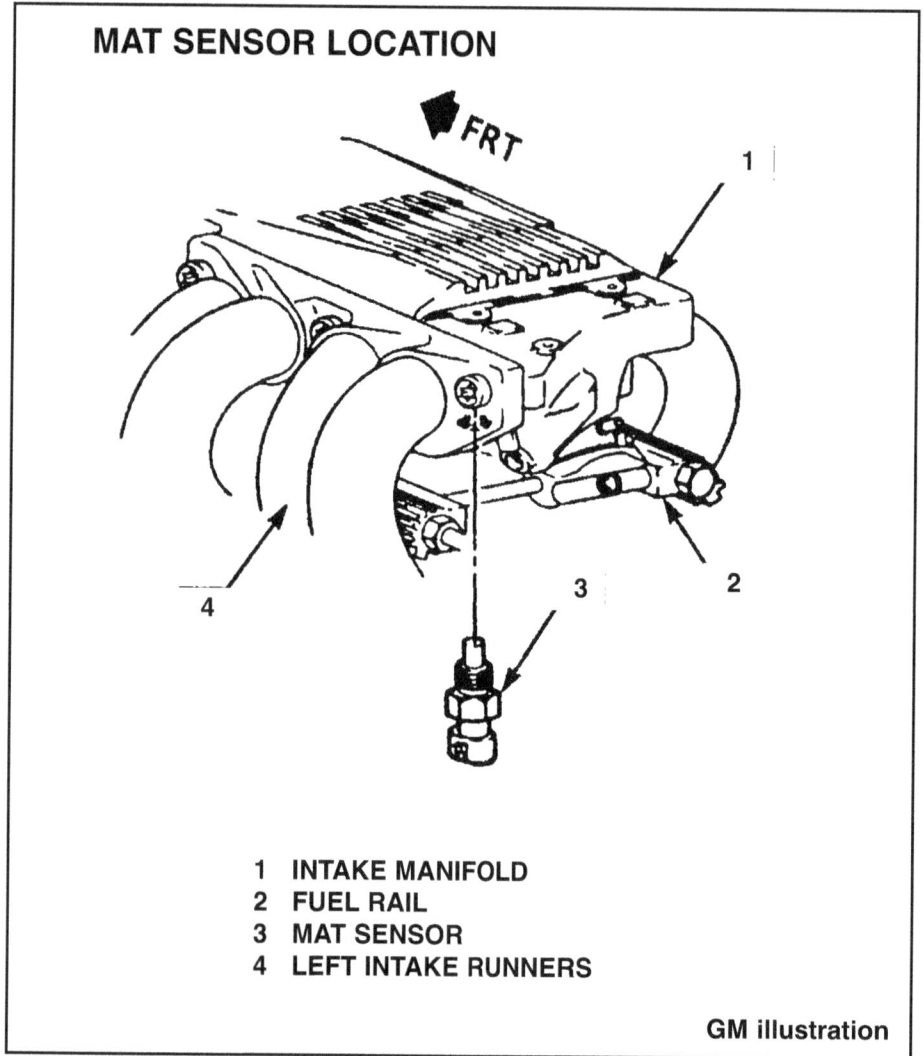

MAT SENSOR LOCATION

1 INTAKE MANIFOLD
2 FUEL RAIL
3 MAT SENSOR
4 LEFT INTAKE RUNNERS

GM illustration

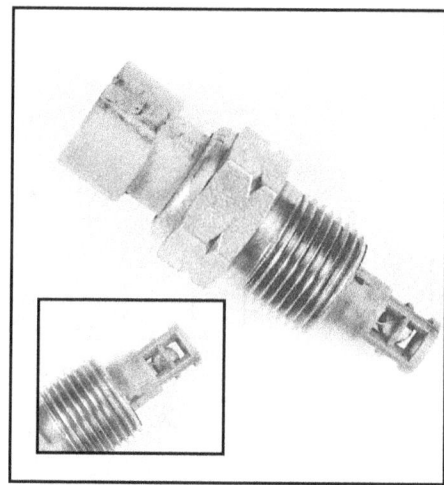

The MAT sensor is installed in the intake air plenum to keep the ECM appraised of changes in inlet air temperature.

electrical resistance with changes in pressure. The sensor returns a voltage signal equal to or less than the reference voltage based on its change in resistance, according to Ohm's Law.

Manifold pressure is an indication of the load placed on an engine. For this reason, the MAP sensor is one of the two most important sensors in the speed density fuel system (the other is the O_2 sensor). All of the ECM's fuel and spark calculations are based on MAP sensor readings.

MANIFOLD AIR TEMPERATURE (MAT) SENSOR

The MAT sensor is similar, if not identical to, the coolant temperature sensor. It is a thermistor and like the CTS, resistance changes as the inverse of temperature changes. It is located in the inlet manifold and is exposed to the incoming air stream.

This sensor supplies the ECM with a voltage signal that is proportioned to the temperatures in the intake manifold. This allows the ECM to correct for changes in air density based on manifold temperatures. For example, when manifold temperature is high, air density is lower and less fuel is required. Conversely, when manifold temperature is low, air density is higher, thus more fuel is required.

MASS AIR FLOW SENSOR (MAF)

The MAF, used only in mass flow fuel systems, takes the place of the MAP sensor in a speed density system, measuring the rate of mass airflow into the engine. This sensor is located between the throttle and the air cleaner.

The MAF is a constant-temperature hot-wire anemometer (an instrument for measuring force, speed, and direction of air). The amount of current necessary to keep a heated wire in the MAS at a constant temperature is proportional to the air flowing across it. A bridge circuit in the sensor produces a voltage output between zero and five volts, which is proportional to airflow. The voltage increases with increased airflow.

In a mass flow fuel system, the MAS measures airflow and uses this value to calculate the appropriate amount of fuel flow and spark advance. Airflow is a measure of load, and for this reason it is used in almost every control decision that the ECM makes.

THE OXYGEN (O_2) SENSOR

The O_2 sensor is mounted in the exhaust manifold or the exhaust system. It is essentially a small variable battery thatt produces a low voltage signal proportioned to the oxygen content of the

32 Chevy TPI Swapper's Guide

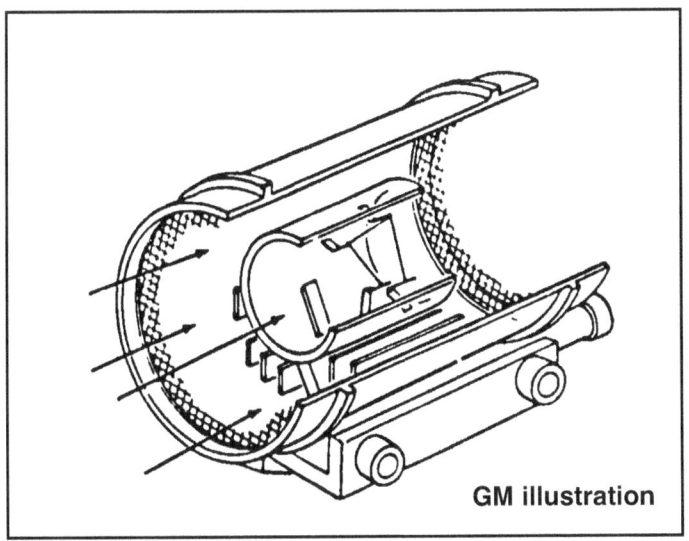

GM illustration

As air enters the MAF, it passes over and cools the hot wire, changing its resistance and requiring additional current flow to maintain the wire's temperature. The current increase is related to the ECM as a voltage signal, and the computer converts it to grams per second of air using pre-programmed information.

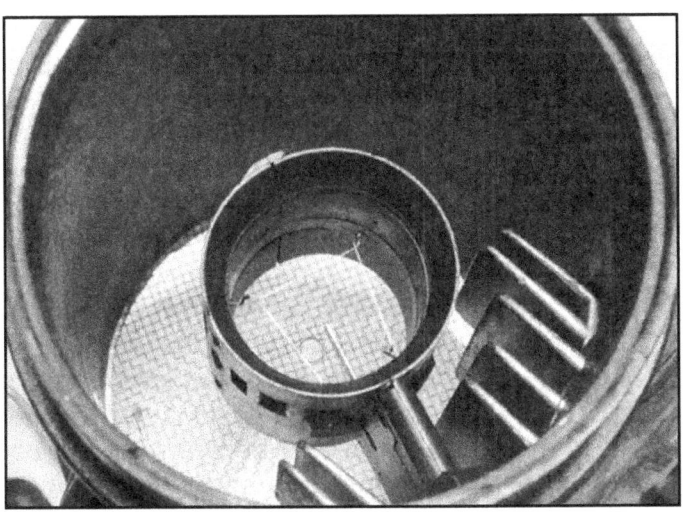

Closeup view shows the very fine, heated wire used to measure the degree of heating or cooling caused by the amount of inlet airflow. Below, a MAF sensor circuit for 5.0L and 5.7L TPI engines.

exhaust. The sensor is constructed with a zirconium/platinum electrolytic element.

The element is a platinum-coated ceramic material. At operating temperature. 600°, the element becomes a semiconductor. The inside of the element is exposed to ambient oxygen as a reference, the outer surface to the engine exhaust. Due to the electrolytic properties of the element, a small voltage is generated that

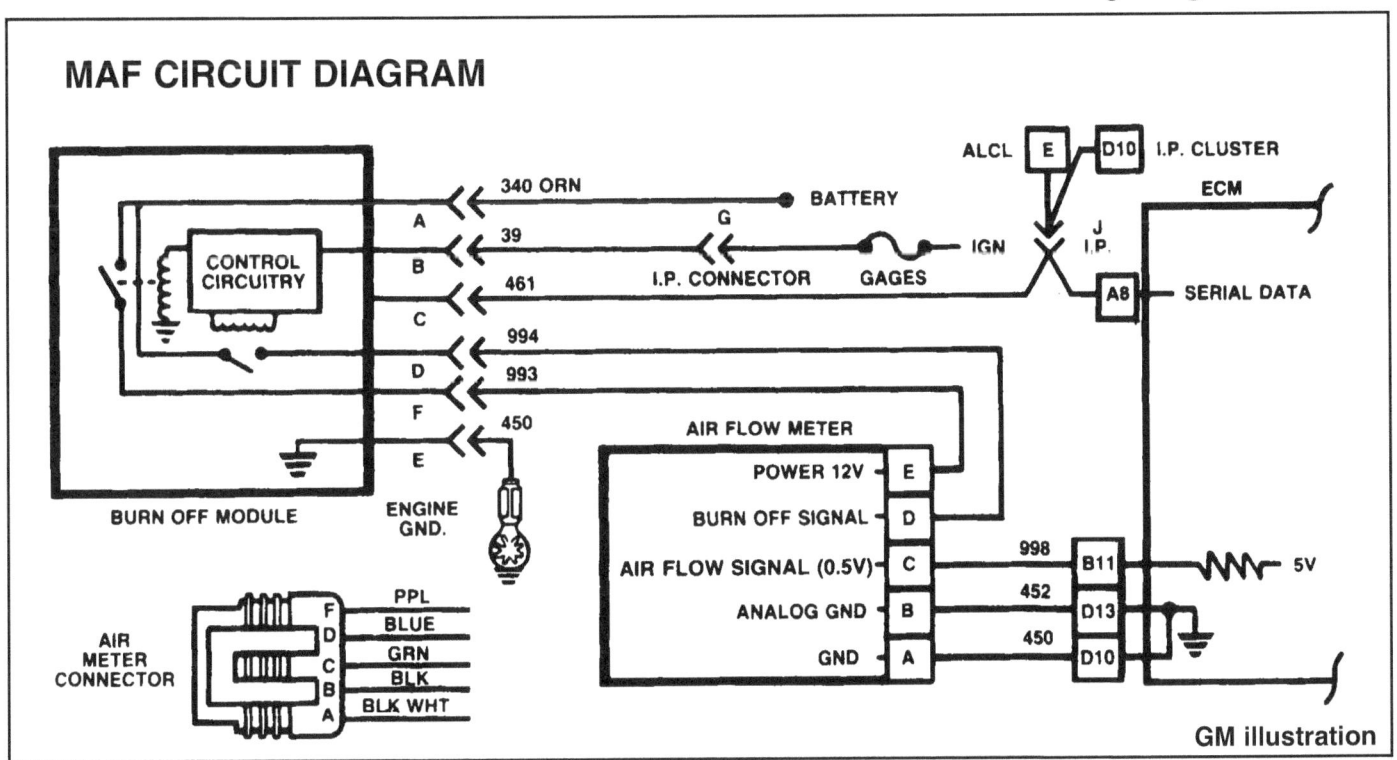

GM illustration

Chevy TPI Swapper's Guide 33

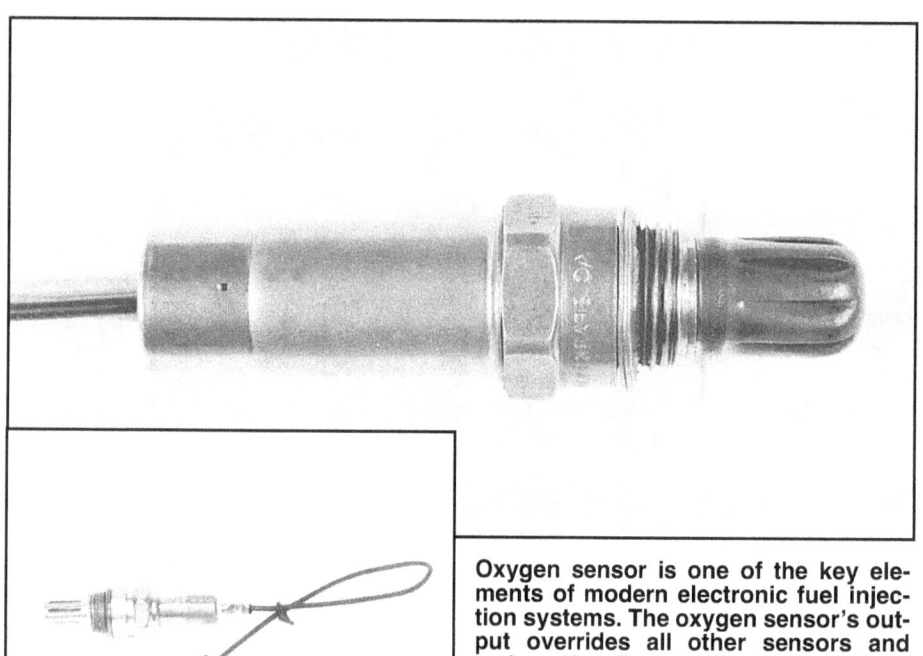

Oxygen sensor is one of the key elements of modern electronic fuel injection systems. The oxygen sensor's output overrides all other sensors and makes the final fuel metering decisions.

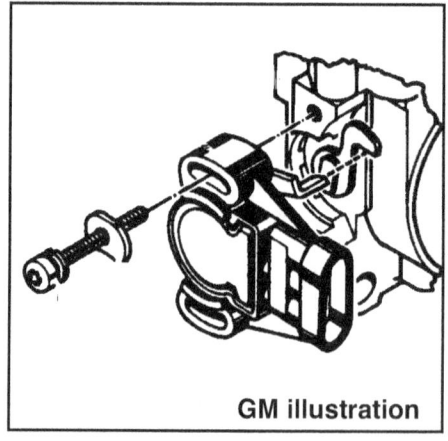

TPS switch engages a tang connedcted to the throttle blades to deliver a direct reading of throttle opening

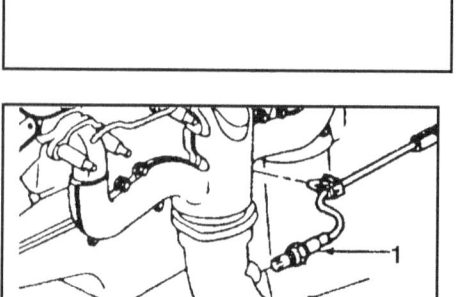

Oxygen sensor must be located as close as possible to the exhaust manifold to ensure quick warm-up for closed-loop operation.

is proportional to the difference between the oxygen content in the exhaust gas and that in the ambient air. A rich mixture has almost no oxygen, which causes the sensor to put out a voltage in excess of 0.5 volt. A lean mixture has some oxygen (approximately 2%) and causes the sensor to output a voltage of less than 0.5 volt.

The voltage output of the sensor is used by the ECM to fine-tune the air/fuel ratio. This fine-tuning is called closed-loop control. The oxygen sensor is the second most important sensor in the fuel system. The corrections from its reading affect all aspects of the fuel system's operation.

THROTTLE POSITION SENSOR (TPS)

The TPS is a potentiometer (an instrument measuring electromotive forces or variable resistance) connected to the throttle shaft. The ECM supplies a five volt reference signal to the TPS—the TPS sends a variable zero to five volt signal back to the ECM. When the throttle is closed the voltage should be near zero; when the throttle is wide open the voltage output of the TPS is near five volts.

The ECM uses the output from the TPS to determine when to add power enrichment (power valve), add acceleration enrichment (pump shot), when to use deceleration fuel shutoff, when to lock and unlock the torque converter clutch, when to

The TPS switch is a potentiometer which returns a variable zero-to-five-volt reference to the ECM to indicate throttle opening. As the arm swings from closed throttle to fully open, the voltage will change from close to zero to nearky five volts.

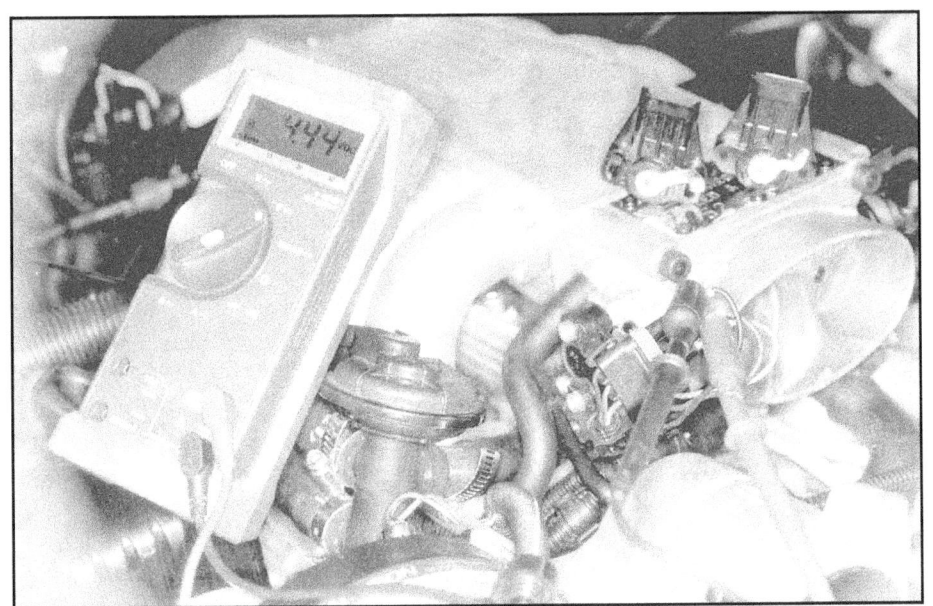

A digital volt meter is used to accurately adjust the TPS switch on the side of the throttle body assembly.

The knock sensor screws into the side of the cylinder block. It is designed to detect the particular type of vibrations that indicate engine knock.

enable or disable the EGR valve, when to allow the carbon canister to purge, and when to turn off the A/C compressor (high load).

VEHICLE SPEED SENSOR (VSS)

The VSS generates a pulse-type output. The VSS rotates a magnet near a coil to generate alternate current (AC) voltage. The magnet is connected to the output shaft of the transmission so that the frequency of the AC signal is proportional to vehicle speed. On speed density-style TPI systems, the ECM processes the VSS signal directly.

The computer uses the VSS in the control process for many functions, including locking and unlocking the torque converter clutch, control of the idle circuit, control of carbon canister purge, and control of mph fuel shut off.

KNOCK SENSOR

The knock sensor, mounted on the engine block, acts like a microphone that is tuned to listen for a specific vibration (sound) which represents spark knock or pre-ignition. The sensor produces an AC signal that increases with the severity of the knock. Thus, this sensor not only detects a knock, but also the severity of the knock. This allows the ECM to retard timing progressively proportional to knock intensity.

REVOLUTIONS PER MINUTE (RPM)

The engine's rpm signal comes directly from the distributor module or from a sensor,

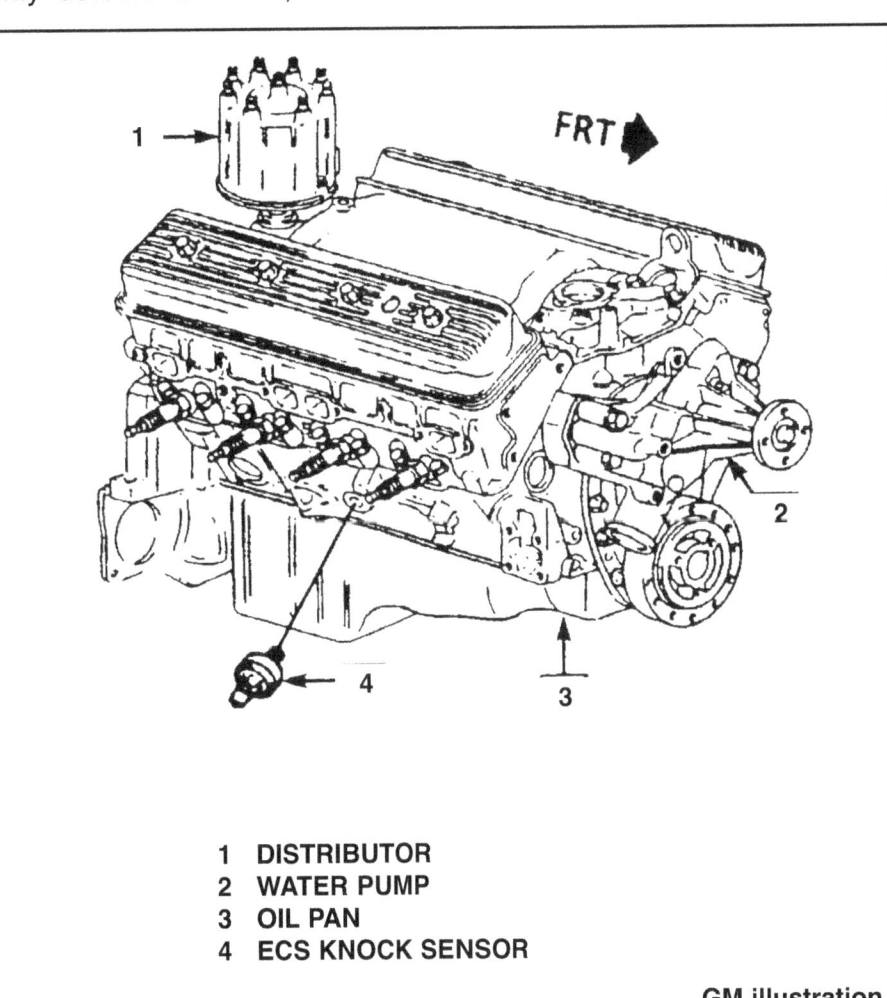

1 DISTRIBUTOR
2 WATER PUMP
3 OIL PAN
4 ECS KNOCK SENSOR

GM illustration

Chevy TPI Swapper's Guide **35**

depending on the type of fuel and ignition system. Engine speed is used by the ECM for just about every operation.

PARK/NEUTRAL POSITION SWITCH

On cars that are equipped with automatic transmissions, a park/neutral position switch is attached to the shift linkage. This unit submits a grounding signal to the ECM whenever the transmission is in park or neutral. It also provides information for the transmission torque converter lockup mode, the idle air control, and the EGR valve. The ECM will operate correctly with a manual transmission PROM if used in an engine swap with an automatic transmission and no park/neutral switch is available. In most cases it is a simple matter to adapt an existing park neutral switch or even fabricate one using the appropriate components and the switch.

If you are doing an engine swap in California, the state requires you to have both a working vehicle speed sensor and a functional Park/Neutral switch. Your vehicle will not be certified without them.

SYSTEM VOLTAGE

The ECM has a built-in voltmeter that measures the system voltage. The ECM must know the system voltage because a change in voltage affects the performance of many of the sensors, most significant, that of the fuel injectors. A calibration table is programmed into the computer's program (on a PROM chip) to compensate for how the injectors' performance changes with a change in voltage.

As shown in the photo above and the illustration below, the idle air control IAC mounts on the bottom of the throttle body and meters air around the throttle blades to control idle speed.

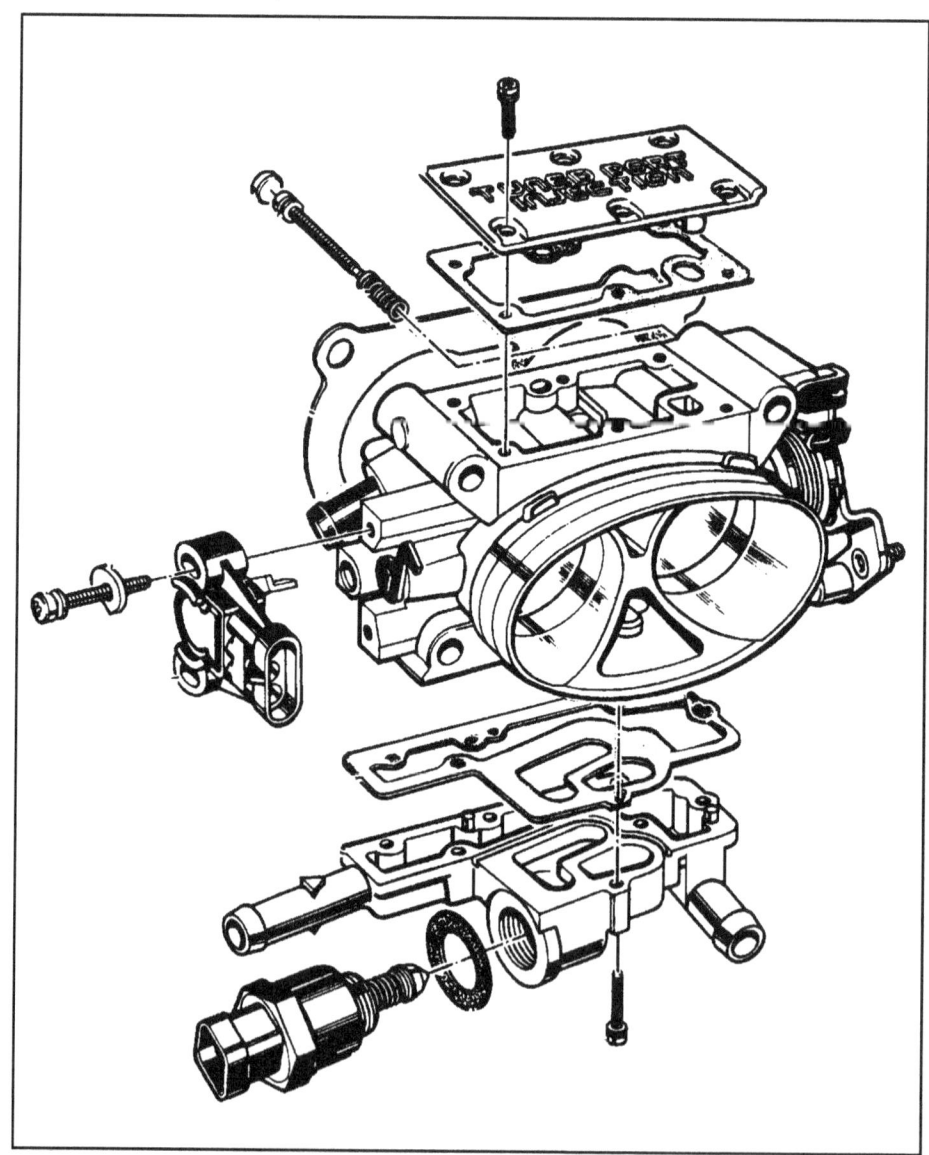

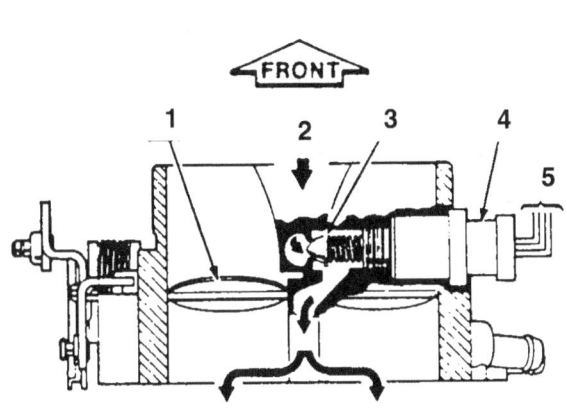

1 THROTTLE VALVE
2 AIR INLET
3 IAC VALVE PINTLE
4 IDLE AIR CONTROL (IAC) VALVE
5 ELECTRICAL INPUT SIGNAL

GM illustration

1 TERMINAL PINS
2 BALL BEARING ASSEMBLY
3 STATOR ASSEMBLY
4 MOTOR ASSEMBLY
5 SPRING
6 PINTLE
7 LEAD SCREW

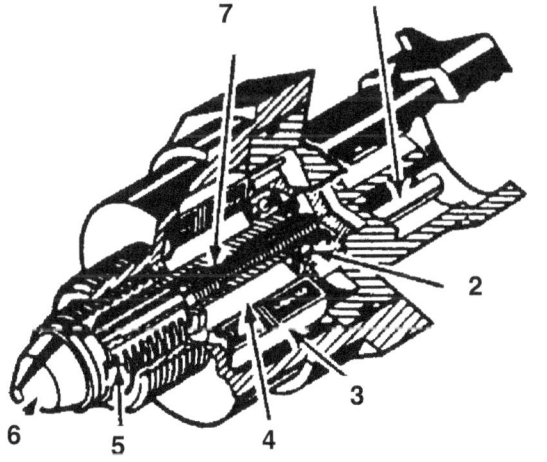

GM illustration

The IAC or idle air control valve mounted in the throttle body is designed to control engine idle speed and prevent stalling due to changes in engine load at start-up. It also provides cold start fast idle during the warmup period. A conical valve called a pintle moves in and out against its seat to control the amount of air being bled past the throttle blades. If RPM is too low, more air is bypassed; if RPM is too high, less air is bypassed. The ECM moves the valve in small steps called counts. Engine idle speed is a function of total airflow calculations based on the IAC valve position, throttle valve opening, PCV flow, and calibrated flow loss to vacuum accessories. If the idle air adjustment is off it can be reset by stopping the engine. Depress the accelerator pedal slightly and start the engine for five seconds, then turn the ignition off for 10 seconds.

OXYGEN SENSOR CONTAMINATION

LEAD
Lead will glaze the sensor making it inaccurate and eventually inoperable. Lead can be introduced by leaded fuel, racing fuel, and some fuel additives.

SILICA
Some RTV silicone gasket sealers emit vapors that will contaminate the oxygen sensor. Tiny sand-like particles in the silicate become imbedded in the surface of the sensor, plugging it up. This causes the sensor to respond slowly or not at all and results in inaccurate or no engine control.

CARBON
Soot deposits or black carbon result from an overrich mixture. Carbon does not harm a sensor and carbon deposits can be burned off by running the engine at a fast idle for two or three minutes or in normal highway driving.

OIL
Oil deposits will eventually plug the sensor and prevent its operation. The sensor will have a dark brown or rust appearance. It is important to maintain good oil control within the engine to prevent oil contamination.

ETHYLENE-GLYCOL
Anti-freeze give the sensor a white pasty appearance and fouls the sensor in the same manner as other contaminants. If anti-freeze is entering the exhaust, you most likely have more serious problems that will require major engine servicing in the near future, if not immediately.

CHEVY TPI Fuel Injection Swapper's Guide
Injector Selection & Tuning

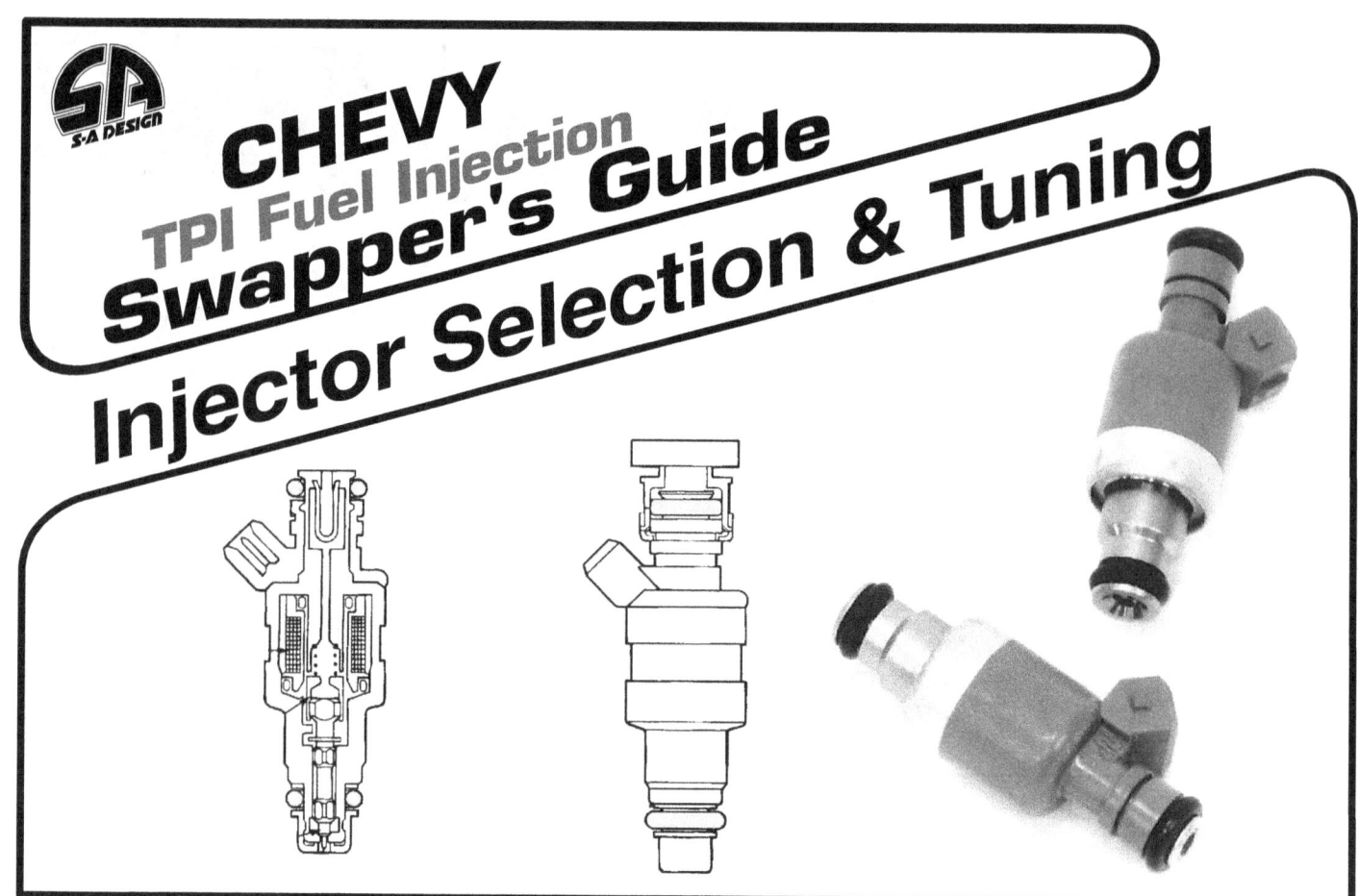

Selecting the correct electronic fuel injector for a high-performance tuned port injected engine is as critical as picking the right cam, carb, or compression ratio. Electronic fuel injectors come in many different types and sizes to meet the varying fuel requirements of most engines. While it may seem complicated at first, matching the proper injector to the engine is ultimately as simple as jet selection, once you know the basics of injector operation. The injector must be capable of flowing enough fuel for optimum power at any given rpm, and it must be compatible with the electronic components of the vehicle's Engine Control Module or ECM. There are two major choices involved when selecting the appropriate electronic fuel injector for a specific application:

1. Injector Flow Rate:

2. Type of Injector: Saturated driver (high impedence) or Peak-and-Hold driver (low impedence).

Electronic fuel injectors must be able to satisfy the fuel needs of an engine at two extremes: wide-open throttle (high fuel flow) and idle (very low fuel flow). The electronic injector is a unique metering device that actually measures fuel flow as it is being delivered. This requires the application of the appropriate-size scale when measuring fuel flow. It would be difficult to measure the length of a house with a micrometer or to measure a thousandth of an inch with a yard stick, yet the typical high-performance fuel injector must be able to measure 24 BSFC/hr. (fuel flow) at the power peak or as little as 0.02 BSFC/hr. at idle.

If an injector is too large for an application, it may not be able to accurately deliver the small amounts of fuel necessary for a smooth, stable idle. If an injector is too small, the engine may suffer from high rpm lean out with disastrous consequences. Clearly, the right injector is critical to the success of an EFI application.

Electronic fuel injectors are not like water faucets that open when flow is desired and remain open until the flow demand is removed. An injector is alternately opened and closed or pulsed according to demand as determined by the ECM and its various sensors. This is typically measured in milliseconds. The electronic pulses that open and close the injector are generated by electrical circuits located in the ECM called drivers.

The percentage of time an injector is open is called the duty cycle. A 20% duty cycle means the injector is open 20% of the time. A 100% duty cycle means the injector is open full time. Electronic fuel injectors are not built to operate at 100% duty cycle except for very short periods of time. When injectors are operated at maximum capacity for any length of time they may overheat, which causes unstable flow and often a permanent shift in the injector's flow rate. Typically, injectors must operate at a maximum duty cycle of 80% to 85%. Overheating an electronically injected engine can also damage the injectors with subsequent loss of power and efficiency.

DETERMINING INJECTOR SIZE REQUIREMENTS

Optimum injector size for a given application is determined by testing the engine on a dyno with a procedure called mapping. The performance of the engine allows you to size the injector accurately based on observed maximum brake horsepower (BHP) and brake specific fuel consumption (BSFC) at peak power. Applying this information to the appropriate formula allows you to size the injector correctly.

$$\frac{(BHP \times BSFC)}{No.\, of\, Injectors \times 0.8} = Injector\, Size$$

The scaler 0.8 adjusts the calculated injector size to produce the fuel necessary for peak power at 80% duty cycle. An accurate BHP figure is critical for proper injector sizing, but not all dynamometers have fuel flow instrumentation, so BSFC is often estimated at approximately 0.45 to 0.50 BSFC/bhphr. for normally aspirated engines.

For example: A V8 engine with a known BSFC of 0.47 makes 425 HP. Applying the formula we derive:

$$\frac{(425 \times 0.47)}{8 \times 0.8} = 31.2\, lbs.\,/\,hr.\, required\, flow$$

You can also calculate the maximum horsepower a given injector size can feed by plugging a known injector size into the formula using either the measured or estimated BSFC.

$$\frac{Flow\, Rate \times No.\, of\, Injectors \times 0.8}{BSFC} = HP$$

or

$$\frac{(50\, lbs.\,/\,hr. \times 8 \times 0.8HP)}{0.47} = 681\, HP$$

Running an engine on a dynamometer to determine its performance statistics isn't practical for most of us so BHP is often estimated by using quarter-mile performance and one of the performance slide rules or "dream wheels." Or if you know the engine's appropriate carburetor size in cfm, the following formula will convert cfm to estimated injector size.

$$\frac{(Carb\, CFM \times 0.44298)}{No.\, of\, Cylinders} = est.\, Injector\, Size$$

This formula only gives an estimated injector size and assumes one injector per cylinder on a normally aspirated engine.

FUEL FLOW VERSUS FUEL PRESSURE

A fuel injector is a precision calibrated orifice. All injectors are rated for flow at a specific fuel pressure, typically 43.5 lbs. 13 bar. Injector flow rate will change if the supply pressure is varied. The equation to convert the static flow of an injector to that of a higher pressure is:

$$Q2 = \sqrt{P2\,/\,P1} \times Q1$$

where: Q2 = New Fuel Flow Rate
Q1 = Original Fuel Flow Rate
P2 = New Fuel Pressure
P1 = Original Fuel Pressure

For example: Calculate the static flow rate of a 24 lbs./hr. injector when the fuel pressure is raised from 32 to 38 psi.

$$26.15 = \sqrt{38\,/\,32} \times 24$$

Higher fuel pressure generally means better fuel atomization, but it also makes the injector work harder when opening. Increasing fuel pressure also slows down an injector's response time. Typical response time is 1.5 to 2.0 milliseconds. When pressure is raised significantly-from 43.5 lbs. 13 bar) to 72.5 lbs. 15 bar), the injectors may have to work so hard that their useful life is drastically shortened. Generally it is safe to raise the fuel flow pressure no more than 10%-15%. Raising the fuel pressure of a stock injection system changes the specific fuel flow calibration of the injector. The computer bases all its calculations on the known calibration of the injector. When the calibration changes due to an increase in fuel pressure, the computer cannot know this without a calibration change (PROM change). Since the injector's flow rate changes, all the computer's original calculations are in error and the fuel curve will experience a shift that may be harmful across most of the engine's operating range. On a turbocharged engine with a linear pressure regulator, extra high pressure exists under boost conditions where fuel pressure rises in proportion to boost. This situation is different from trying to run a normally aspirated engine with the idle pressure cranked up to 50-plus psi. Don't do it.

INJECTOR COMPATIBILITY

In addition to selecting the correct injector size. tile chosen injector must~ be electronically compatible with the computer which controls it. There are two kinds of injector control circuits (drivers):

1. Saturated (high impedence or voltage mode-type}

2. Peak-and-Hold (low impedence or current mode type)

Depending on the type of driver, an injector is referred to as either a saturated injector or a peak-and-hold injector. Saturated injectors have a higher electrical resistance (22 to16 ohms) than peak-and-hold injectors (2-5 ohms). An injector's resistance may be measured with an ohmmeter across its two terminals. Resistance dictates the compatibility of injectors and ECM drivers.

Most U.S. passenger cars use a 12-volt saturated injector that uses 12 volts to open and close the injectors. These are high-resistance injectors that maintain low current flow in the injectors and drivers to keep them cool and promote longer life. Saturated circuits generally have slightly slower response time that limits their operating range.

Peak-and-hold injectors are more exotic and have a greater dynamic range, but require more amperage to operate. It is very important not to replace a saturated injector with a peak-and-hold injector because

TUNED PORT Fuel Injection Tips & Tricks

CALCULATING INJECTOR SIZE QUICK SUMMARY

HOW TO CALCULATE THE PROPER SIZE INJECTOR FOR YOUR COMBINATION

An injector consists of a solenoid that moves an internal plunger when the magnetic windings are energized by the application of voltage. A sized orifice is opened when the plunger is activated, allowing pressurized fuel to flow through the created opening. The critical element is the injector's ability to maintain linear fuel flow from very narrow pulse widths to very wide pulse widths, so that the dynamic range of fuel delivery remains accurate for any given rpm and load requirement. The injector's metering orifice is designed to spray the fuel in a cone-shaped pattern of 15 to 30 degrees F for optimum fuel atomization.

Fuel flow is controlled by varying the pulse width or duty cycle of the injectors. Pulse width is the time in milliseconds that the injector is open, while duty cycle is the injector's overall percentage of open time. A 70 percent duty cycle means that the injector is open 70% of the injector's maximum cycling time.

Ultimately, to find the optimum injector size for a given application you have to test it. You can map it out on a dyno, sizing the injector based on observed maximum brake horsepower (BHP) and brake specific fuel consumption (BSFC) at peak power. You can also use a wide band oxygen sensor that tells you the air/fuel ratio at the load points you're tuning for. The following formulas will get you close to the correct size injector for wide open throttle performance.

$$\frac{(BHP \times BSFC)}{No.\ of\ Injectors \times 0.8} = Injector\ Size\ (Flow\ Rate)$$

The scaler 0.8 adjusts the calculated injector size to produce the fuel necessary for peak power at 80% duty cycle. An accurate BHP figure is critical for proper injector sizing, but not all dynamometers have fuel flow instrumentation, so BSFC is often estimated at approximately 0.5 lbs./BHP/hr. for normally aspirated engines.

For example, look at a 350 engine with a known BSFC of 0.49 making 350 horsepower. Applying the formula we derive:

$$\frac{350 \times 0.49}{8 \times 0.8} = 17.15\ lbs.\,/\,hr.\ (required\ injector\ flow\ rate)$$

You can also calculate the maximum horsepower a given injector size can feed by plugging a known injector size into the formula using either the measured or estimated BSFC.

$$\frac{Flow\ Rate \times No.\ of\ Injectors \times 0.8}{BSFC} = HP$$

$$or\ \frac{50\ lbs./hr. \times 8 \times 0.8}{0.49} = 653.06\ HP$$

Running an engine on a dynamometer to determine its performance statistics isn't practical for most of us, so BHP is often estimated by using quarter-mile performance and one of the performance slide rules or "dream wheels." Or you can calculate the cfm flow of the engine using assumptions about volumetric efficiency.

Then use the following formula to convert cfm to estimated injector size.

$$\frac{CFM \times 0.44298}{No.\ of\ Cylinders} = Estimated\ Injector\ Size$$

This formula only gives an estimated injector size and assumes one injector per cylinder on a normally aspirated engine.

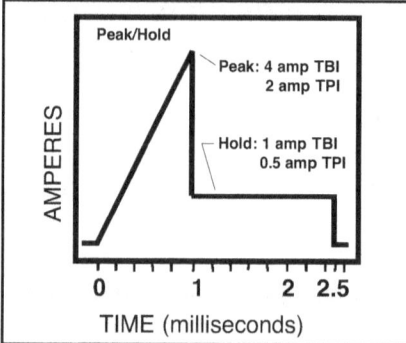

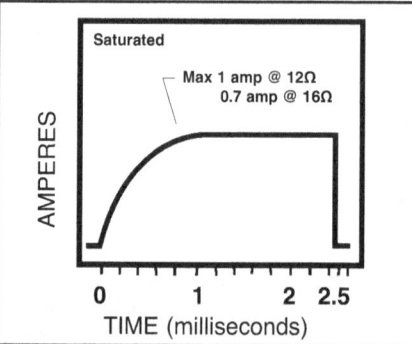

Compare the typical current levels and response curves for saturated injectors and peak-and-hold injectors above. Peak-and-hold injectors use a large surge of current to kick the injector off its seat, and then maintain the minimum amount of current required to hold the injector open. Saturated injectors use less current and a slower response time to ensure greater durability.

Pintle type (left) uses a small orifice with a pulsed pintle. Multec type has a ball-and-seat inside with a special director plate to gain a better spray pattern.

the additional amperage required to operate the peak-and-hold injector can destroy the ECM's drivers. The higher (peak) current level generates more force for opening the injector and the lower (hold) current improves closing response by reducing the hold force. It is possible to replace a peak-and-hold injector with a saturated injector since the amperage required to operate a saturated injector is lower and within the range of the peak-and-hold injector's drivers.

Most racing injection systems use a peak-and-hold injector. These low-resistance drivers are also known as current limiting. Twelve volts are still delivered to the injector, but because the resistance is low, current in the driver circuit is high. The peak current is used to kick the injector off its seat quickly, then the lower current holds it open until the ECM closes it. There are two basic drivers for peak-and-hold systems: 4 amp peak/1 amp hold, and 2 amp peak/0.5 amp hold. Although this type of driver is rated up to 5 amps, it will not draw that amount. A lower current limit is deliberately set to protect the circuitry.

Use Ohm'sLaw to determine the current in a given injector and driver. Ohm's law states that current is equal to voltage divided by the resistance in ohms:

If I=E+R then E=IxR
where: E=Voltage
I=Current (amps)
R=Resistance (ohms)

A saturated 12-volt injector with a resistance of 12 ohms has a current of 1 amp to keep the circuit cool. A peak-and-hold injector with 2 ohms resistance and 12 volts supplied will draw a current of 6 amps. This much current creates considerable heat, making peak-and-hold injectors more vulnerable. However, this current is precisely what allows the racing fuel system to flow large amounts of fuel and still have exceptional response.

BALANCING INJECTOR FLOW FOR MAXIMUM PERFORMANCE

Having a balanced set of injectors in your engine combination does two things. First, it lets you know the actual fuel flow to the individual cylinders. Second, it ensures that each cylinder is getting the same amount of fuel as the others, assuming the rail pressure is the same at each injector. When you start super-tuning your tuned port injection system both of these parameters are critical.

MSD RACING INJECTORS

PN	Injector Resistance (ohms)	Driver Type	Fuel Flow
2012	2.0	2/0.5 peak & hold	34 lbs./hr. @ 43.5 psi
2013	12.0	12v saturated	50 lbs./hr. @ 43.5 psi
2014	2.0	4/1 peak & hold	72 lbs./hr. @ 43.5 psi
2015	2.0	4/1 peak & hold	96 lbs./hr. @ 43.5 psi
2018	12.0	012v saturated	38 lbs./hr. @ 43.5 psi

Because it takes a certain amount of fuel to support a certain amount of horsepower, you have to know the total fuel flow capacity of your injectors. Brake Specific Fuel Consumption is a value derived by dividing the amount of fuel an engine consumes by the horsepower it is generating. BSFC = fuel lbs./hr./horsepower. Modern, efficient, normally aspirated engines, such as the tuned port Chevy, usually have a BSFC of .50 or slightly less at the torque peak. So as you saw in the section on fuel-injection basics, you can use this fuel-consumption-to-horsepower ratio to determine how much fuel you'll need from your injectors to support a certain amount of horsepower.

The second issue—ensuring that each cylinder receives the same amount of fuel—is important when trying to get every last bit of power from your engine. If an engine has uneven distribution of the air/fuel mixture between cylinders, the leaner cylinders are more prone to detonate. As a result, you or the computer has to, retard the timing for the mixture of the leanest cylinder. This most often occurs on carbureted cars, but it also happens to fuel-injected cars if the injectors get clogged or if they just weren't built right at the factory. Basically, if one cylinder is down on power, the rest of the cylinders

INJECTOR DUTY CYCLE: WHAT IS IT?

We stated earlier that fuel flow is controlled by varying the pulse width or duty cycle of the injectors. Pulse width is the time in milliseconds that the injector is open, while duty cycle is the injector's overall percentage of open time. A 70 percent duty cycle means that the injector is open 70 percent of the injector's maximum cycling time. Great. But what does maximum cycling time mean?

You could call it the injector's redline. Maximum cycling time is how quickly the injector can open, fire a pulse of fuel, close and be ready to open and fire another pulse of fuel. The limiting factor here is the injector's response time. As we said earlier typical response times are in the .0015- to .002-second range. In order for an injector to fire every .010 second, i.e., every 10 milliseconds, the duty cycle, which is the actual pulse width of the injector, can only be .008 or .0085 second, i.e., 8.0 or 8.5 milliseconds, depending on the response time of the injector. (Some injectors have quicker response times, making them more useful for high-performance applications). This is the reasoning behind using a scale factor when you calculate fuel injector sizes for your engine combination.

This whole injector sizing thing gets a little misleading at this point, probably because it's easy to assume that .010 second is all the time an injector can hang open. It isn't. If it were, you wouldn't be able to get the raw flow number in lb./hr. from a flow bench. In these tests, the injector is simply locked open, and stays open, as long as the computer tells it to. Of course, we run into the question of whether the computer and injector drivers on the fuel management system are up to the task, but that is a different question. (For more information on this subject, see the sidebar Calculating Injector Size.)

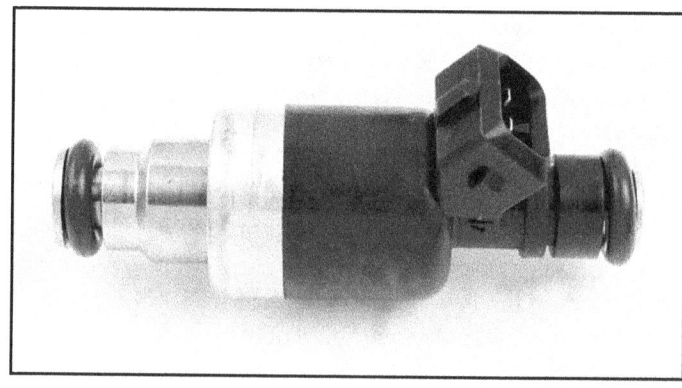
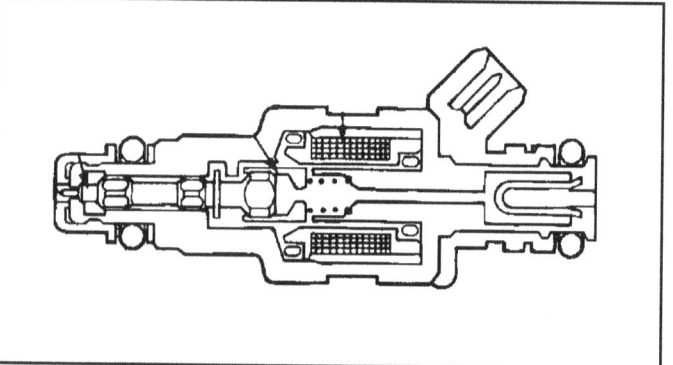
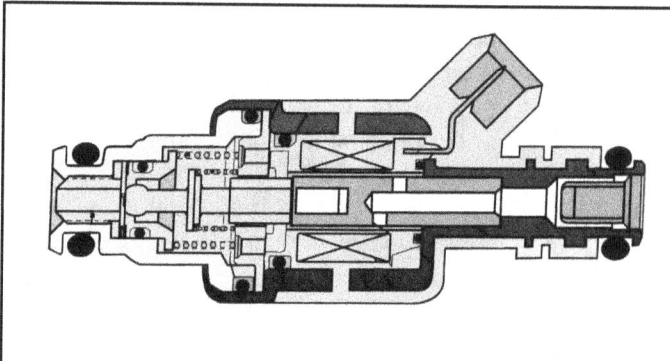

Original TPI injectors were the pintle type where fuel is metered by moving a small pintle in and out of a sized orifice. Both 305 and 350 engines used 12v saturated injectors with 16 ohms of resistance. The 5.0L injector delivers 19 lbs./hr. at 36 psi and the 5.7L injector delivers 22 lbs./hr. at 43.5 psi.

GM Multec injector, built by Rochester Products, uses a stainless steel ball-and-seat valve with a director plate that delivers a more precise spray pattern while remaining less sensitive to poor fuel qualities that cause clogging. These are the same types of injectors offered by MSD for high-performance applications.

TUNED PORT Fuel Injection Tips & Tricks

WHEN YOU NEED A LARGER INJECTOR

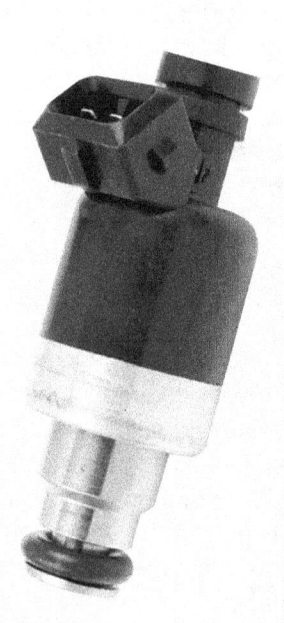

If your TPI engine has been extensively modified, larger injectors will be required to ensure adequate fuel delivery. However, upgrading to a larger injector to meet horsepower requirements also requires recalibration of the ECM. Since the ECM is programmed with information about the original injectors, its calculations will be in error when controlling larger injectors. While it is easier and more cost effective to raise the fuel pressure, this is a mistake. Many tuners try this, but keep in mind that raising the fuel pressure more than 15% will usually skew the fuel curve enough to harm performance unless a calibration change is made.

Before aftermarket companies began offering specific injectors for performance applications, enthusiast tried to swap injectors from other performance applications such as Ford Thunderbird Turbo Coupes and injected 5.0L Mustangs. But these injectors are incompatible with the stock GM injector drivers and problems occurred with idle and high-speed operation. Now it is possible to closely match the injector to your requirements. For a substantial power increase, you can substitute and 38 lb. MSD saturated injector which has the same current draw and up to 40% more available fuel flow. This injector would still require a calibration change, but it is fully compatible with you existing hardware.

Keep in mind that even with a compatible injector, bigger is not always better. Higher flowing injectors without a calibration change will rarely yield a performance gain, and may even net a performance loss. Under closed loop control, the computer will try to compensate for the greater fuel deliver during each injector pulse. It does this by decreasing the injector on-time to reduce the amount of fuel being delivered. Generally, the ECU will probably be able to control the injector efficiently if the injector flow rate is no more than 10 to 20 percent greater than stock. Beyond this, you need a calibration change or even a different ECM to avoid excessive unburned hydrocarbons, and possible catalytic converter damage.

are brought to that level by the computer retarding timing. In this situation, you're losing a lot more power than you should.

Several types of injector dynos or test benches are available for evaluating and correcting fuel injector flow rates and spray patterns, They allow the operator to observe the behavior of an injector under different fuel pressures, duty cycles, pulse widths and frequencies. You can learn some interesting things about injector performance and selection.

For example; at 85 percent duty cycle many injectors freeze in between opening and closing; they sort of flutter and reduce fuel flow by half. This is really good information to have if you're pushing your combination right to the limit. If you step over it and get to the point where the injectors flutter, you can lean out and get into detonation right at the worst possible time—full throttle, high r.p.m.

MSD INJECTOR SELECTOR COMPUTER SOFTWARE

MSD Competition fuel injectors are individually balanced to a wide open static flow rate of 1.5-3%. Race engines need this kind of precision, but MSD even applies this standard to its stock replacement 5.0L (PN 2016) and 5.7L (PN 2017) injectors.

MSD's PC software program makes easy work of selecting the proper injector for your application. It allows you to enter 12 basic engine parameters that the program will evaluate and suggest the appropriate injector. The software needs to know the following information to properly select an injector.

- Displacement
- Max RPM
- Turbo/Supercharger, yes or no
- Boost pressure
- Compressor efficiency
- Intercooler efficiency
- Intercooling temperature
- Inlet air temperature
- Number of injectors
- Estimated volumetric efficiency
- Air fuel ratio
- Brake Specific (BSFC)

FUEL INJECTION FORMULAS

The following formulas are useful for determining injector size requirements for a given horsepower rating.

LBS./HR. @ FUEL PRESSURE

$$F_2 = \left(\frac{P_2}{F_1}\right) 0.5 \times P_1$$

where:
F_2 = New Fuel Flow Rate
F_1 = Original Fuel Flow Rate
P_2 = New Fuel Pressure
P_1 = Original Fuel Pressure

Example: $\left(\dfrac{40\ psi}{24\ lbs/hr}\right) 0.5 \times 30\ psi = 25\ lbs/hr$

INJECTOR SIZE @ HORSEPOWER (Assumes 80% duty cycle)

$$\frac{BHP \times BSFC}{No.\ of\ Injectors \times 0.8} = lbs/hr$$

HP INJECTOR SIZE SUPPORTS (Assumes 80% duty cycle)

$$\frac{Flow\ Rate \times No.\ of\ Injectors \times 0.8}{BSFC} = HP$$

ESTIMATED INJECTOR SIZE
(Assumes one injector per cylinder; normally aspirated)

$$\frac{CFM \times 0.44298}{No.\ of\ Cylinders} = Estimated\ Injector\ Size$$

OEM INJECTOR IDENTIFICATION

Year	CID	OE Mfg.	OE Mfg. Part No.	GM P/N	Lucas Service P/N
1985	305	AC	5235047	17110872	5207002
1985 - 86	305	Bosch	0280150222	17110872	5207002
1985 - 86	305	Lucas	5720D570	10077513	5207002
1985 - 86	350	Lucas	5720D810	10077514	5207011
1985 - 88	305	Lucas	5720D780	10108480	5207002
1985 - 88	350	Lucas	5720D810	10108481	5207011
1986	350	AC	5235211	17111418	5207011
1987 - 88	305	AC	5235301	17111960	5207002
1987 - 88	350	AC	5235302	17111961	5207011
1989	305	AC	5235434	17112092	5207002
1989	305	AC	5235435	17112093	5207002
1989	350	AC	5235436	17112094	5207011
1989	350	AC	5235437	17112095	5207011

TPI FUEL RAIL SELECTION GUIDE

Year	ID No.	Body	Engine Size	Injector Type
1985-87	17085052	F	5.0L	Bosch
1985-87	17087264	F	5.0L	Multec
1989	17089024	F	5.0L	Rochester
1990-91	17090100	F	5.0L	Rochester
1985	17085050	Y	5.7L	Bosch
1986-87	17085019	Y, F	5.7L	Bosch
1986-87	17086106	Y, F	5.7L	Bosch
1987-88	17087265	Y, F	5.7L	Bosch
1987	17087266	Y, F	5.7L	Multec
1988	17088065	Y, F	5.7L	Multec
1989	17089025	Y, F	5.7L	Multec
1989	17089026	Y, F	5.7L	Rochester
1990-91	17080101	Y, F	5.7L	Rochester
1990-91	17080102	Y, F	5.7L	Rochester

F = Camaro/Firebird
Y = Corvette

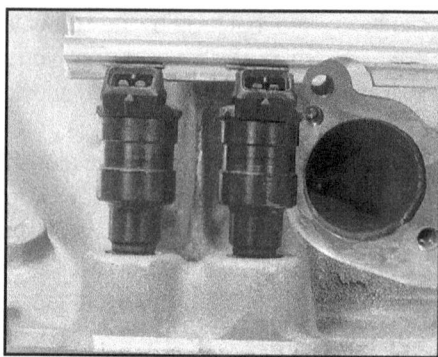

Injectors are held in place by the fuel rail which is screwed securely to the intake manifold. An O-ring at the top and bottom of the injector seals it to the fuel rail and intake manifold.

Bottom view shows injector tips peeking through into each intake port. Slots are milled in the port to keep the spray pattern directed toward the back of the valve and into the primary air flow to ensure good atomization. Note spray pattern diagram below.

Enter the parameters and the program calculates the values and recommends the appropriate injector for your application. MSD's software includes on-line help functions and calculates in U.S. or metric units. It requires an IBM™ PC/XT/AT or equivalent computer, a monitor with CGA/EGA/VGA or Hercules graphics, and 256K RAM. It is available in both 3.5 and 5.25-inch floppy disks.

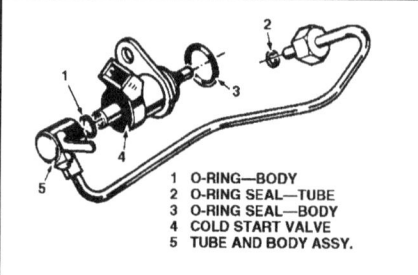

1 O-RING—BODY
2 O-RING SEAL—TUBE
3 O-RING SEAL—BODY
4 COLD START VALVE
5 TUBE AND BODY ASSY.

Cold-start valve at left is used to provide start-up enrichment on TPI equipped engines through 1988.

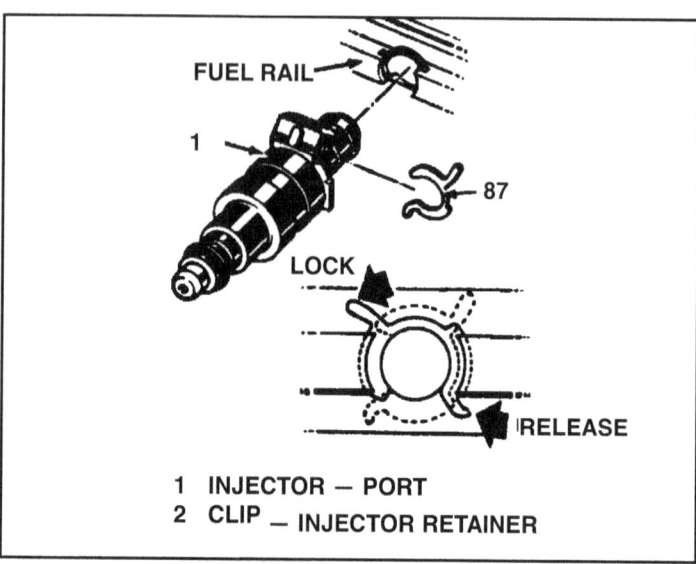

Each injector is locked into the fuel rail with these small locking tabs. Simply flip them over to unlock the injector for removal.

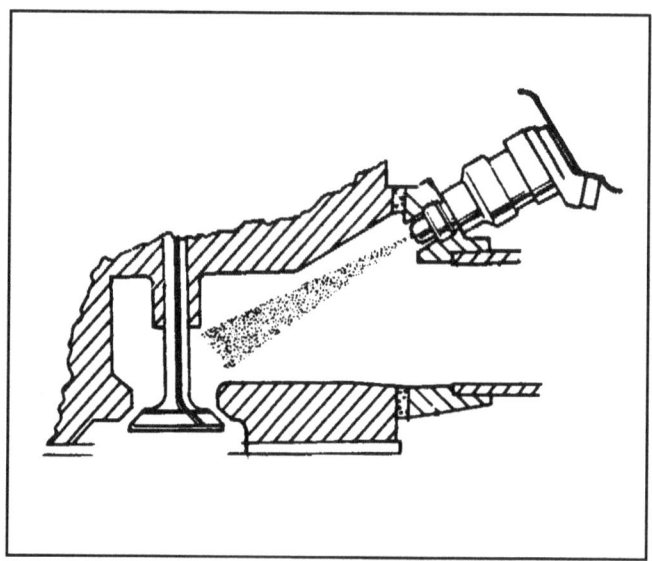

This illustration shows how the injector is aimed at the back of the valve for optimum atomization.

Chevy TPI Swapper's Guide

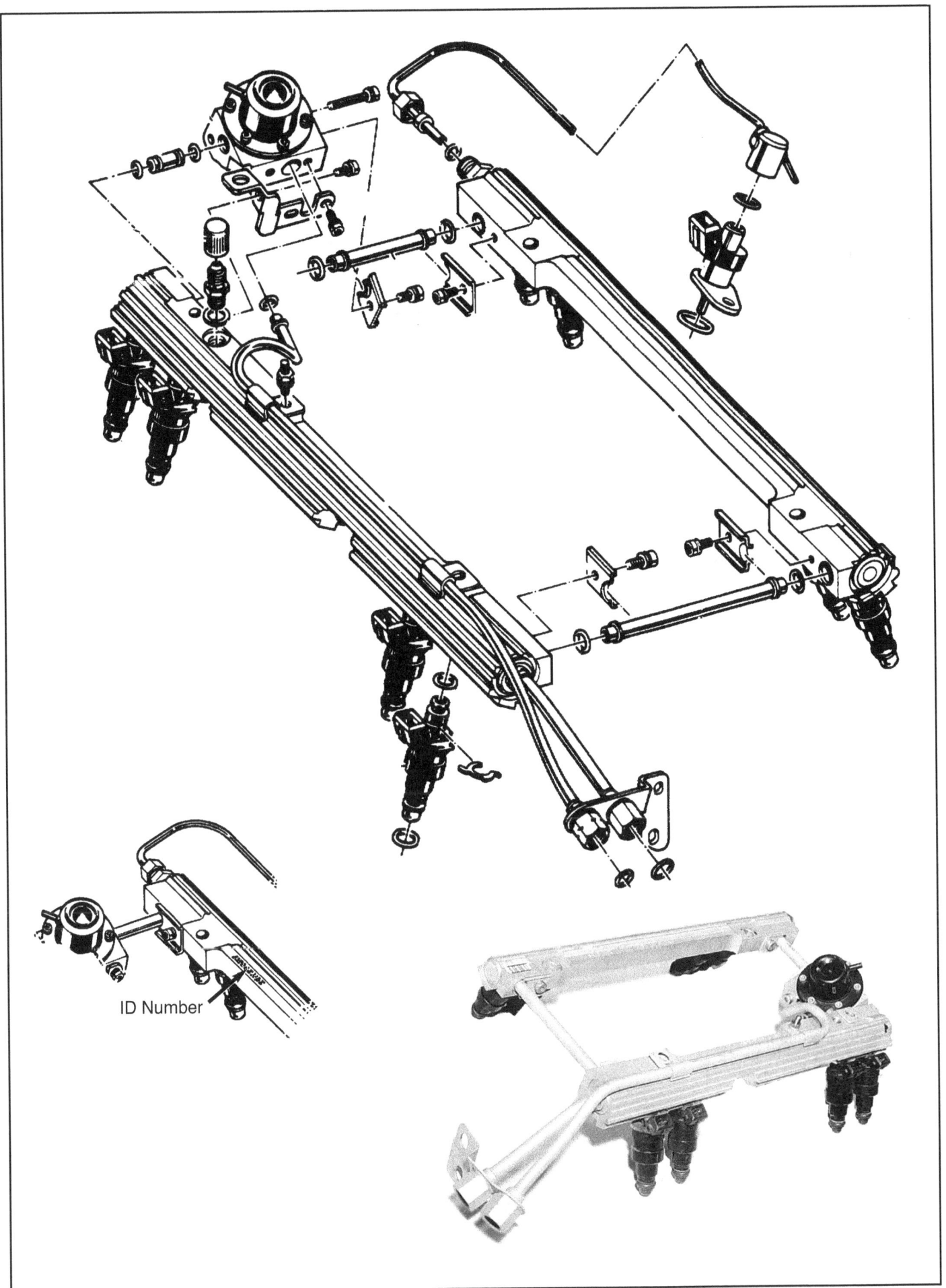

ID Number

Chevy TPI Swapper's Guide

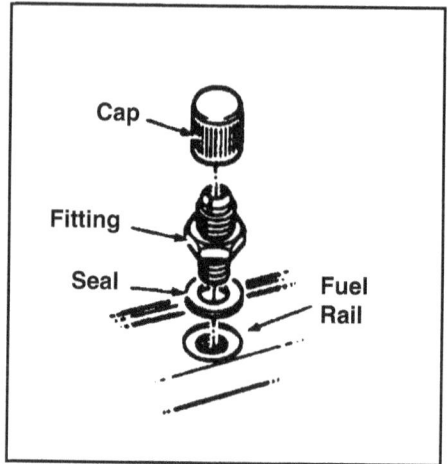

Fuel pressure test port is used to check rail pressure and bleed the system for maintenance.

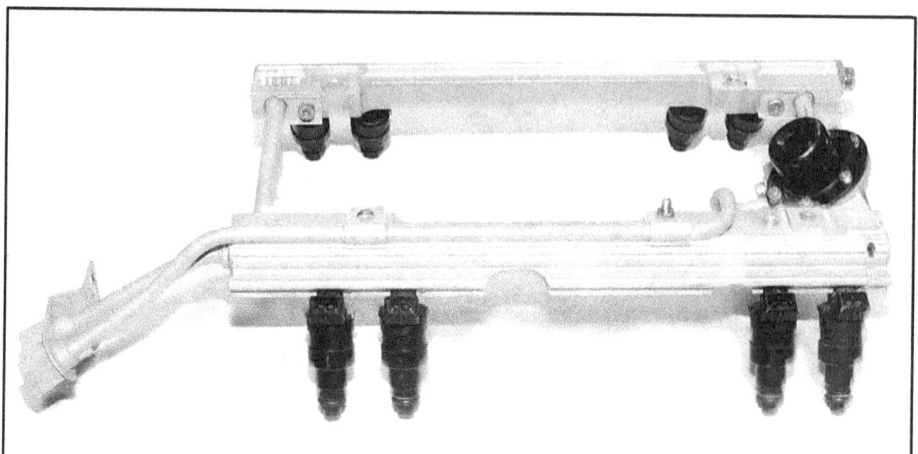

One reason for purchasing MSD injectors and accessories is the fact that they are full compatible components, both with the factory system and other MSD pieces. Injectors are balanced and tested to ensure equal flow rates. Moreover, MSD is also a reliable source for all the specialized sensors and small hardware components required to make a tuned port injection system operate smoothly and efficiently in your car.

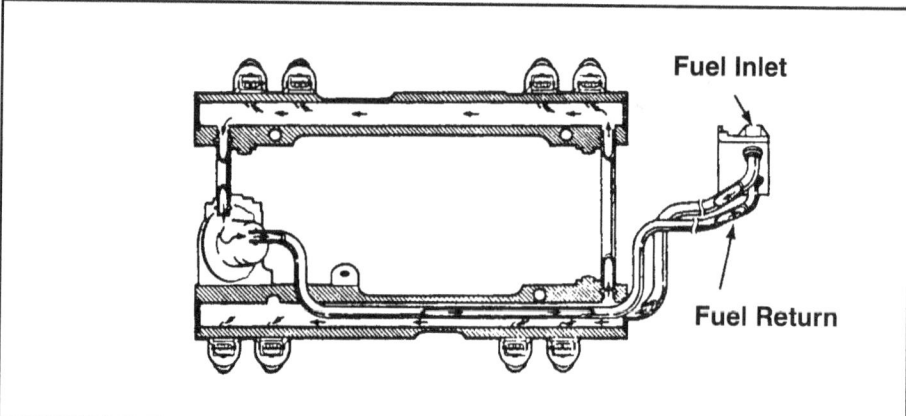

Fuel flow through the fuel rail shows how the rail is pressurized to all injectors. When each bank of injectors is energized, fuel is dispersed to those cylinders.

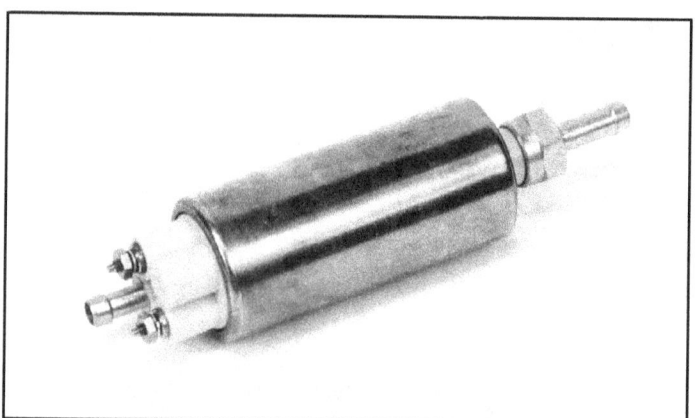

MSD high-volume fuel pump and fuel regulator are designed to deliver adequate fuel flow for modified applications where additional fuel volume may be required for maximum performance.

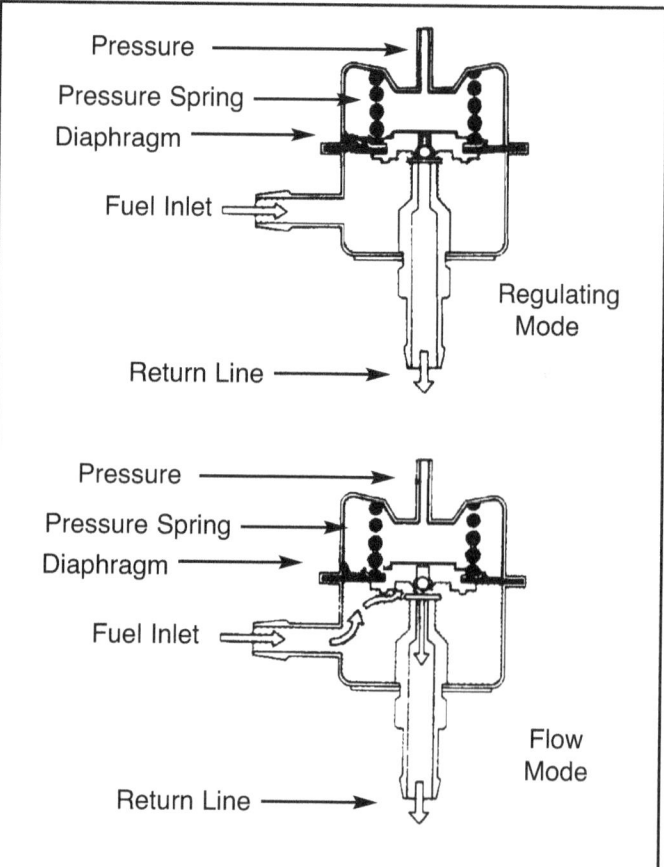

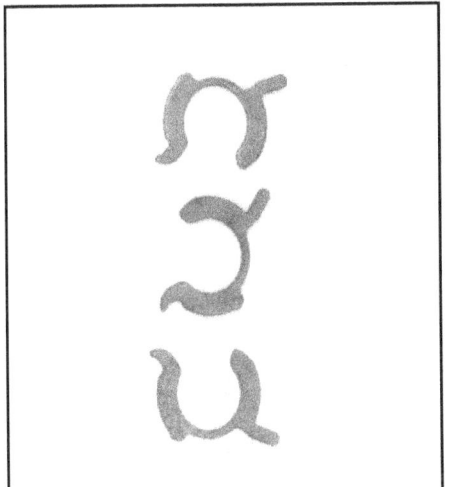

MSD also offers replacement injector retaining locks for fuel rails that have been damaged or pirated.

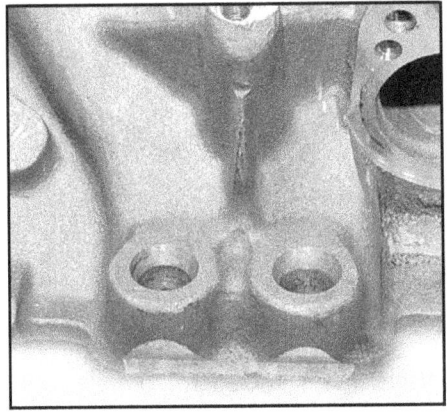

MSD injectors have the appropriate O-rings to seal properly in the intake manifold injector mount holes.

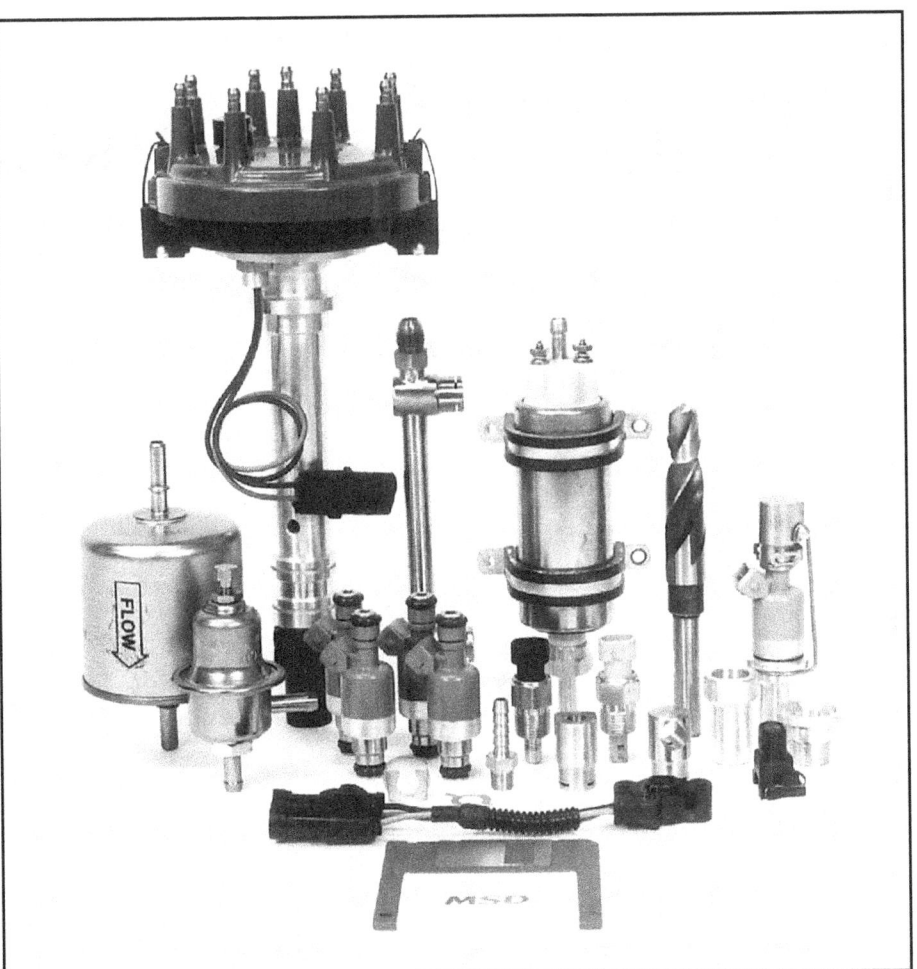

MSD Fuel Management systems offer everything you're likely to need to upgrade and tune your TPI-equipped vehicle. Fully compatible fuel pumps, fuel filters, harnesses, injectors, distributors, and hardware are all available to TPI tweakers and tuners. MSD Injector Selector computer software also is available to help you select the perfect injector for your application.

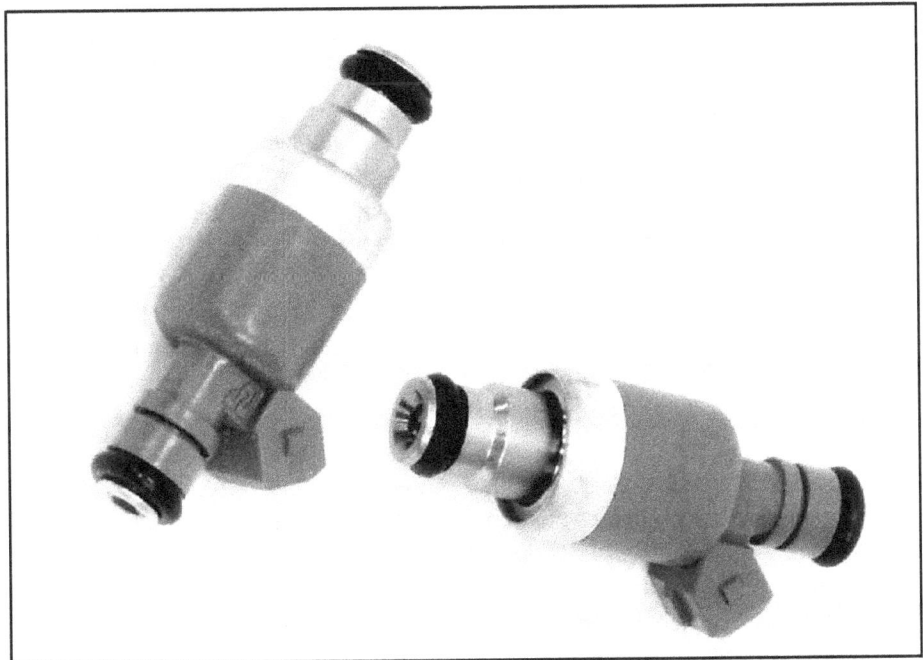

MSD Competition Fuel Injectors are available in flow rates to power high-performance racing engines from 250 to 1300 horsepower (V8). Manufactured by AC/Rochester, these MULTEC™ design injectors feature stainless steel "ball and seat" metering with six hole metering orifices delivering a fully atomized 10° to 15° spray pattern.

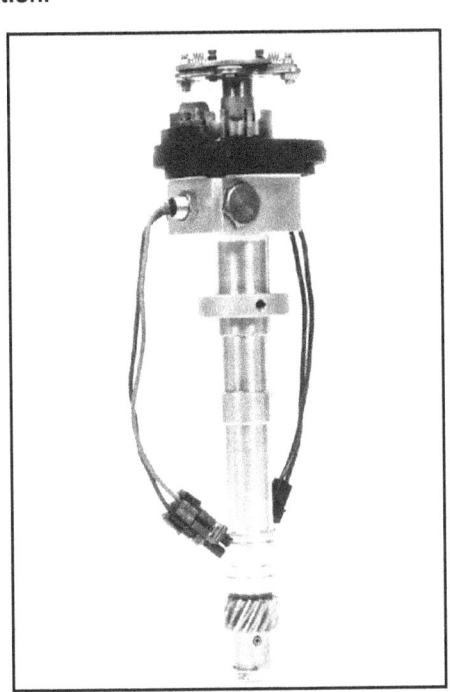

MSD's adjustable sync billet distributor provides both an injector syncronization signal and a magnetic ignition trigger signal with all the other great features of an MSD billet distributor.

CHEVY TPI Fuel Injection Swapper's Guide
Troubleshooting Guide

Diagnostics are typically handled through the ALDL or Assembly Line Data (Diagnostic) Link located under the dash.

Diagnostic circuit checks are an organized testing approach for identifying fuel injection problems. Driver complaint's typically fall into three categories.

— Steady "Service Engine "Soon" light
— Drivability problems
— Engine "Cranks But Will Not Run"

1. A steady "Service Engine Soon" light with the ignition "On" and engine stopped, confirms battery and ignition voltage to the ECM.

2. Ground the diagnostic terminal by jumpering terminal "A" to "B" in the ALDL connector located below the instrument panel or whatever location you have chosen for it in your TPI equipped vehicle.

The ECM will cause the "Service Engine Soon" light to flash Code 12, indicating that the ECM diagnostics are working properly. Code 12 will flash three times followed by any other trouble codes that the system has stored in memory. Starting with the lowest code, each code will flash three times, and then start over again with Code 12. If there are no other codes, Code 12 will flash until the diagnostic terminal jumper is disconnected or the engine is started.

3. Record all stored codes except Code 12. If the problem is "Engine Cranks But Will Not Run", proceed to Chart A-3.

4. If no additional codes were recorded, see Section "B" for drivability symptoms and recommended service procedures. Depending on the severity of the problem, the "Field Service Mode" may be helpful in diagnosis. With the engine running and the diagnostic terminal grounded, the ECM will respond to the oxygen sensor signal voltage and use the "Service Engine Soon" light to display this information as follows:

A. "Closed Loop" confirms that the oxygen sensor signal is being used by the ECM to control fuel delivery and that the system is working normally. Signal voltage will swing quickly from below .35 to above .55 volts.

B. "Open Loop" indicates that oxygen sensor voltage signal is not usable to the ECM. Signal voltage is at a constant value between .35 to .55 volts.

System will flash "Open Loop" from 30 second to two minutes after the engine starts, or until the oxygen sensor reaches normal operating temperature. If the system fails to go "Closed Loop", use the Code 13 chart.

C. "Service Engine Soon" light "OUT" indicates that the exhaust is lean. O2 sensor voltage will be less than .35 volts and steady. Use the Code 44 chart.

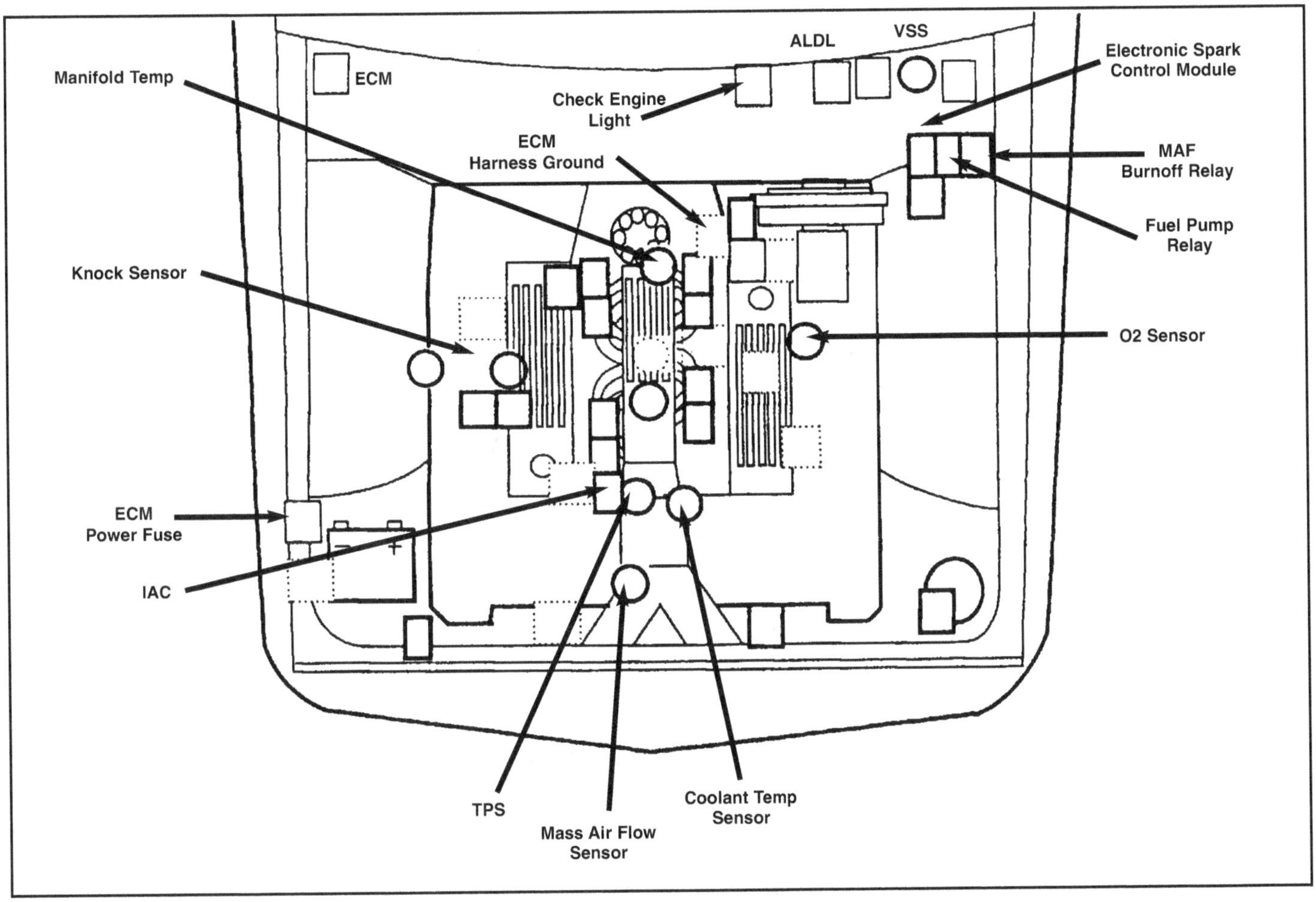

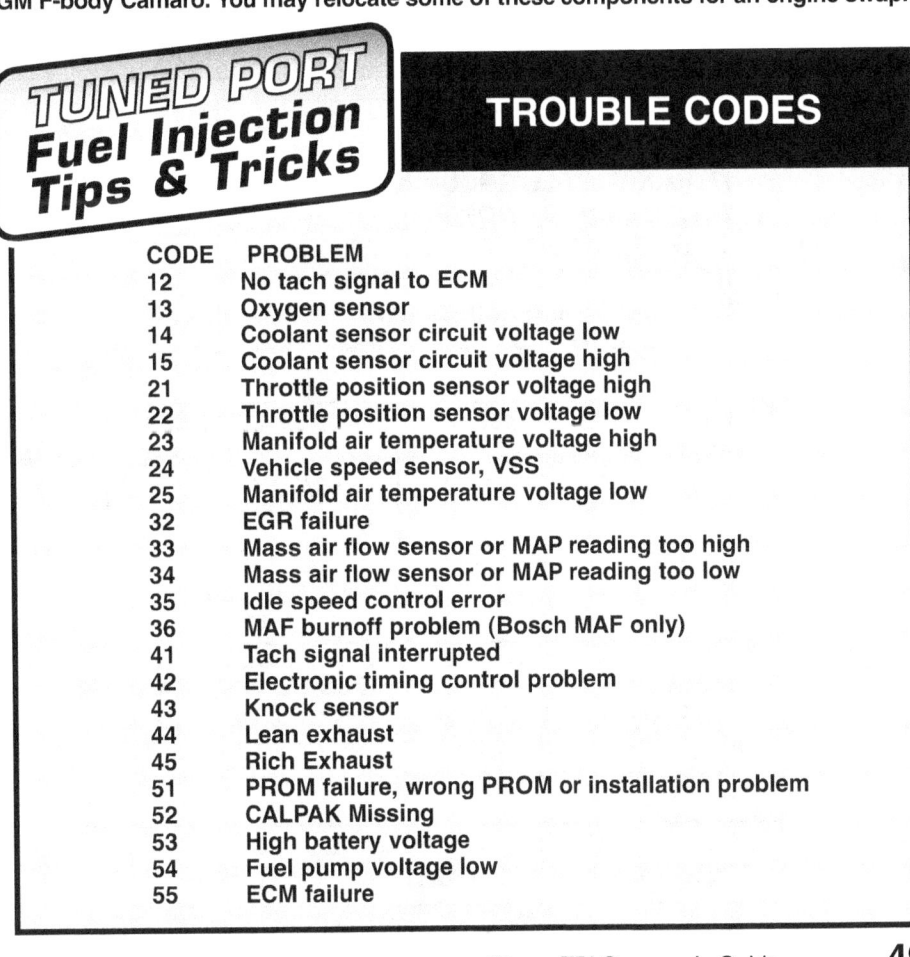

Typical component locations on a standard GM F-body Camaro. You may relocate some of these components for an engine swap.

D. "Service Engine Soon" light "ON" steady indicates that exhaust is rich. Sensor signal voltage will be above .55 volts and steady. Use the Code 45 chart.

5. Road test of the system using the "Field Service Mode" should be done only at steady road speeds. Because the vehicle operates differently in the "Field Service Mode", the following conditions may be observed and should be considered normal.

—Acceleration -Light may be "ON" too long due to acceleration enrichment.
—Deceleration -Light may be "OFF" too long due to decel enleanment or fuel cut-off.
— Idle -Light may be "ON" too long with idle below 1200 rpm.

6. Clearing codes. Ignition "OFF". Remove continuous battery fuse for 30 second. Fuse and holder are located near the battery.

TROUBLE CODES

CODE	PROBLEM
12	No tach signal to ECM
13	Oxygen sensor
14	Coolant sensor circuit voltage low
15	Coolant sensor circuit voltage high
21	Throttle position sensor voltage high
22	Throttle position sensor voltage low
23	Manifold air temperature voltage high
24	Vehicle speed sensor, VSS
25	Manifold air temperature voltage low
32	EGR failure
33	Mass air flow sensor or MAP reading too high
34	Mass air flow sensor or MAP reading too low
35	Idle speed control error
36	MAF burnoff problem (Bosch MAF only)
41	Tach signal interrupted
42	Electronic timing control problem
43	Knock sensor
44	Lean exhaust
45	Rich Exhaust
51	PROM failure, wrong PROM or installation problem
52	CALPAK Missing
53	High battery voltage
54	Fuel pump voltage low
55	ECM failure

Chevy TPI Swapper's Guide

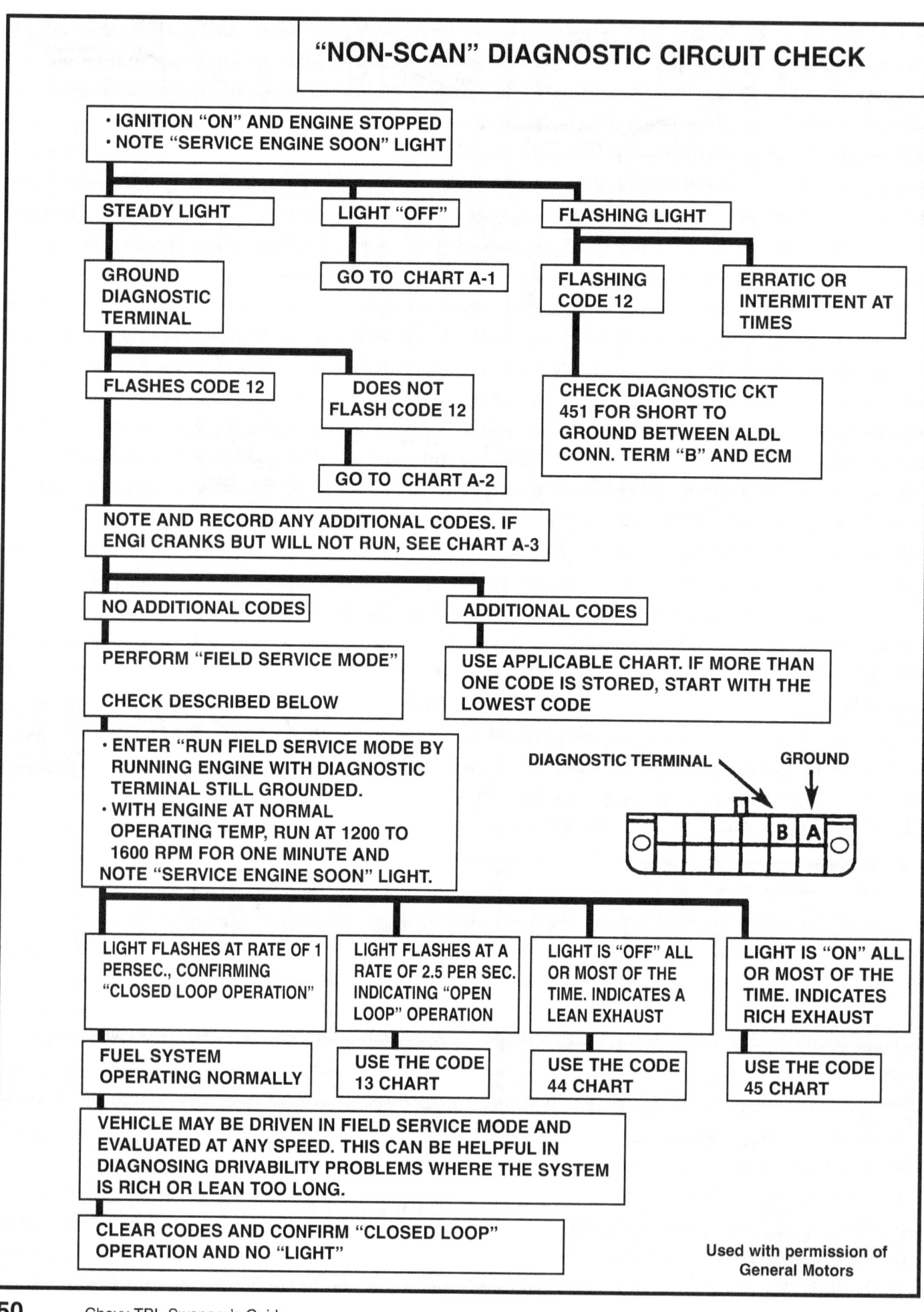

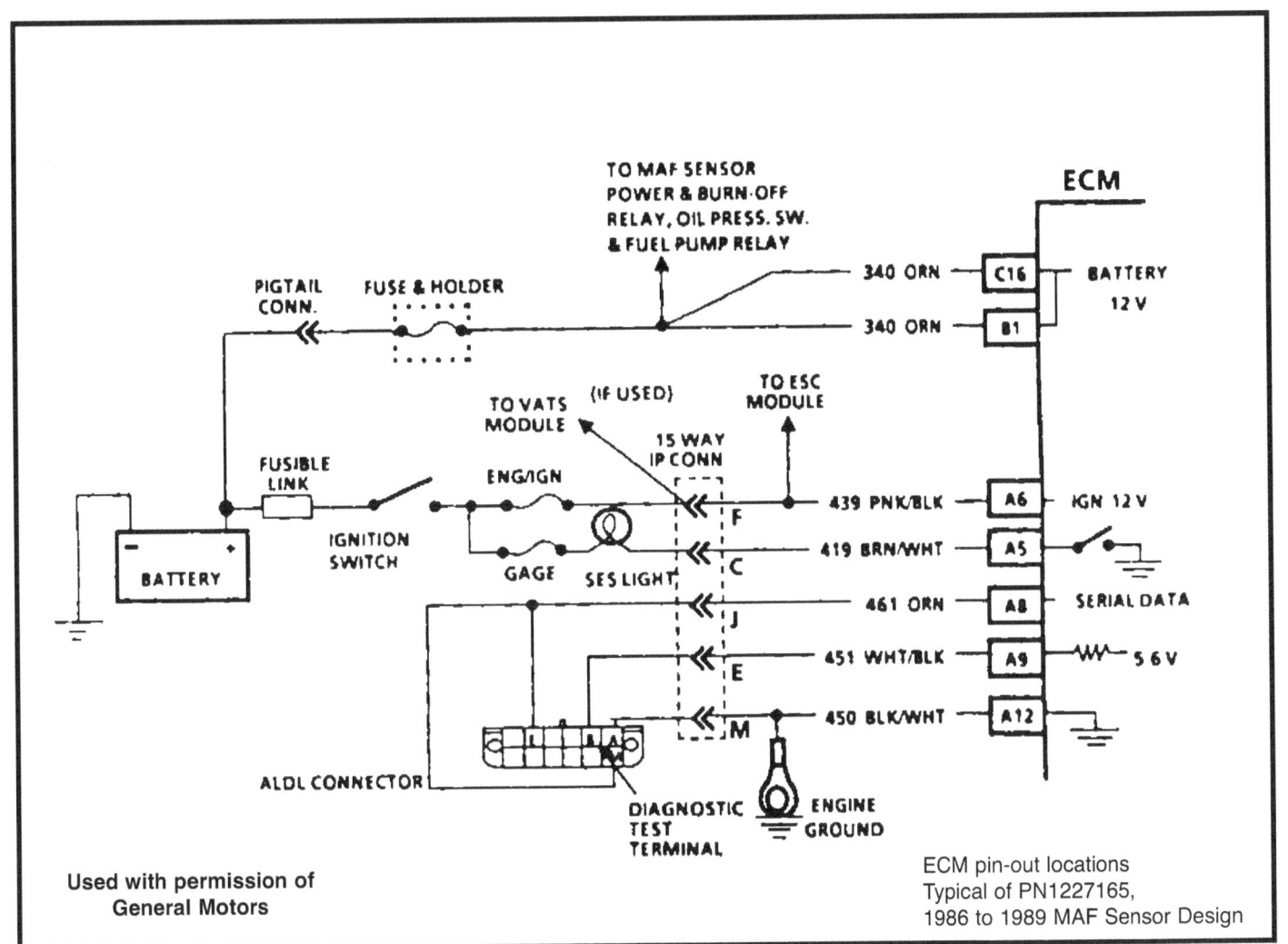

CHART A-1
NO "SERVICE ENGINE SOON" LIGHT

Circuit Description:

There should always be a steady "Service Engine Soon" light when the ignition is "ON" and the engine stopped. Ignition voltage is supplied directly to the light bulb. The electronic control module (ECM) will control the light and turn it "ON" by providing a ground path through CKT 419 to the ECM.

Test Description:

Numbers below refer to circled numbers on the diagnostic chart.

1. If the fuse holder is blown, refer to the facing page of Code 54 for complete circuit.

2. Using a test light connected to 12 volts, probe each of the system ground circuits to be sure a good ground is present. Refer to ECM terminal end view in front of this section for ECM pin locations of ground circuits.

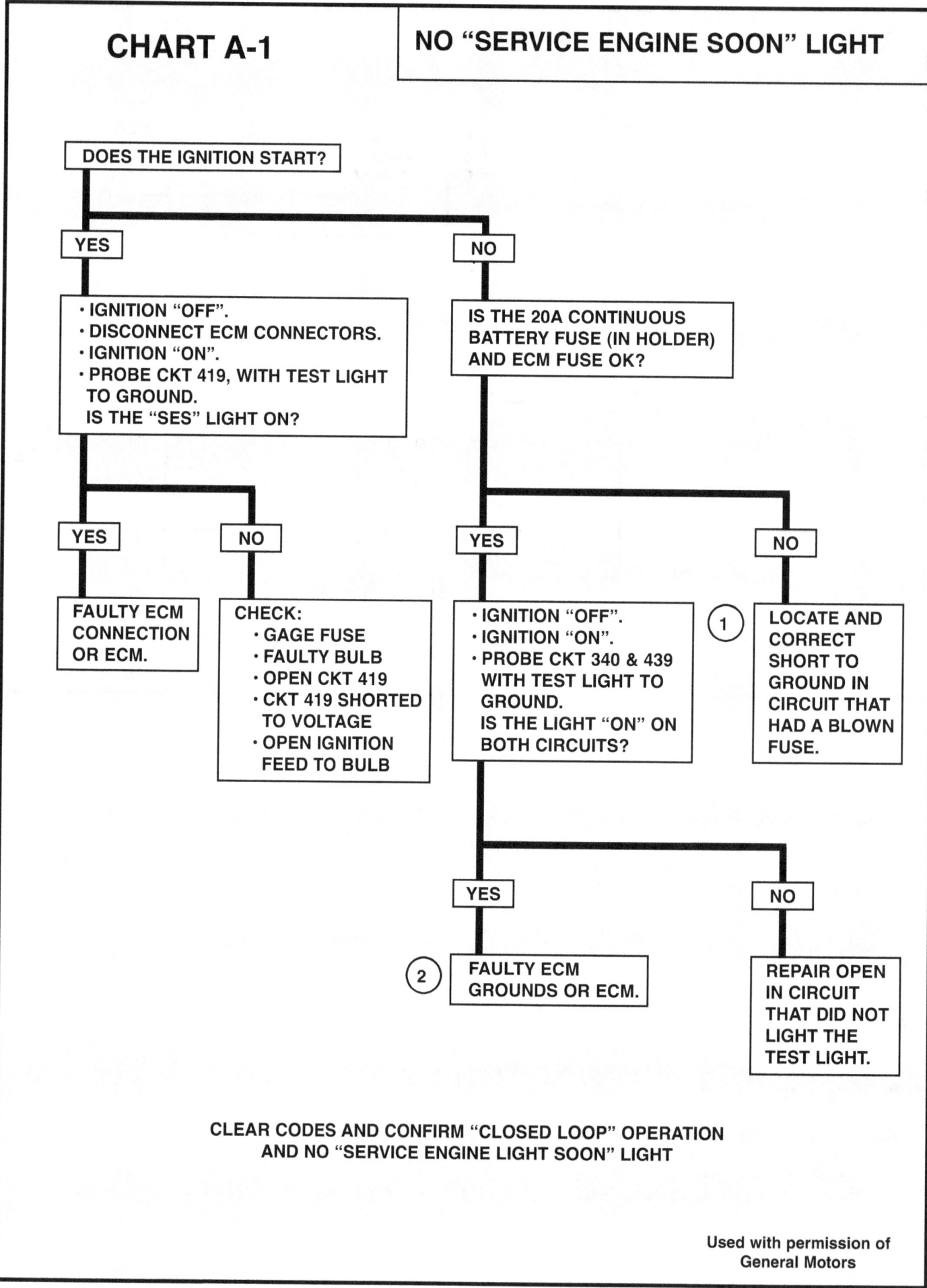

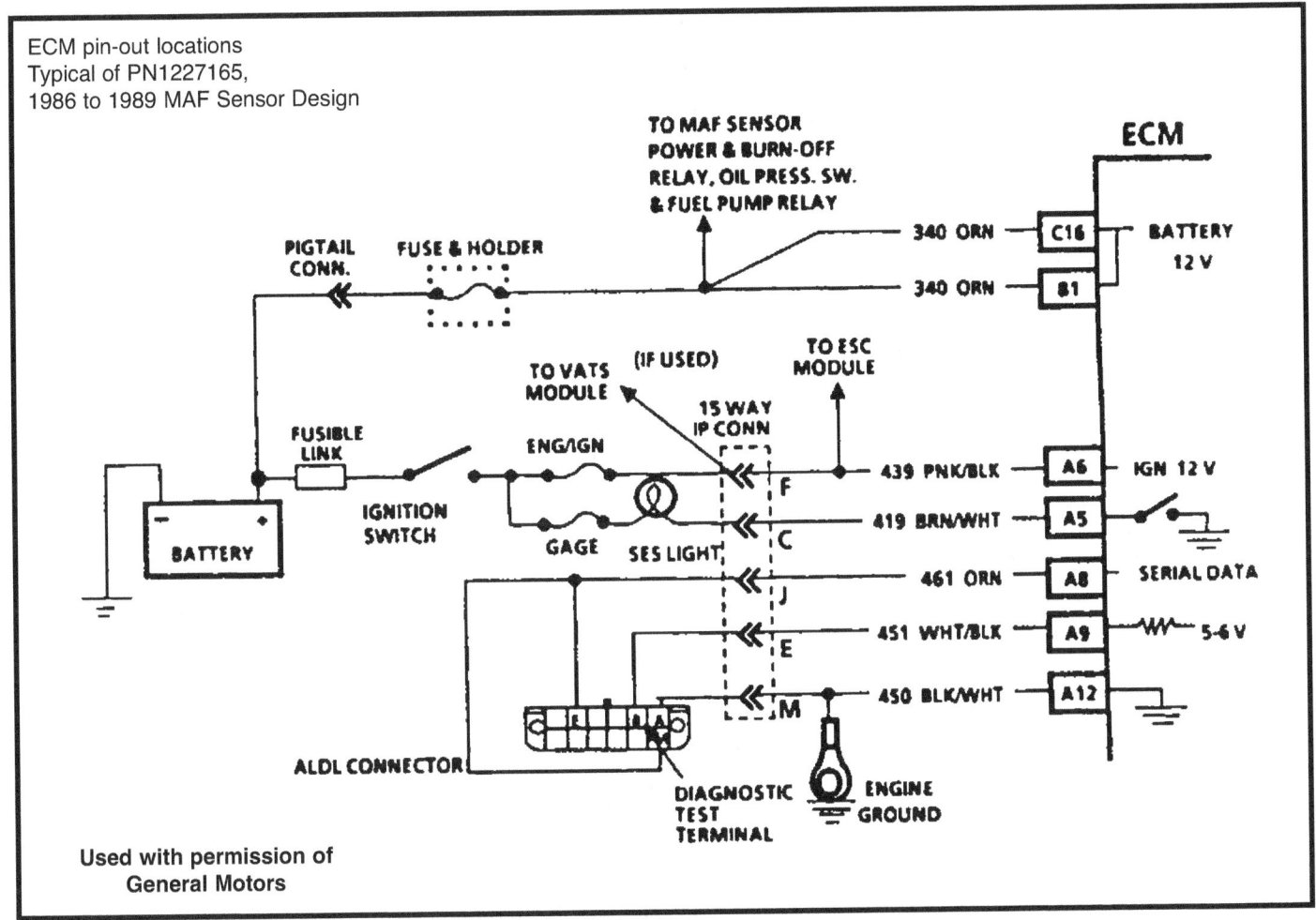

ECM pin-out locations
Typical of PN1227165,
1986 to 1989 MAF Sensor Design

Used with permission of General Motors

CHART A-2
NO ALDL DATA OR WON'T FLASH CODE 12
"SERVICE ENGINE SOON" LIGHT ON STEADY

Circuit Description:

There should always be a steady "Service Engine Soon" light when the ignition is "ON" and engine stopped. Ignition voltage is supplied to the light bulb. The electronic control module (ECM) will turn the light "ON" by grounding CKT 419 at the ECM.

With the diagnostic terminal grounded, the "SES" light should flash a Code 12, followed by any trouble code(s) stored in memory.

A steady light suggests a short to ground in the light control CKT 419, or an open in diagnostic CKT 451.

Test Description:

Numbers below refer to circled numbers on the diagnostic chart.

1. If the light goes "OFF" when the ECM connector is disconnected, them CKT 419 is not shorted to ground. Also, check the connector terminals physically for proper connect at this time.

2. This step will check for an open diagnostic CKT 451.

3. At this point the "Serive Engine Soon" light wiring is OK. The problem is a faulty ECM or Mem-Cal. If a Code 12 did not flash, the ECM should be replaced using the original Mem-Cal. Replace te Mem-Cal only after trying an ECM, as a defective Mem-Cal is an unlikely cause of this problem.

Chevy TPI Swapper's Guide   53

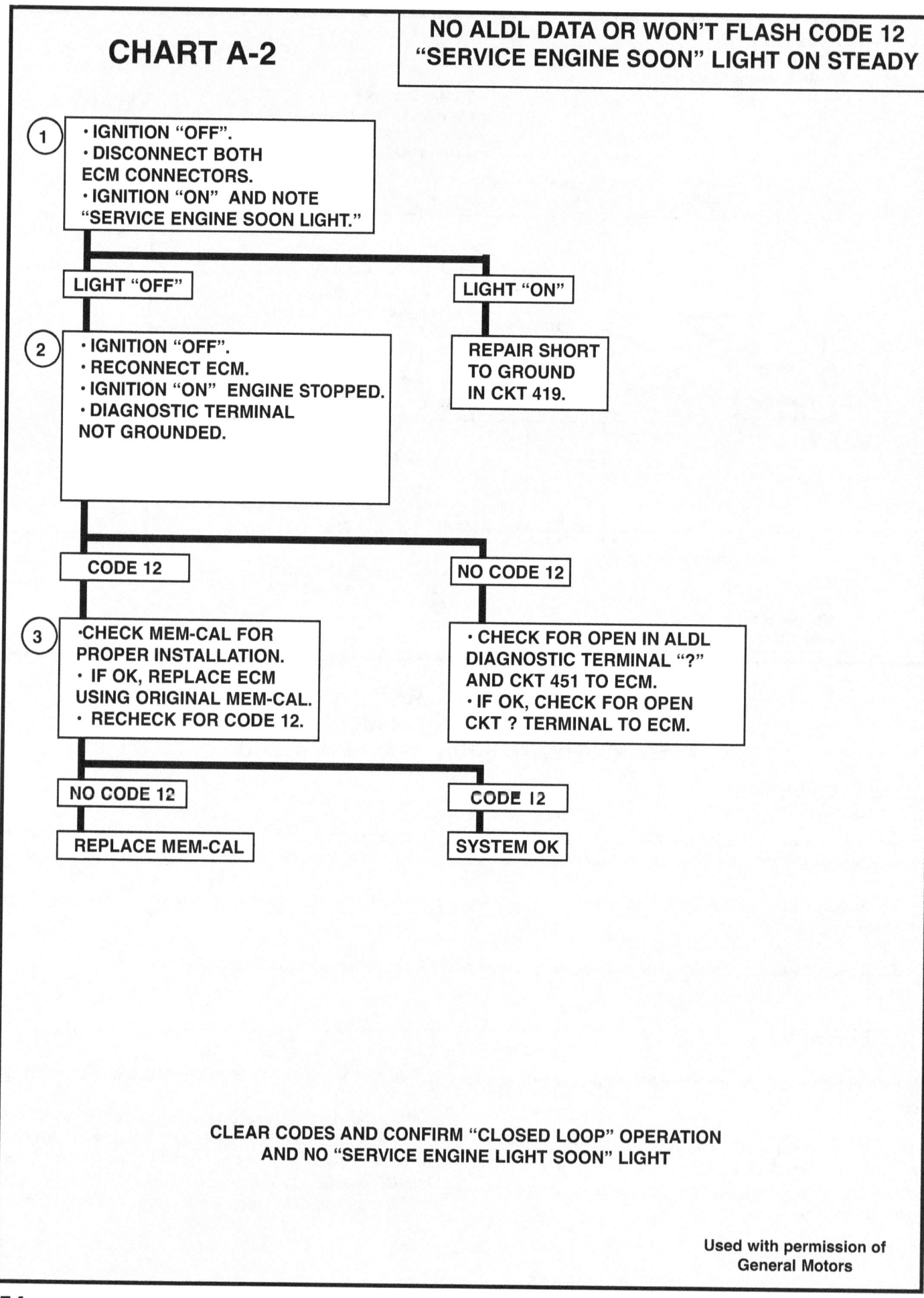

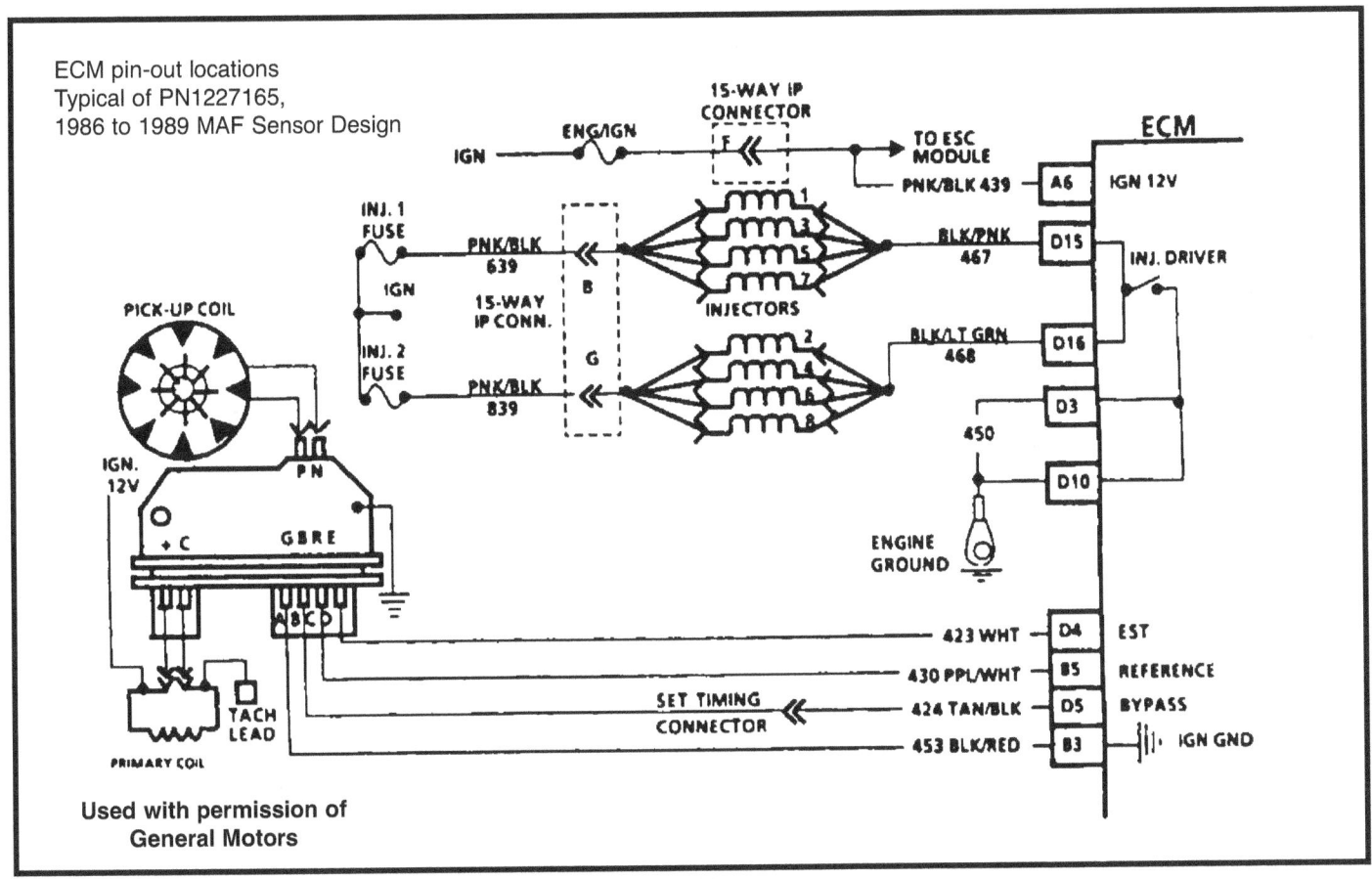

ECM pin-out locations
Typical of PN1227165,
1986 to 1989 MAF Sensor Design

Used with permission of General Motors

CHART A-3
(Page 1 of 2)
ENGINE CRANKS BUT WON'T RUN

Circuit Description:

Battery condition and cranking speed are OK and there is adequate fuel in the tank. If engine starts but immediately stalls, review "Fuel System and Voltage levels to ECM.

Test Description:

Numbers below refer to circled numbers on the diagnostic chart.

1. A "Service Engine Soon" light "ON" is a basic check for ignition and battery supply to the electronic control module (ECM).

2. No spark indicates a basic HEI problem.

3. This test will determine if the ECM is receiving the reference signal and controlling the injectors. If the test light "blinks" while cranking, the ECM control should be considered OK. How bright the test light "blinks" is not important. However, if the test light should be a J-34730-2 or equivalent (6.3V bulb).

Diagnostic Aids:

An EGR valve sticking open can cause a low air/fuel ratio during cranking.

Unless engine enters "Clear Flood" at the first indication of a flooding condition, it can result in a no start.

Check for fouled plugs.

If the TPS is sticking or binding in the wide open throttle position, the ECM will be in the "Clear Flood" mode.

A defective MAF sensor may cause no start or a stall after start. Tp determine if the sensor is causing the problem, disconnect it. The ECM will then use a default value for the sensor, and if the condition is corrected and the connections are OK, replace the sensor.

Also check that injectors on both sides of engine will cause a light to "blink".

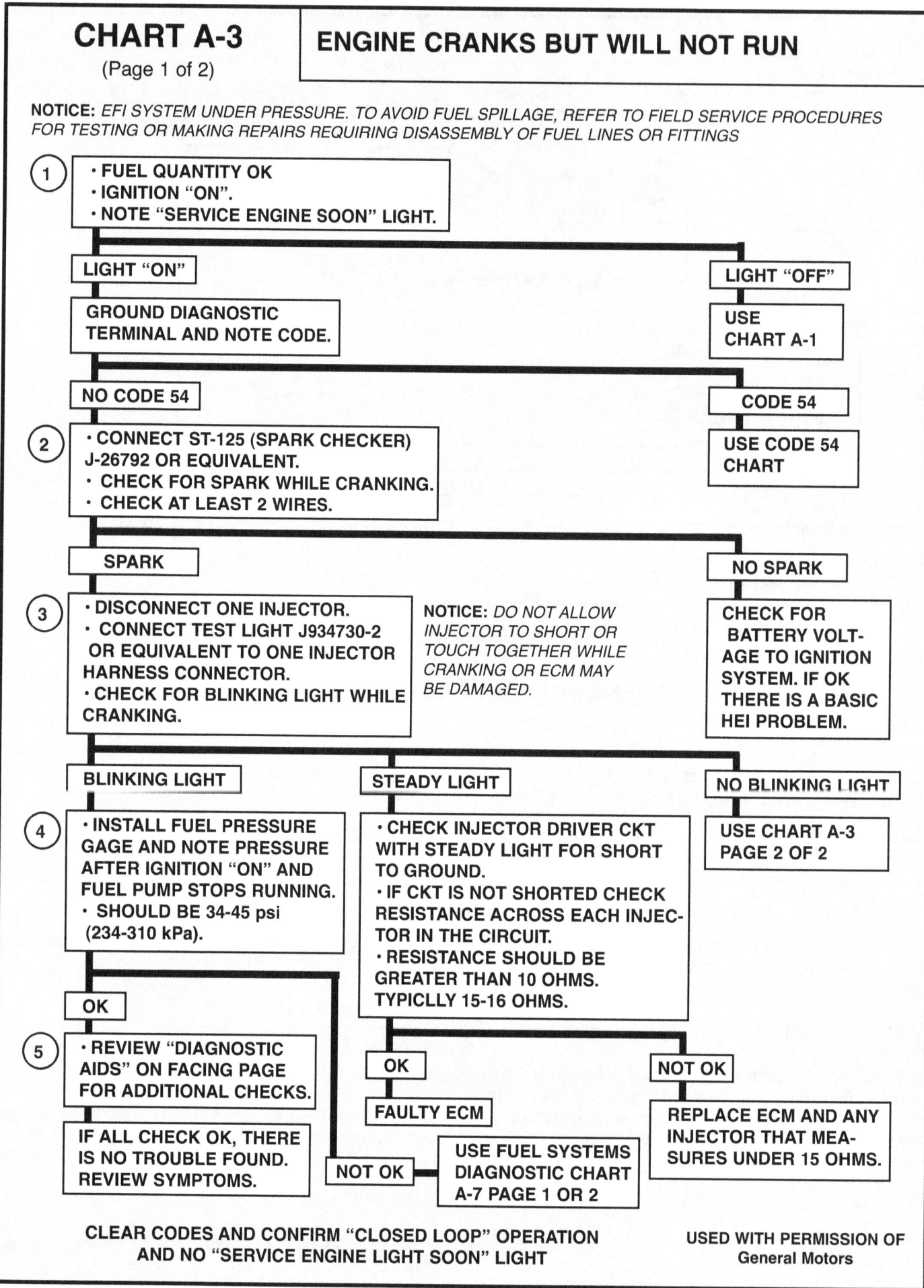

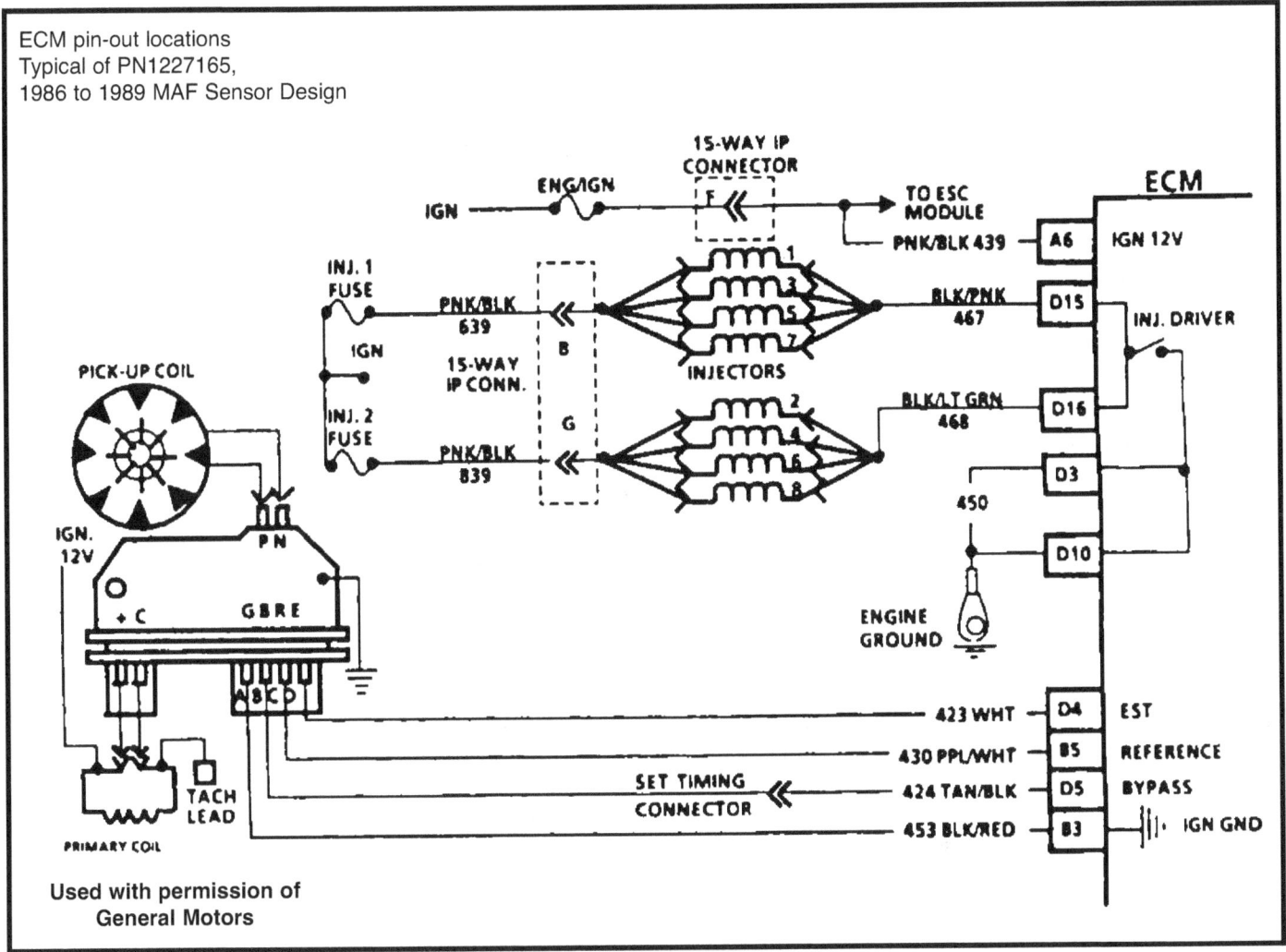

CHART A-3
(Page 2 of 2)
ENGINE CRANKS BUT WON'T RUN

Test Description:

Numbers below refer to circled numbers on the diagnostic chart.

6. Checks for 12 volt supply to Injectors.

7. This test will determine if the distributor module is not generating the reference pulse or if the wiring or ECM are at fault. By touching CKT 430 with a test light, a reference signal is being generated. If the test light (J34730-2) blinks at the injector, then the ECM and wiring are OK.

8. If the ECM is seeing a high TPS voltage it may be in the clear flood mode. Disconnecting the TPS will allow the ECM to use a default value and turn the injectors "ON". If the TPS ground wire and connections are OK the TPS should be replaced.

9. Each time the test light touches CKT 430, the ECM should turn "ON" the fuel pump for 2 seconds.

10. All checks made to this point would indicate that the ECM is at fault. However, there is a possibility of CKT 467 or 468 being shorted to a voltage source either in the engine harness or in an injector.

To test for this condition:
Disconnect the ECM connectors and injectors.

Ignition "ON"

Probe CKTs 467 and 468 with a test light connected to the ground. There should be no light. If light is present, repair short to voltage.

If OK, check harness for terminals shorted together and check each injector resistance.

Resistance should be 15 to 16.5 ohms.

If all are OK, check ECM ground circuits before replacing ECM.

Chevy TPI Swapper's Guide **57**

"NON-SCAN" DIAGNOSTICS

CHART A-3 (Page 2 of 2) — ENGINE CRANKS BUT WILL NOT RUN

NOTICE: *EFI SYSTEM UNDER PRESSURE. TO AVOID FUEL SPILLAGE, REFER TO FIELD SERVICE PROCEDURES FOR TESTING OR MAKING REPAIRS REQUIRING DISASSEMBLY OF FUEL LINES OR FITTINGS*

FROM CHART A-3 PAGE 1

NO BLINKING LIGHT

(6)
- IGNITION "ON".
- PROBE INJECTOR HARNESS TERMINALS WITH A TEST LIGHT TO GROUND.
- LIGHT SHOULD BE "ON" AT BOTH TERMINALS.

LIGHT "ON" BOTH

(7)
- RECONNECT J-34730-2 OR EQUIVALENT TEST LIGHT TO INJECTOR HARNESS.
- DISCONNECT DISTRIBUTOR 4-WAY CONNECTOR.
- MOMENTARILY TOUCH HARNESS CONNECTOR TO TERMINAL CKT 430 WITH TEST LIGHT TO 12 VOLTS.

INJECTOR LIGHT "BLINKS" → FAULTY IGNITION MODULE OR CONNECTION.

LIGHT "ON" ONE
DUE TO INJECTORS WIRED IN PARALLEL THERE SHOULD BE A LIGHT ON BOTH TERMINALS.

IF NOT, THE PROBLEM IS IN THE HARNESS TO THE TESTED INJECTOR.

NO LIGHT → REPAIR OPEN IN INJECTOR FEED CIRCUIT.

NO BLINKING LIGHT AT INJECTOR

(8)
- DISCONNECT TPS.
- REPEAT TEST.

NO BLINKING LIGHT

LIGHT BLINKS → REPLACE TPS

(9) REPEAT TEST AND OBSERVE FOR FUEL PUMP RUNNING FOR 2 SECONDS OR FUEL PUMP RELAY CLICK.

OK
- RECONNECT INJECTOR(S)
- IGNITION "OFF"
- DISCONNECT ECM.
- IGNITION "ON"
- PROBE TERMINALS "D15"

NOT OK
- OPEN OR GROUNDED CKT 430.
- FAULTY CONNECTION AT "B5" OR FAULTY ECM.

LIGHT → **(10)** REFER TO FACING PAGE, STEP 10.

NO LIGHT → OPEN CKT 467 OR 468

CLEAR CODES AND CONFIRM "CLOSED LOOP" OPERATION AND NO "SERVICE ENGINE LIGHT SOON" LIGHT

Used with permission of General Motors

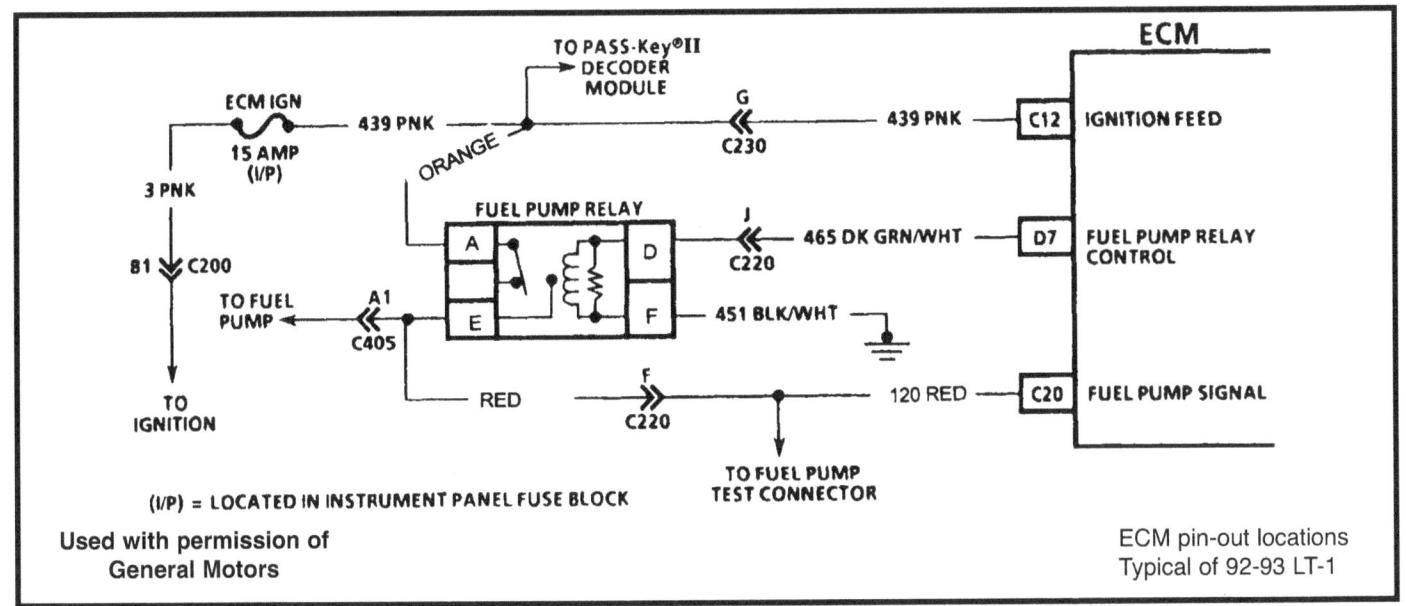

CHART A-5
FUEL PUMP RELAY CIRCUIT
TYPICAL OF ALL TPI

Circuit Description:

When the ignition switch is turned "ON", the Engine Control Module (ECM) will turn "ON" the in-tank fuel pump. It will remain "ON" as long as the ECM is receiving ignition low resolution reference pulses from the ignition system.

If there are no reference pulses, the ECM will shut "OFF" the fuel pump about 2-3 seconds after key "ON".

The pump will deliver fuel to the fuel rail and injectors, then to the pressure regulator, where the system pressure is controlled to 284-325 kPa (41-47 psi). Excess fuel is then returned to the fuel trank.

When the engine is stopped, the fuel pump can be turned "ON" by removing the fuel pump relay connector and jumpering the orange and red wires in the relay connector. Improper fuel system pressure will result in one or all of the following symptoms:

    Cranks won't run.
    DTC 44 and 64.
    DTC 45 and 65.
    Cuts out, may feel like ignition problem.
    Poor fuel economy, loss of power.

Test Description:

Numbers below refer to circled numbers on the diagnostic chart.

1. The fuel pump relay is located on a separate branch of the ECM harness. Check for 12-volt supply to the fuel pump relay. Check ECM IGN fuse for being open. If fuse is open, check CKT 439 for being grounded. If ECM IGN fuse was OK, check CKT 4398 for being open.

2. The test lid illuminate for 2 seconds when the ignition was turned "ON".

A Tech 1 can also be used to enable the fuel pump relay control circuit.

Chevy TPI Swapper's Guide

"NON-SCAN" DIAGNOSTICS

CHART A-5 — FUEL PUMP RELAY CIRCUIT — TYPICAL OF ALL TPI

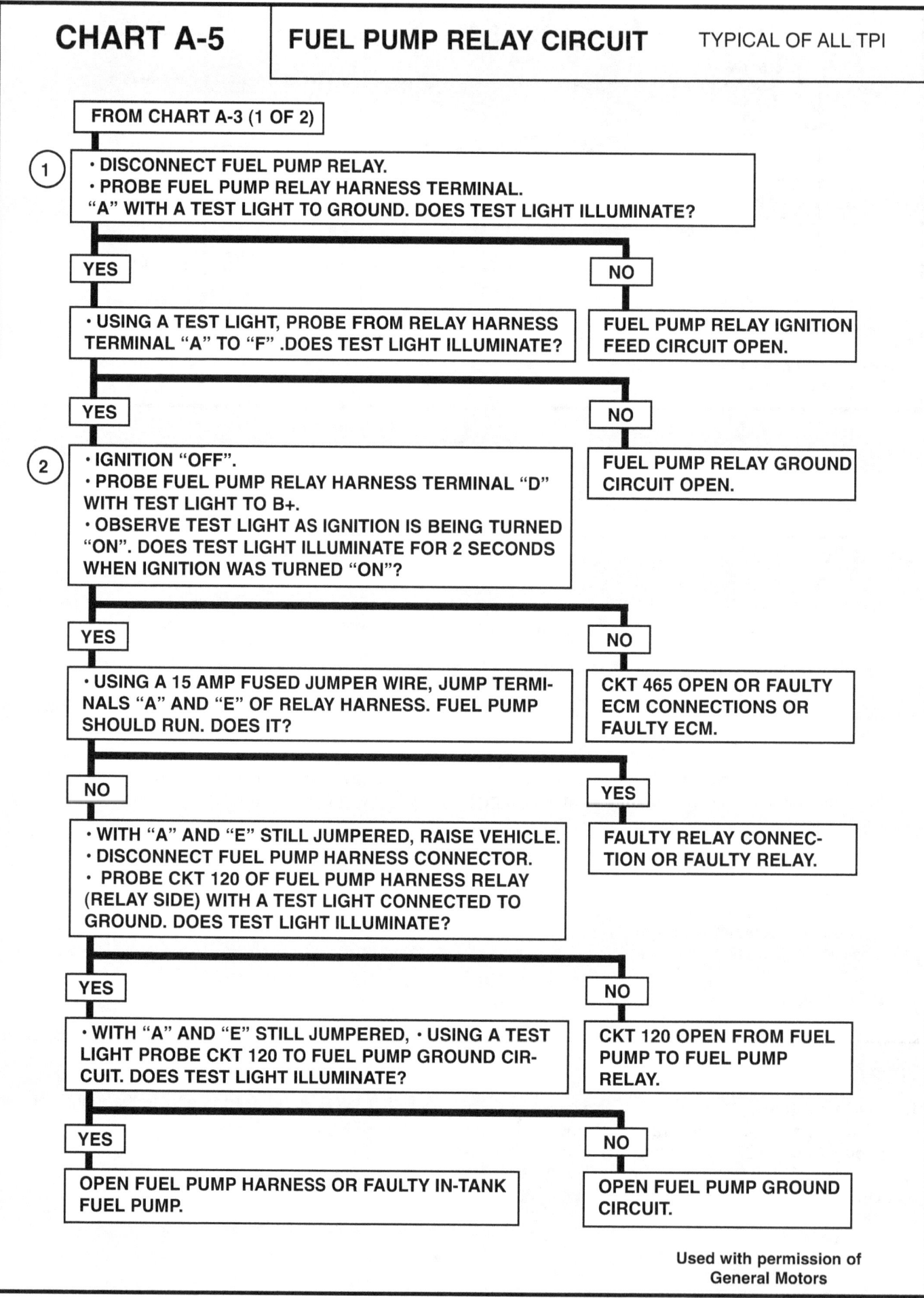

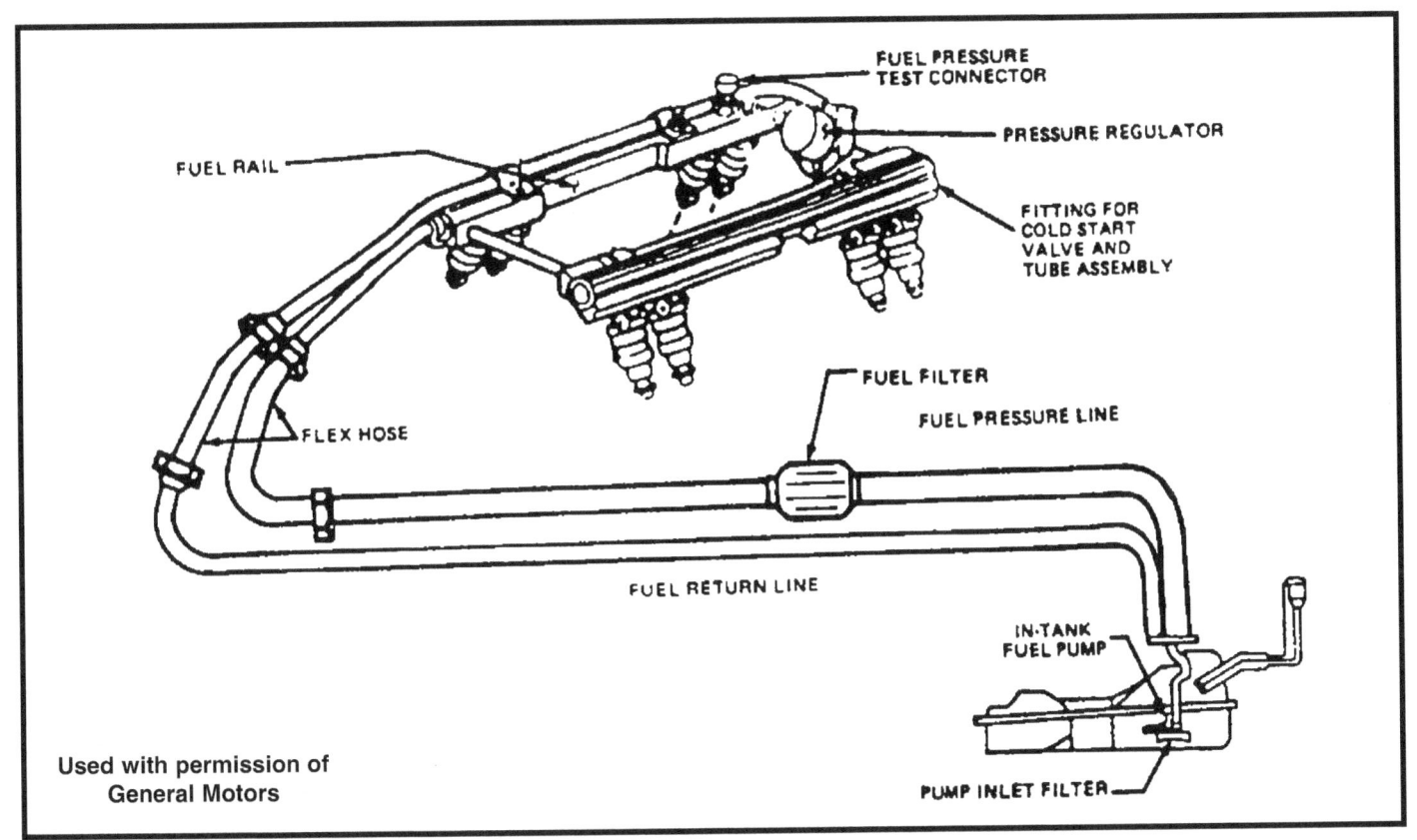

CHART A-7
(Page 1 of 2)
FUEL SYSTEM DIAGNOSIS

Circuit Description:

When the ignition switch is turned "ON", the Engine Control Module (ECM) will turn "ON" the in-tank fuel pump. It ill remain "ON" as long as the engine is cranking or running, and the ECM is receiving reference pulses. If there are no reference pulses, the ECM will shut "OFF" the fuel pump within 2 second after ignition "ON" or engine stops.

The pump will deliver fuel to the fuel rail and injectors, then to the pressure regulator, where the system pressure is controlled to 234-325 kPa (34-47 psi). Excess fuel is then returned to the fuel trank.

Test Description:

Numbers below refer to circled numbers on the diagnostic chart.

1. Wrap a shop towel around the fuel pressure connector to absorb any small amount of fuel leakage that may occur when installing the gage. Ignition "ON" pump pressure should be 280-325 kPa (40.5-47 psi). This pressure is controlled by spring pressure within the regulator assembly.

2. When the engine is idling, the manifold pressure is low (high vacuum) and is applied to the fuel regulator diaphragm. This will offset the spring and result in a lower fuel pressure. This idle pressure will vary somewhat depending on barometric pressure, however, the pressure idling should be less indicating pressure regulator control.

3. Pressure that continues to fall is caused by one of the following:
   In-tank fuel pump check valve not holding.
   Pump coupling hose or pulsator leaking.
   Fuel pressure regulator valve leaking.
   Injector(s) sticking open.

4. An injector sticking open can best be determined by checking for a fouled or saturated spark plug(s). If a leaking injector can not be determined by a fouled or saturated spark plug the following procedure should be used:
   Remove Plenum, and remove fuel rail bolts.
   Follow the procedures in the Fuel Control Section of this manual, but leave fuel lines connected.

CAUTION: BE SURE INJECTOR(S) ARE NOT ALLOWED TO SPRAY ON ENGINE AND THAT INJECTOR RETAINING CLIPS ARE INTACT. THIS SHOULD BE CAREFULLY FOLLOWED TO PREVENT FUEL SPRAY ON ENGINE WHICH WOULD CAUSE A FIRE HAZARD.

Pressurize the fuel system and observe injector nozzles.

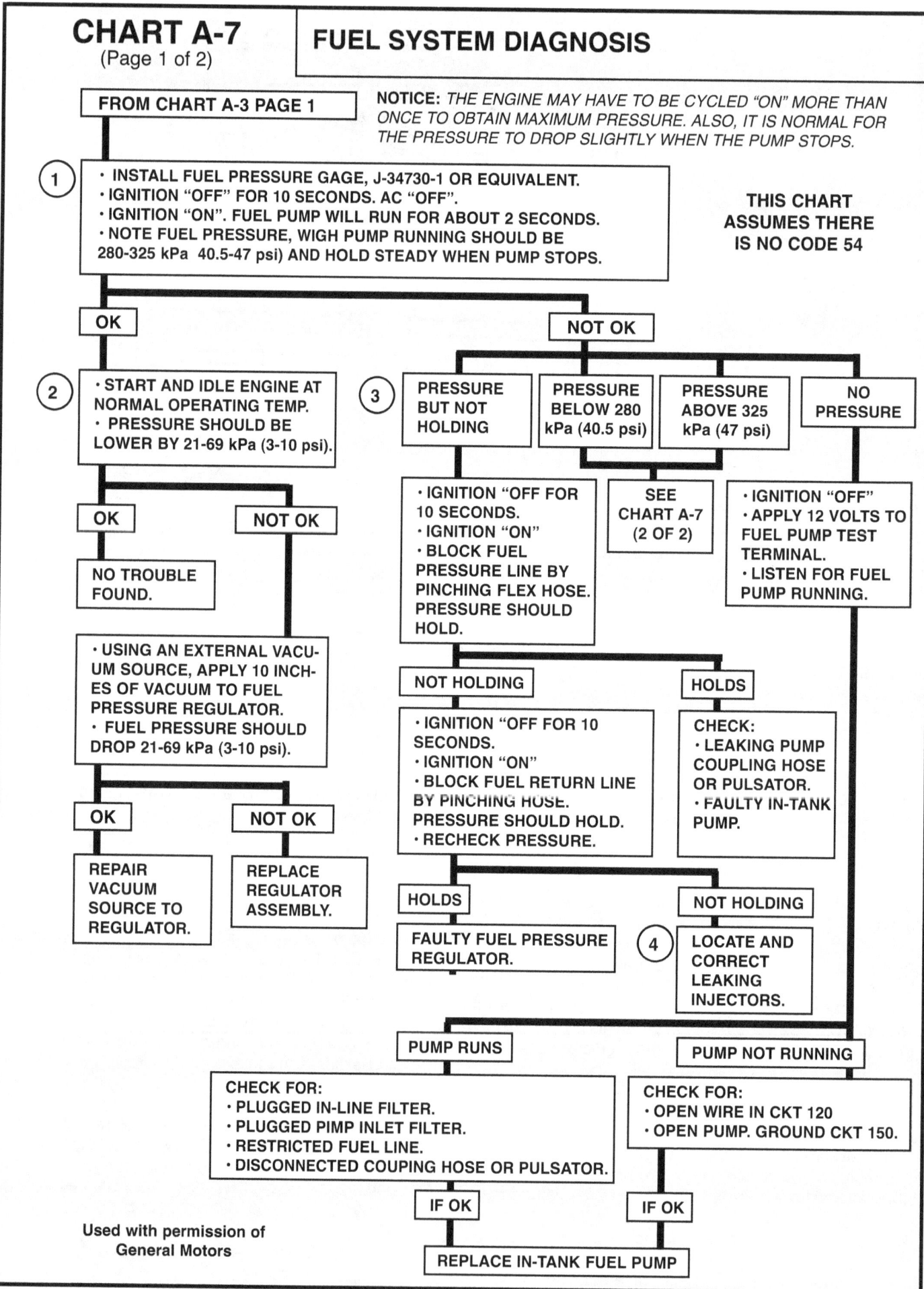

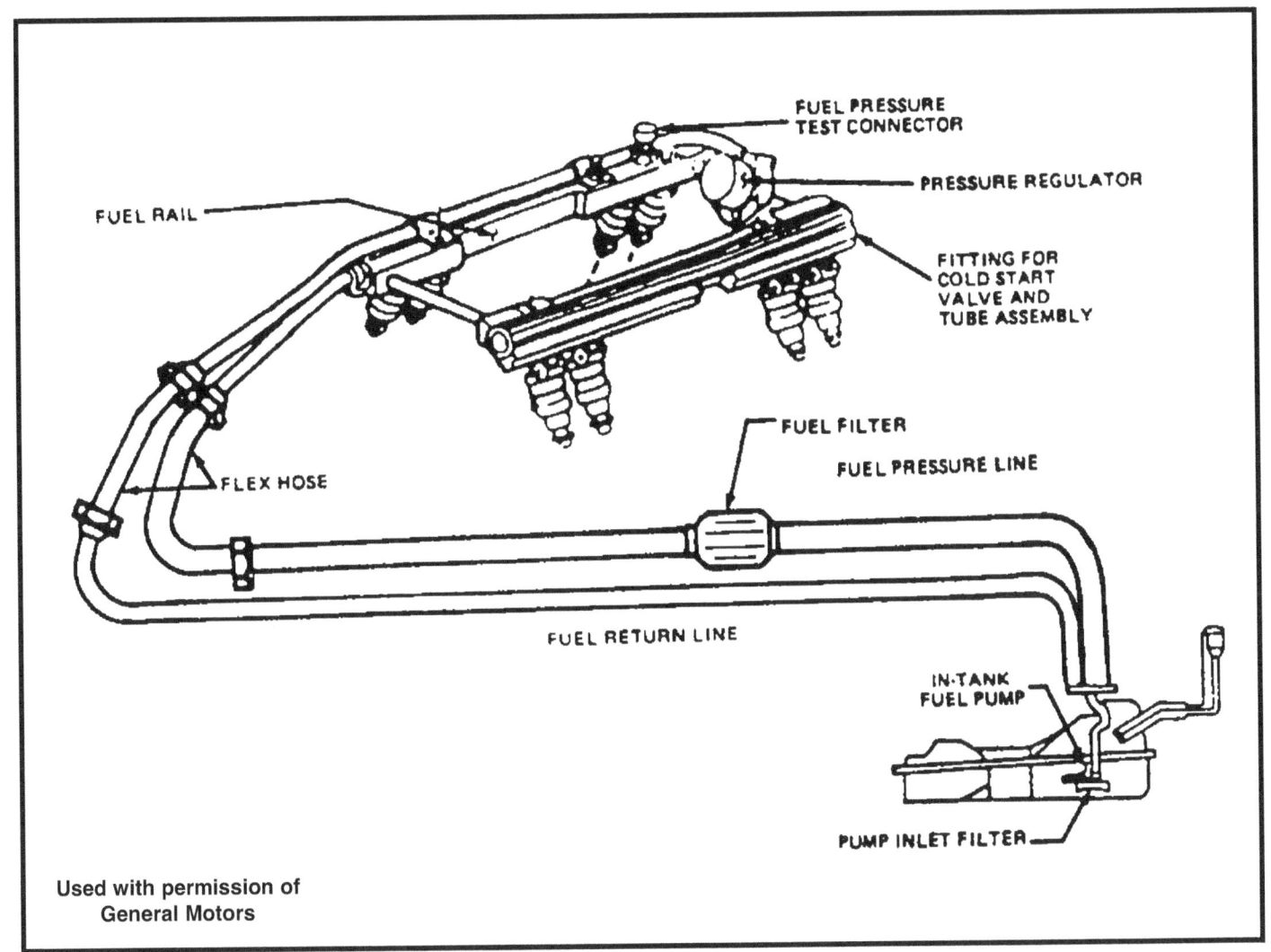

CHART A-7
(Page 2 of 2)
FUEL SYSTEM DIAGNOSIS

Test Description:

Numbers below refer to circled numbers on the diagnostic chart.

1. Pressure fuel less than 280 kPa (40.5 psi) falls into two areas:

   Regulated pressure less than 280 kPa (40.5 psi). Amount of fuel to injectors OK but pressure is too low. System will be lean running and may set Code 44. Also, hard starting cold and overall poor performance.

   Restricted flow causing a pressure drop. Normally, a vehicle with a fuel pressure of less than 165 kPa (24 psi at idle will not be driveable.

   However, if the pressure drop occurs only while driving, the engine will normally surge then stop running as pressure begins to drop rapidly. This is most likely caused by a restricted fuel line or plugged filter.

2. Restricting the fuel return line allows the fuel pump to develop its maximum pressure (dead head pressure). When battery voltage is applied to the fuel pump test terminal, fuel pressure should be above 414 kPa (60 psi).

3. This trest determines if the high fuel pressure condition is due to restricted fuel return line or a pressure regulator problem.

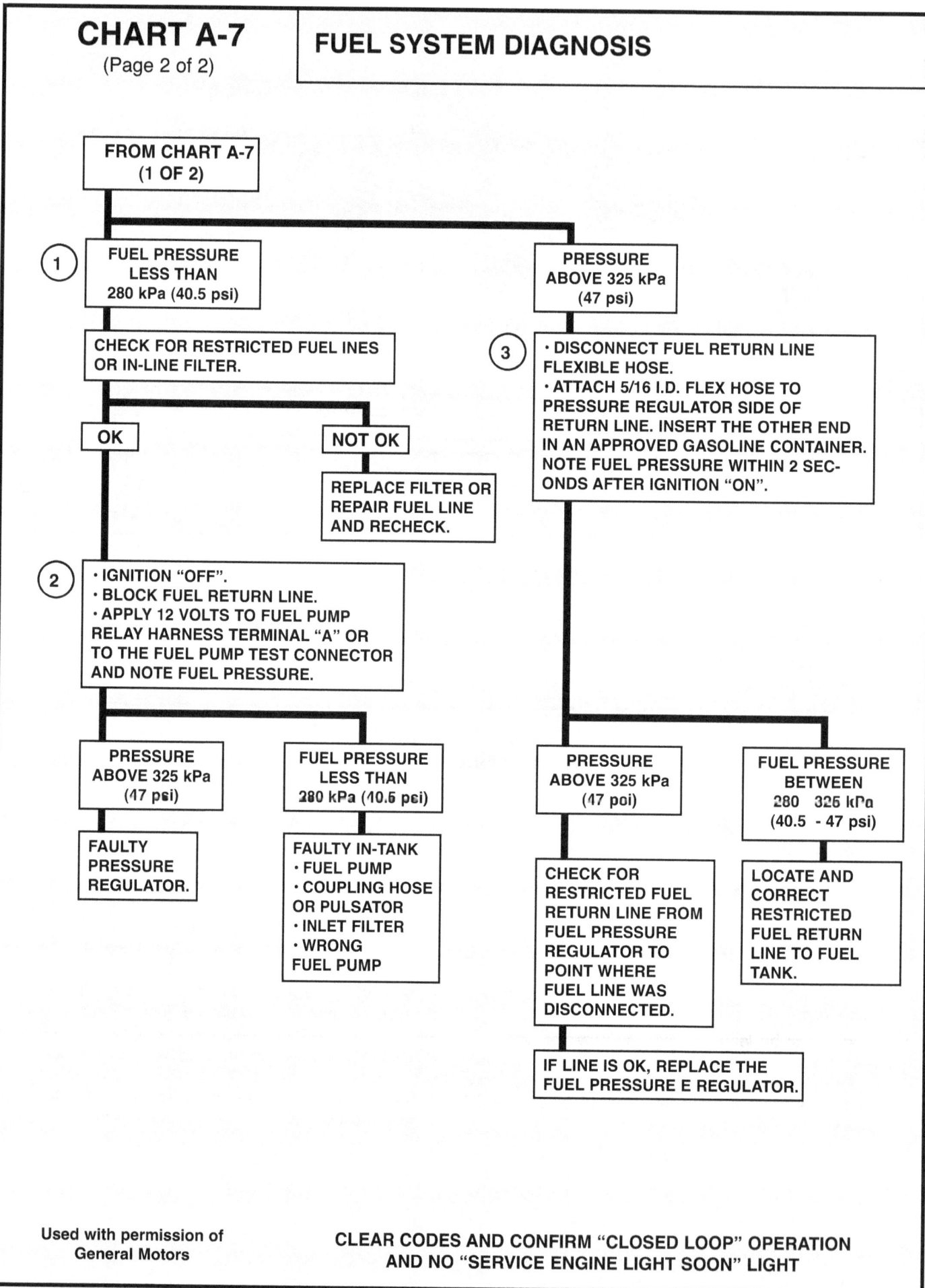

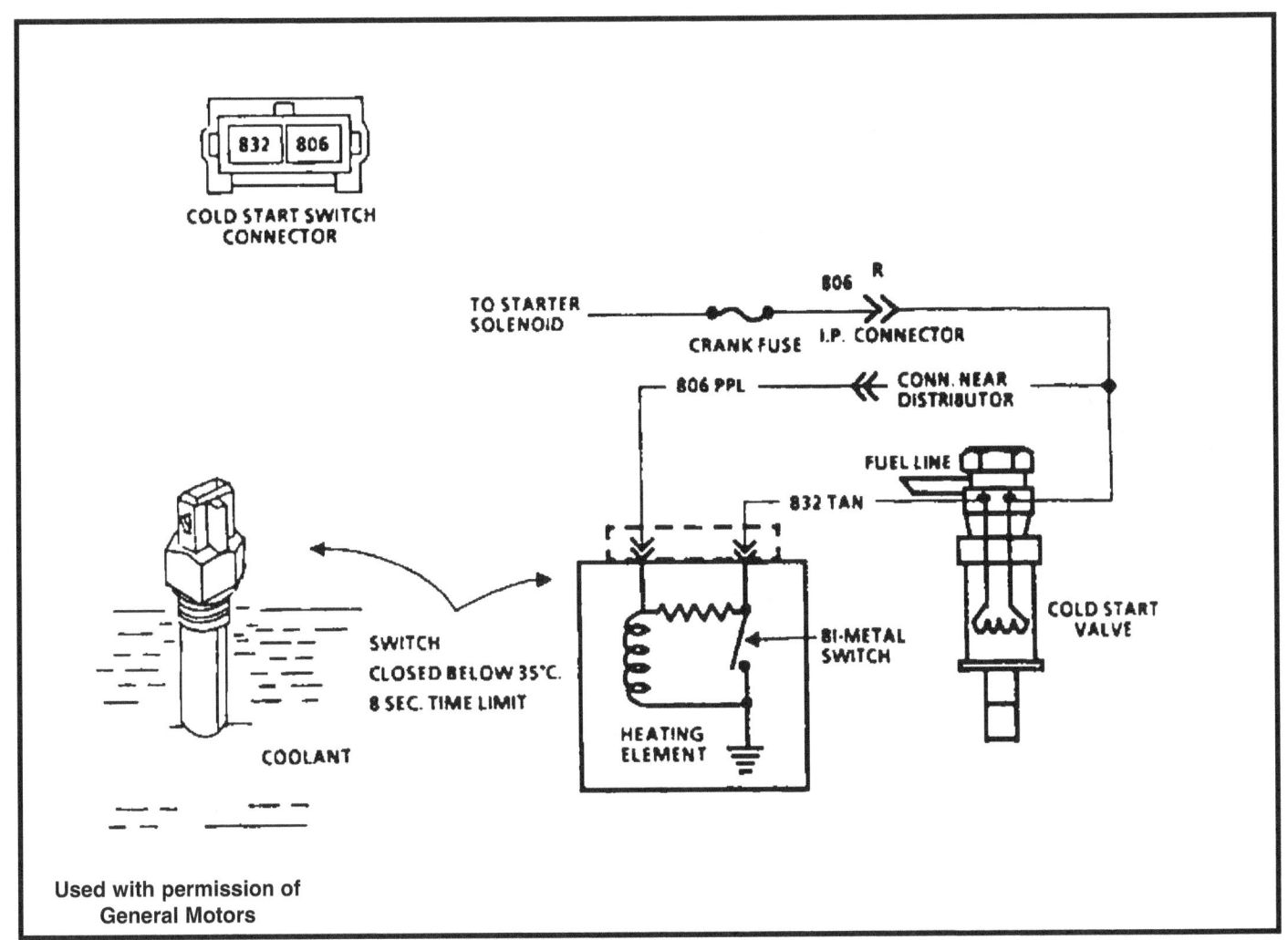

CHART A-9
COLD START VALVE CIRCUIT TEST
USED ON 1985 TO 1988 TPI'S ONLY

Circuit Description:

The cold start valve is used to provide additional fuel during the crank mode to improve cold start-ups. This circuit is important when engine coolant temperature is low because the other injectors are not pulsed "ON" long enough to provide the needed amount of fuel to start.

Tho circuit is activated only in the crank mode. The power is supplied directly from the starter solenoid and is protected by a fuse. The system is controlled by a cold start fuel injection switch which provides a ground path for the valve during cranking when engine coolant is below 35°C (95°F).

The cold start fuel injection switch consists of a bimetal material which opens at a specified coolant temperature. This bimetal is also heated by the winding in the terminal switch which allows the valve to stay "ON" for 8 seconds at -20°C (-4°F) coolant. The time the switch will stay closed varies inversely with coolant temperature. In other words, as the coolant temperature goes up, the cold start valve "ON" time will go down.

Test Description:

Numbers below refer to circled numbers on the diagnostic chart.

1. Disconnecting the distributor 4-way connector will disable the other injectors. The amount of pressure drop depends on the temperature of the engine. this test could also be performed by removing the two injector fuses.

2. This test will determine the continuity through the switch to ground.

"NON-SCAN" DIAGNOSTICS

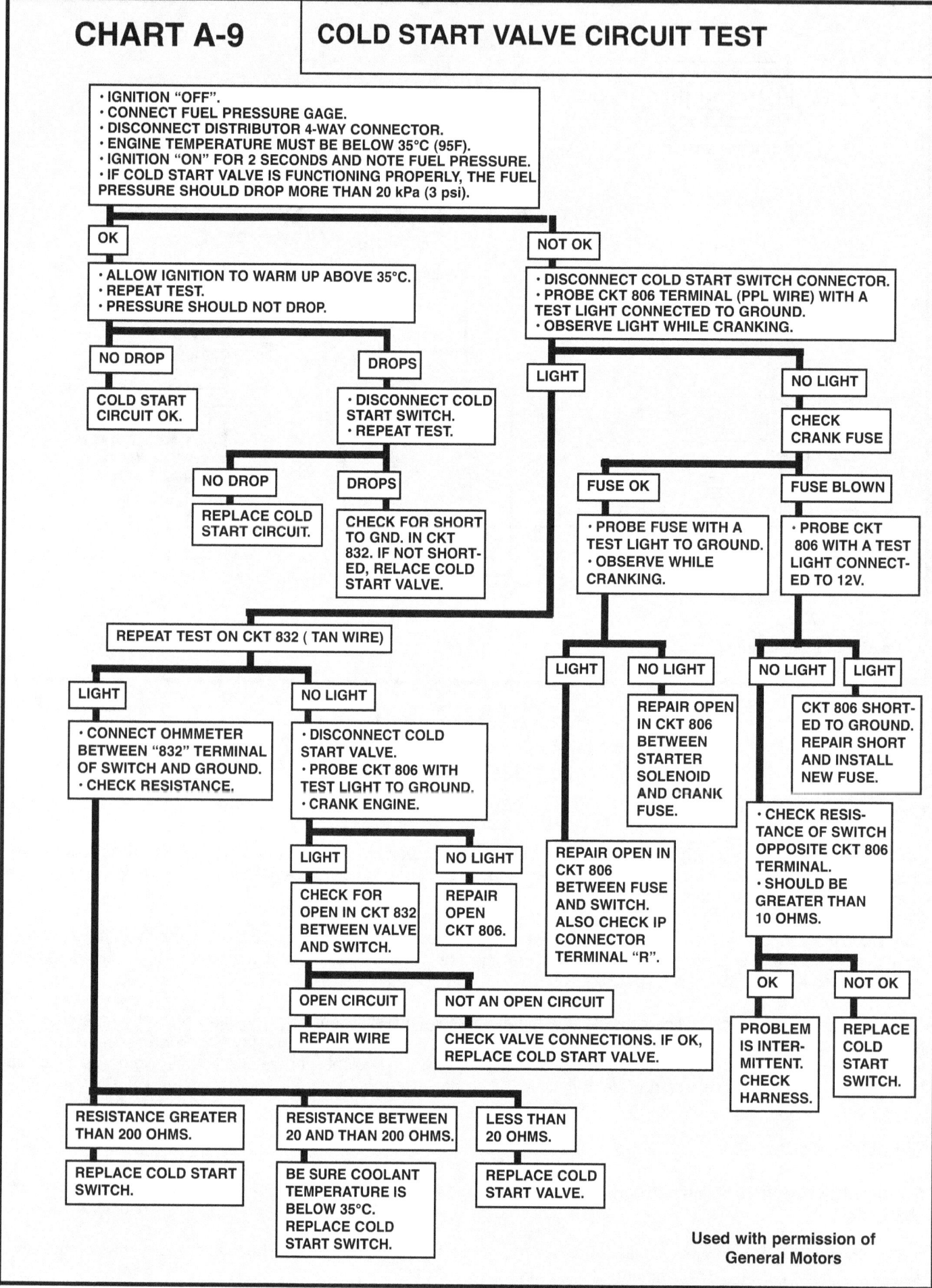

Used with permission of General Motors

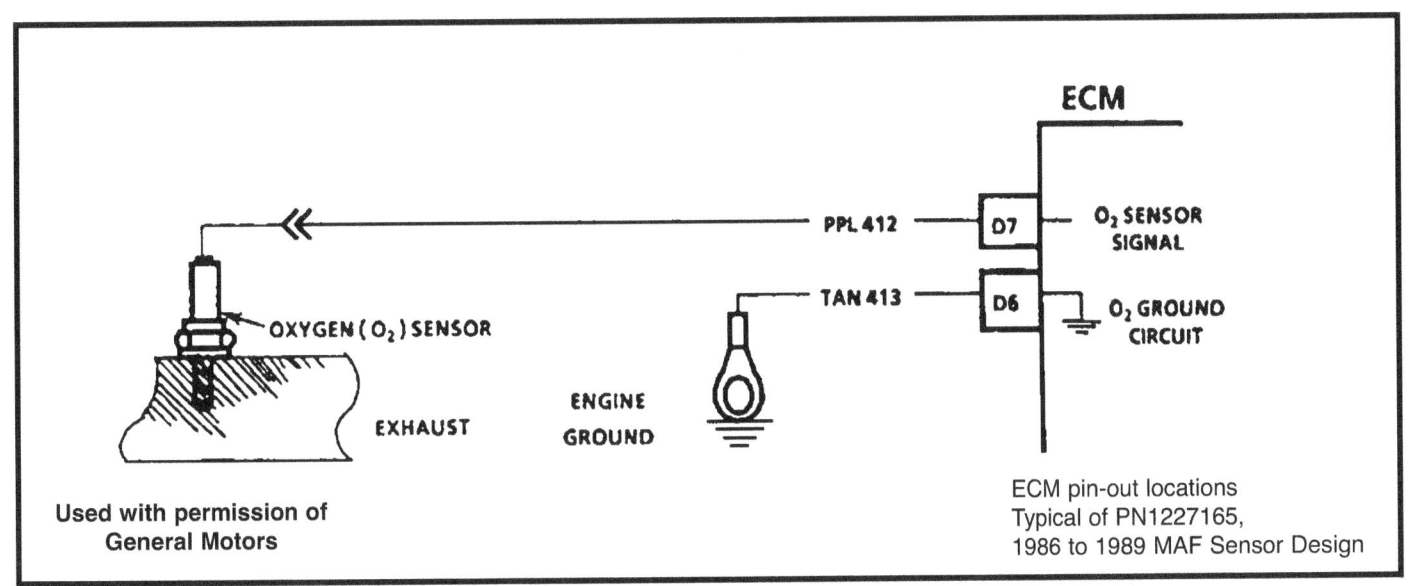

CODE 13
OXYGEN SENSOR CIRCUIT, TPI & LT-1 LEFT BANK
(OPEN CIRCUIT)

Circuit Description:

The electronic control module (ECM) supplies a voltage of about .45 volt between terminals "D7" and "D6". (If measured with a 10 megaohm digital voltmeter, this may read as low as .32 volts.) The O-2 sensor varies the voltage within a range of about 1 volt if the exhaust is rich, down through about .10 volt if the exhaust is lean.

The sensor is like an open circuit and produces no voltage when it is below below 360°C (600°F). An open sensor circuit or cold sensor senses "Open Loop" operation.

Test Description:

Numbers below refer to circled numbers on the diagnostic chart.

1. Code 13 WILL SET:

   Engine at normal operating temperature (above 70°C).

   At least 2 minutes engine time after start.

   O-2 signal voltage steady between .35 and .55 volts.

   Throttle position sensor (TPS) signal above 5% (about .3 volts above closed throttle voltage).

   All conditions must be met for about 60 seconds.

   If the conditions for a Code 13 exist, the system will not go "Closed Loop".

2. This will determine if the sensor is at fault or the wiring or ECM is the cause of the Code 13.

3. This step verifies no additional code stored and that Code 13 is intermittent.

4. In doing this test, use only a high impedence digital volt ohmmeter. This test checks the continuity of CKTs 412 and 413. If CKT 413 is open, the ECM voltage on CKT 412 will measure over .6 volt (600mV).

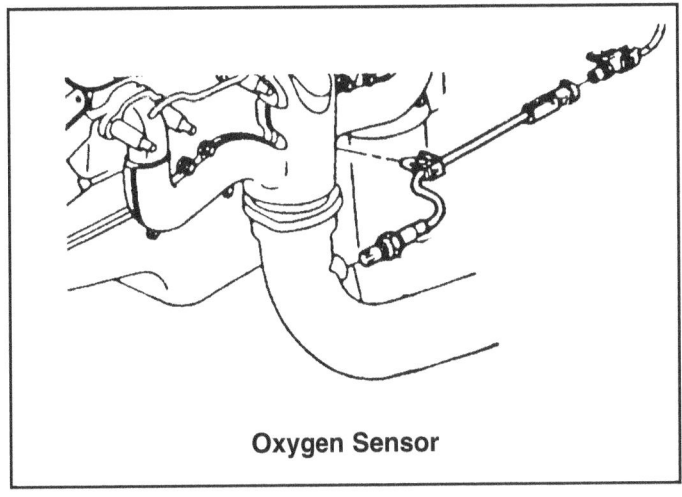

Oxygen Sensor

"NON-SCAN" DIAGNOSTICS

CODE 13   OXYGEN SENSOR CIRCUIT (OPEN CIRCUIT)

(1)
- ENGINE AT NORMAL OPERATING TEMPERATURE.
- GROUND DIAGNOSTIC TERMINAL TO ENABLE "FIELD SERVICE MODE"
- RUN ENGINE ABOVE 1200 RPM FOR 1 MINUTE AND NOTE "SERVICE ENGINE SOON" LIGHT.

FLASHING "OPEN LOOP".

FLASHING "CLOSED LOOP".

(2)
- IGNITION "OFF".
- DIAGNOSTIC TERMINAL GROUNDED.
- DISCONNECT OXYGEN SENSOR CONNECTOR AND JUMPER HARNESS CONNECTOR SIGNAL CKT 412 TO GROUND.
- START ENGINE AND IMMEDIATELY NOTE "SERVICE ENGINE SOON" LIGHT.
- IT SHOULD FLASH "OPEN LOOP" FOR ABOUT 1-4 SECONDS, THEN GO "OFF" FOR AT LEAST 30 SECONDS.

(3) CODE 13 IS INTERMITTENT. IF NO ADDITIONAL OTHER CODE IS STORED, REFER TO "INTERMITTENTS" IN SECTION OR "DIAGNOSTIC AIDS" ON FACING PAGE WHERE APPLICABLE.

OK

FAULTY OXYGEN SENSOR CONNECTOR OR SENSOR.

NOT OK

(4)
- IGNITION "ON", ENGINE "OFF"
- CHECK VOLTAGE OF CKT 412 AT O_2 SENSOR HARNESS CONNECTOR USING A DVM. IT SHOULD BE .3-.6V (300-600mV).

.3-.6 VOLT (300-600mV)	OVER .6 VOLT (600mV)	LESS THAN .3 VOLT (300mV)
FAULTY ECM.	OPEN CKT 413, FAULTY ECM CONNECTION OR ECM.	OPEN CKT 412, FAULTY ECM CONNECTION OR ECM.

FIELD SERVICE MODE:
- ENGINE RUNNING, DIAGNOSTIC TERMINAL GROUNDED.
- "OPEN LOOP", "SERVICE ENGINE SOON" LIGHT FLASHES AT A RATE OF 2.5 TIMES PER SECOND.
- "CLOSED LOOP, "SERVICE ENGINE SOON" LIGHT FLASHES AT A RATE OF 1 TIME PER SECOND.

Used with permission of General Motors

CLEAR CODES AND CONFIRM "CLOSED LOOP" OPERATION AND NO "SERVICE ENGINE LIGHT SOON" LIGHT

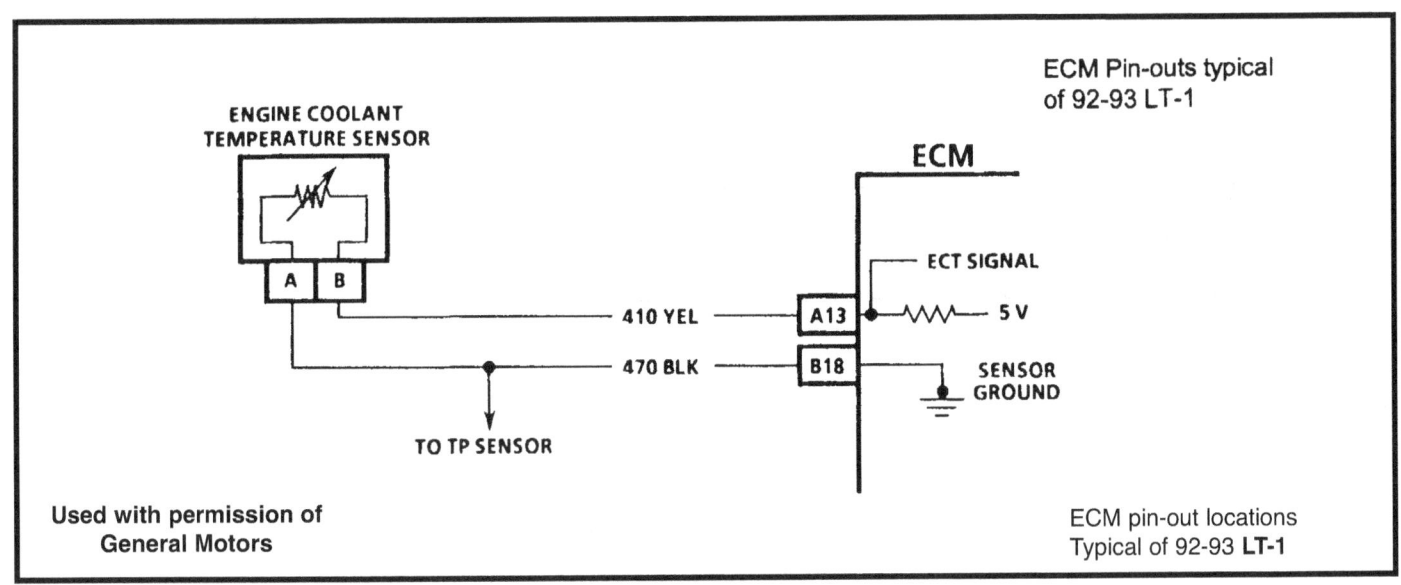

DTC 14
ENGINE COOLANT TEMPERATURE (ECT) SENSOR CIRCUIT (HIGH TEMPERATURE INDICATED) TYPICAL OF ALL TPI & LT-1

Circuit Description:

The Engine Coolant Temperature (ECT) sensor uses a thermistor to control a signal voltage to the ECM. The ECM applies a voltage on CKT 410 to the sensor. When the engine coolant is cold, the sensor (thermistor) resistance is high, therefore the ECM will sense a high signal voltage. As the engine coolant warms, the sensor resistance becomes less, and the voltage drops. At normal engine temperature (85°C - 95°C or 185°F - 203°F) the voltage will measure about 1.5 to 2.0 volts.

Test Description:

Numbers below refer to circled numbers on the diagnostic chart.

1. DTC 14 will set if:

    Signal voltage indicates an engine coolant temperature above 130°C (266°F).

2. This test will determine if CKT 410 is shorted to ground, which will cause the condition for a DTC 14.

Diagnostic Aids:

Check harness routing for a potential short to ground in CKT 410.

Tech 1 displays engine coolant temperature in degrees celsius and fahrenheit. After engine is started, the temperature should rise steadily, reach normal operating temperature, and then stabilize when thermostat opens.

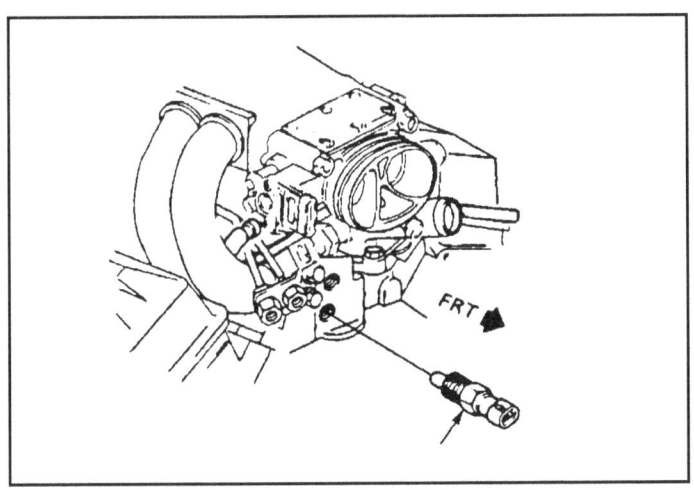

Chevy TPI Swapper's Guide

"NON-SCAN" DIAGNOSTICS

DTC 14 — **ENGINE COOLANT TEMPERATURE (ECT) SENSOR CIRCUIT**
(HIGH TEMPERATURE INDICATED) TYPICAL OF TPI & LT-1

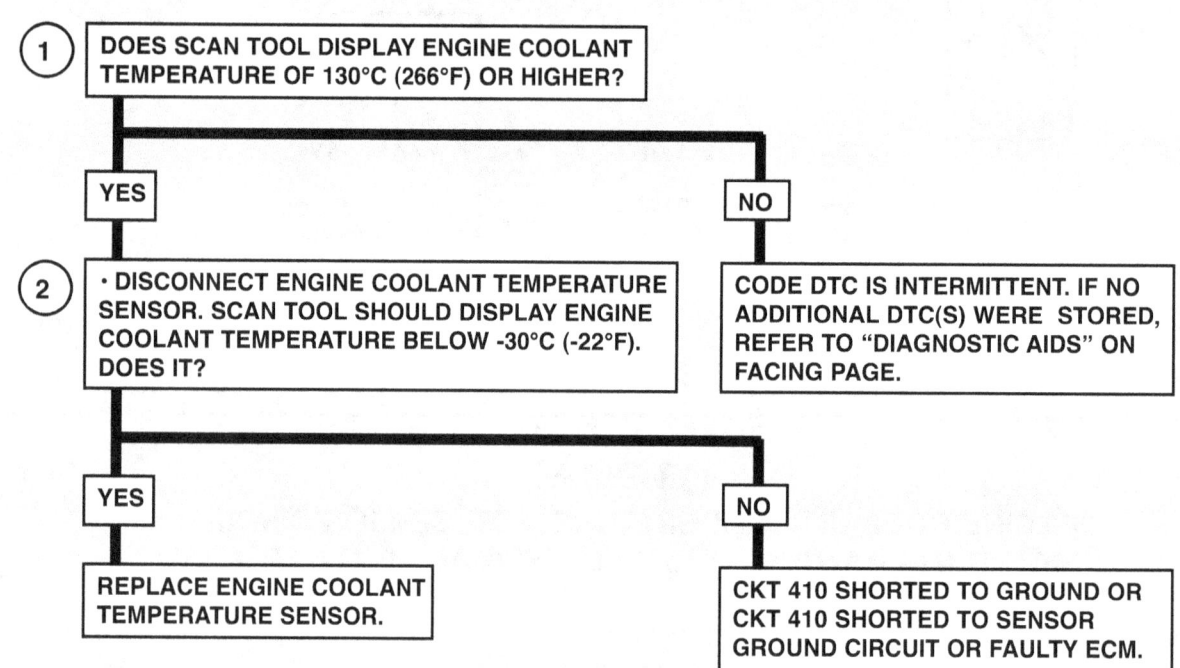

DIAGNOSTIC AID

ENGINE COOLANT TEMPERATURE SENSOR		
TEMPERATURE VS. RESISTANCE VALUES (APPROXIMATE)		
°C	°F	OHMS
100	212	177
90	194	241
80	176	332
70	158	467
60	140	667
50	122	973
45	113	1188
40	104	1459
35	95	1802
30	86	2238
25	77	2796
20	68	3520
15	59	4450
10	50	5670
5	41	7280
0	32	9420
-5	23	12300
-10	14	16180
-15	5	21450
-20	-4	28680
-30	-22	52700
-40	-40	100700

Used with permission of General Motors

"AFTER REPAIRS," REFER TO DTC CRITERIA ON FACING PAGE AND CONFIRM DTC DOES NOT RESET.

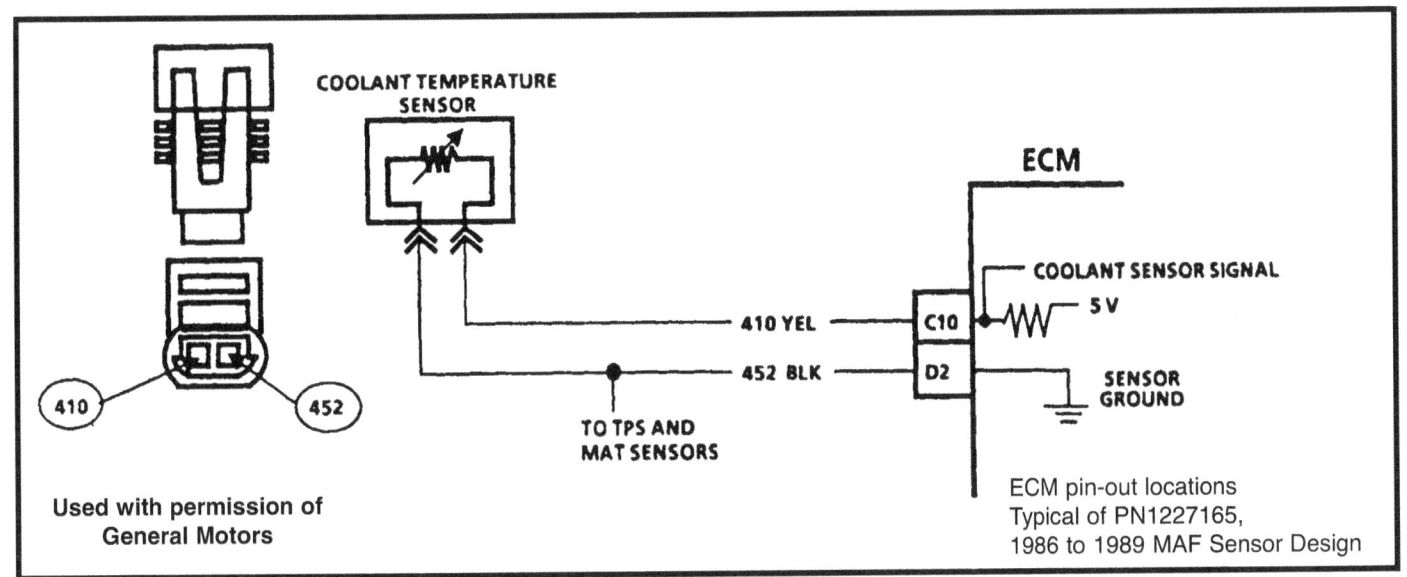

CODE 15
COOLANT TEMPERATURE SENSOR CIRCUIT
(LOW TEMPERATURE INDICATED)

Circuit Description:

The coolant temperature sensor uses a thermistor to control the signal voltage to the ECM. The ECM applies a voltage on CKT 410 to the sensor. When the engine is cold, the sensor (thermistor) resistance is high, therefore the ECM will see high signal voltage.

As the engine warms, the sensor resistance becomes less, and the voltage drops. At normal engine operating temperature (85°C - 95°C) the voltage will measure about 1.5 to 2.0 volts at the ECM.

Test Description:

Numbers below refer to circled numbers on the diagnostic chart.

1. CODE 15 will set if:

   Signal voltage indicates a coolant temperature less than -44°C (-47°F) for 3 seconds.

2. This test simulates a Code 14. If the ECM recognizes the low signal and sets a Code 14 the ECM and wiring are OK. If Code 15 repeats, the problem is an open CKT 410, 452, a poor connection at the ECM or sensor, or a faulty ECM.

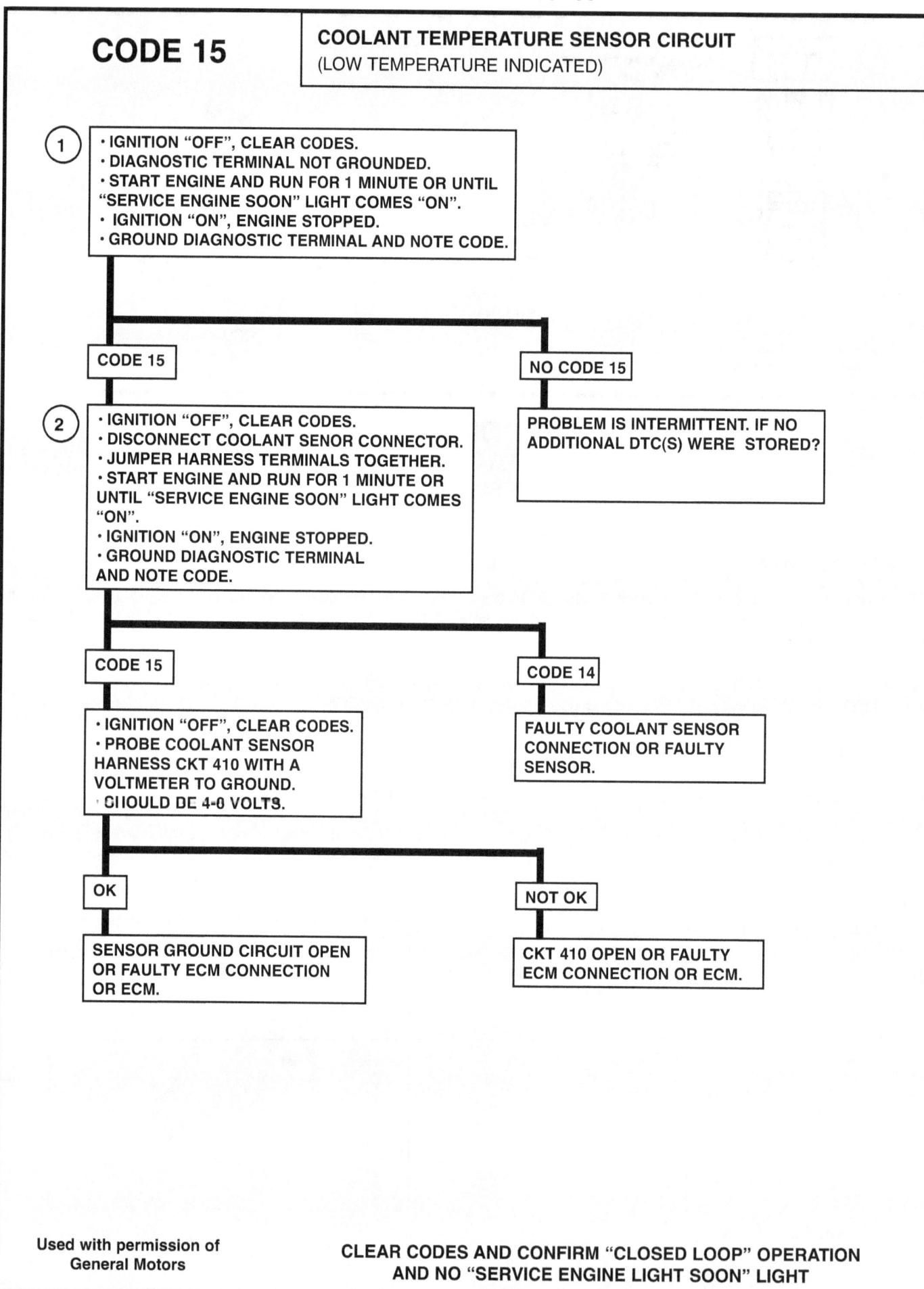

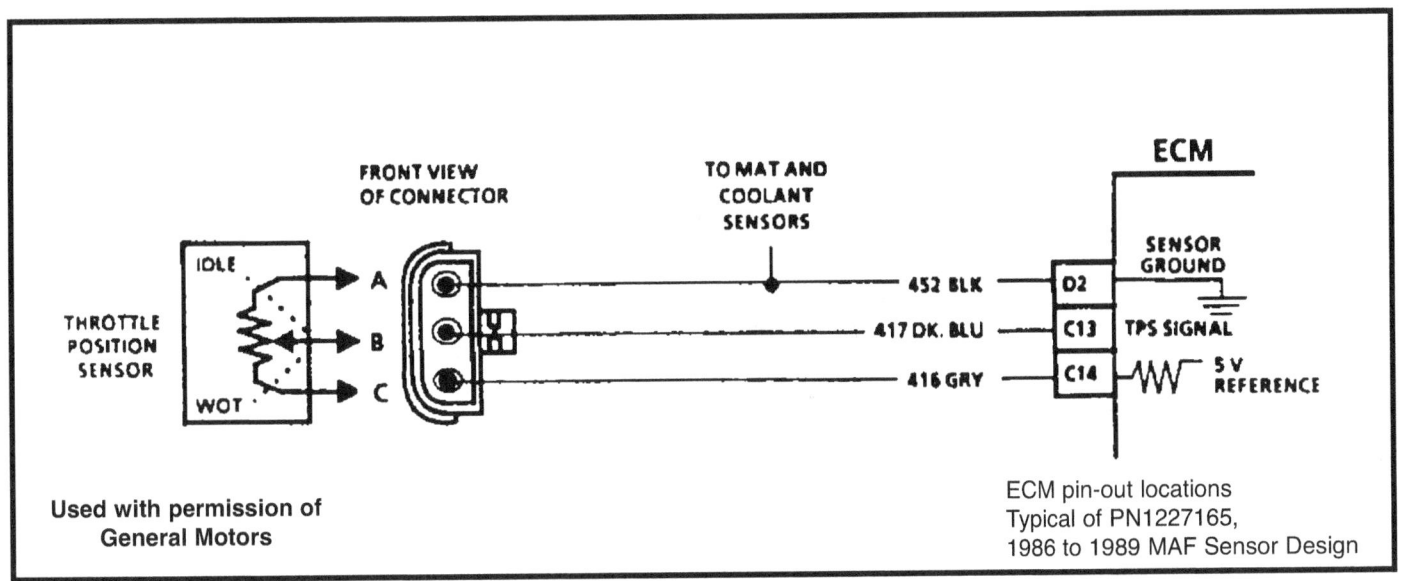

CODE 21
THROTTLE POSITION SENSOR
(SIGNAL VOLTAGE HIGH)

Circuit Description:

The throttle position sensor (TPS) provides a voltage signal that changes, relative to the throttle blade. Signal voltage will vary from about .5 at idle to about 5 volts at wide open throttle (WOT).

The TPS signal is one of the most important inputs used by the electronic control module (ECM) for fuel control and for most of the ECM control outputs.

Test Description:

Numbers below refer to circled numbers on the diagnostic chart.

1. CODE 21 will set if:

   TPS signal voltage is greater than 2.5 volts.
   Engine is running.
   Air flow is less than 15 gm/sec.
   All conditions met for 3 seconds.

OR

TPS signal over 4.5 volts with ignition on.

With throttle closed, the TPS should read less than .62 volts. If not, check adjustment.

2. With the TPS sensor disconnected, the TPS voltage should go low, if the ECM and wiring are OK.

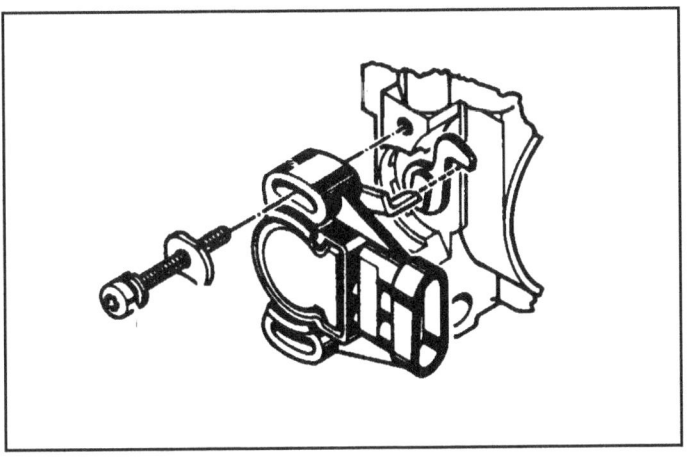

Chevy TPI Swapper's Guide

"NON-SCAN" DIAGNOSTICS

CODE 21
THROTTLE POSITION SENSOR (TPS) CIRCUIT
(SIGNAL VOLTAGE HIGH)

(1)
- ENGINE AT NORMAL OPERATING TEMPERATURE.
- DIAGNOSTIC TERMINAL NOT GROUNDED.
- IGNITION "OFF", CLEAR CODES.
- START ENGINE AND IDLE IN NEUTRAL, AC OFF, FOR ONE MINUTE OR UNTIL "SERVICE ENGINE SOON" LIGHT COMES "ON".
- IGNITION "ON", ENGINE STOPPED.
- GROUND DIAGNOSTIC TERMINAL AND NOTE CODE.

CODE 21 → **(2)**
- DIAGNOSTIC TERMINAL NOT GROUNDED.
- IGNITION "OFF", CLEAR CODES.
- DISCONNECT SENSOR.
- START ENGINE AND IDLE IN NEUTRAL, AC OFF, FOR ONE MINUTE OR UNTIL "SERVICE ENGINE SOON" LIGHT COMES "ON".
- IGNITION "ON", ENGINE STOPPED.
- GROUND DIAGNOSTIC TERMINAL AND NOTE CODE.

NO CODE 21 STORED
PROBLEM IS INTERMITTENT.

CODE 22
- PROBE TPS SENSOR GROUND CIRCUIT AT HARNESS CONNECTOR WITH TEST LIGHT TO 12 VOLTS.

CODE 21
CHECK CKT 417 SHORTED TO A VOLTAGE SOURCE OR FAULTY ECM.

LIGHT "ON"
FAULTY TPS CONNECTION OR SENSOR.

LIGHT "OFF"
OPEN SENSOR GROUND CKT FAULTY CONNECTION OR FAULTY ECM.

Used with permission of General Motors

CLEAR CODES AND CONFIRM "CLOSED LOOP" OPERATION AND NO "SERVICE ENGINE LIGHT SOON" LIGHT

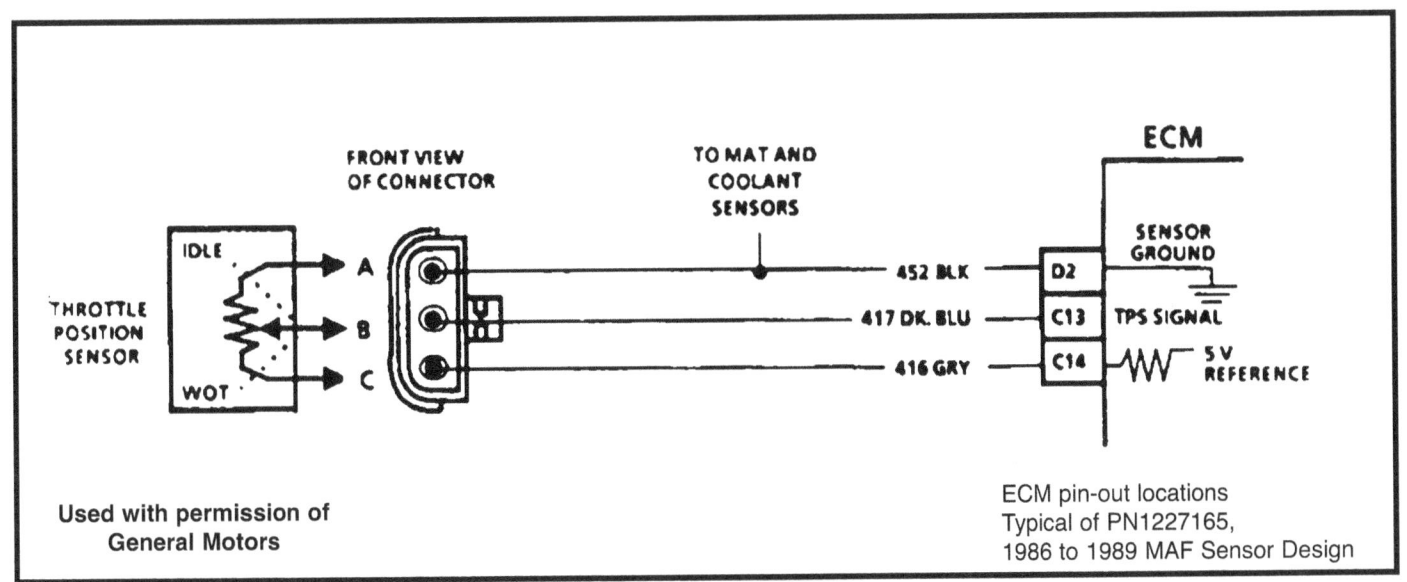

CODE 22
THROTTLE POSITION SENSOR (TPS) CIRCUIT
(SIGNAL VOLTAGE LOW)

Circuit Description:

The throttle position sensor (TPS) provides a voltage signal that changes, relative to the throttle blade. Signal voltage will vary from about .5 at idle to about 5 volts at wide open throttle (WOT).

The TPS signal is one of the most important inputs used by the electronic control module (ECM) for fuel control and for most of the ECM control outputs.

Test Description:

Numbers below refer to circled numbers on the diagnostic chart.

1. CODE 22 will set if:

   Engine running.
   TPS signal voltage is less than about .2 volt for 3 seconds.

2. Simulates Code 21: (high voltage) if the ECM recognizes the high signal voltage the ECM and wiring are OK.

3. Checks for reference voltage from the ECM.

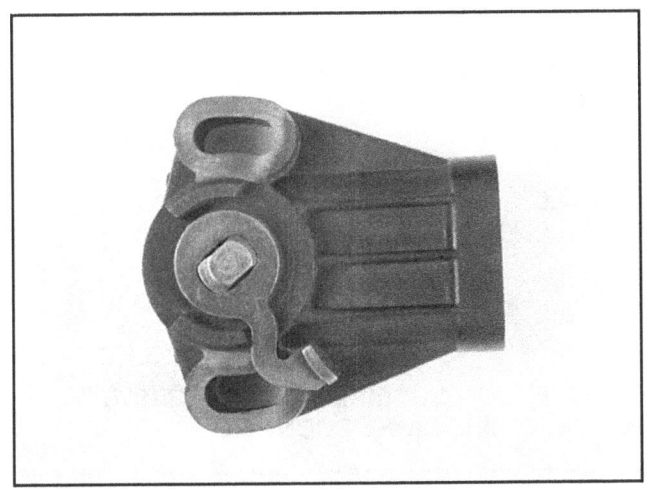

Chevy TPI Swapper's Guide

"NON-SCAN" DIAGNOSTICS

CODE 22

THROTTLE POSITION SENSOR (TPS) CIRCUIT
(SIGNAL VOLTAGE LOW)

(1)
- ENGINE AT NORMAL OPERATING TEMPERATURE.
- DIAGNOSTIC TERMINAL NOT GROUNDED.
- IGNITION "OFF", CLEAR CODES.
- START ENGINE AND IDLE IN NEUTRAL, AC OFF, FOR ONE MINUTE OR UNTIL "SERVICE ENGINE SOON" LIGHT COMES "ON".
- IGNITION "ON", ENGINE STOPPED.
- GROUND DIAGNOSTIC TERMINAL AND NOTE CODE.

CODE 22

NO CODE 22
PROBLEM IS INTERMITTENT.

(2)
- DIAGNOSTIC TERMINAL NOT GROUNDED.
- IGNITION "OFF", CLEAR CODES.
- DISCONNECT TPS AND JUMPER 5V REFERENCE CIRCUIT TO TPS SIGNAL CIRCUIT AT HARNESS CONNECTOR.
- START ENGINE AND IDLE IN NEUTRAL, AC OFF, FOR ONE MINUTE OR UNTIL "SERVICE ENGINE SOON" LIGHT COMES "ON".
- IGNITION "ON", ENGINE STOPPED.
- GROUND DIAGNOSTIC TERMINAL AND NOTE CODE.

CODE 22
- REMOVE JUMPER.
- CHECK FOR 5V REFERENCE SIGNAL FROM ECM AT TPS HARNESS CONNECTOR "C" TO GROUND USING DIGITAL VOLTMETER (J-34029-A) OR EQUIVALENT.

CODE 21
IF TPS IS ADJUSTABLE, ADJUST TO SPECIFICATION (SEE SECTION "C". IF ADJUSTMENT IS NOT POSSIBLE, REPLACE TPS.

4-6 VOLTS
OPEN OR SHORT TO GROUND IN SIGNAL CIRCUIT, FAULTY ECM CONNECTOR TERMINAL OR ECM.

BELOW 4 VOLTS
OPEN OR SHORT TO GROUND IN 5V REFERENCE CIRCUIT, FAULTY ECM CONNECTOR TERMINAL OR ECM.

Used with permission of General Motors

CLEAR CODES AND CONFIRM "CLOSED LOOP" OPERATION AND NO "SERVICE ENGINE LIGHT SOON" LIGHT

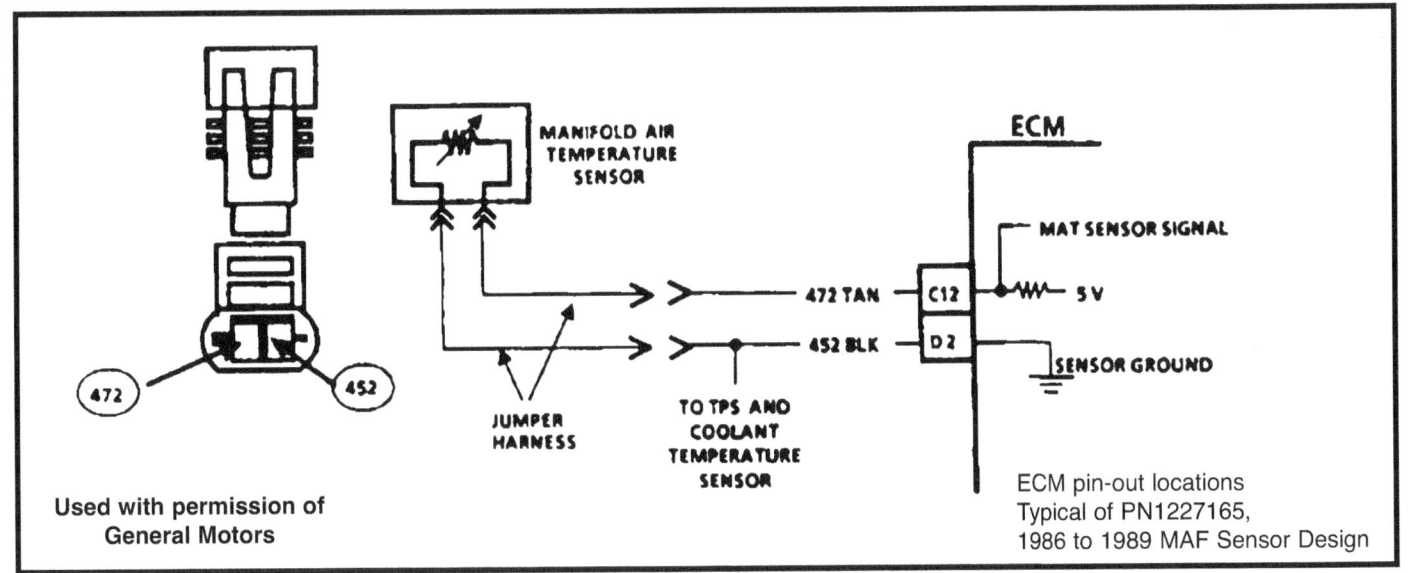

Used with permission of General Motors

ECM pin-out locations Typical of PN1227165, 1986 to 1989 MAF Sensor Design

CODE 23
MANIFOLD AIR TEMPERATURE (MAT) SENSOR CIRCUIT
(LOW TEMPERATURE INDICATED)

Circuit Description:

The manifold air temperature (MAT) sensor uses a thermistor to control the signal voltage to the electronic control module (ECM). The ECM applies a voltage (about 5 volts) on CKT 472 to the sensor. When the air is cold, the sensor (thermistor) resistance is high, therefore the ECM will see a high signal voltage. If the sir is warm, the sensor resistance is low, therefore the ECM will see a low voltage.

Test Description:

Numbers below refer to circled numbers on the diagnostic chart.

1. CODE 23 will set if:

A signal voltage indicates a manifold air temperature below -30°C (-22°F) for 12 seconds.

Time since engine start is 4 minutes or longer.

No vehicle speed sensor (VSS) (vehicle not moving).

A Code 23 will set, due to an open sensor, wire or connection. This test will determine if the wiring and the ECM are OK. The MAT sensor is difficult to reach and this test can be performed by disconnecting the MAT jumper harness connector after removing coil from engine.

2. If the resistance is greater than 25,000 ohms replace the sensor.

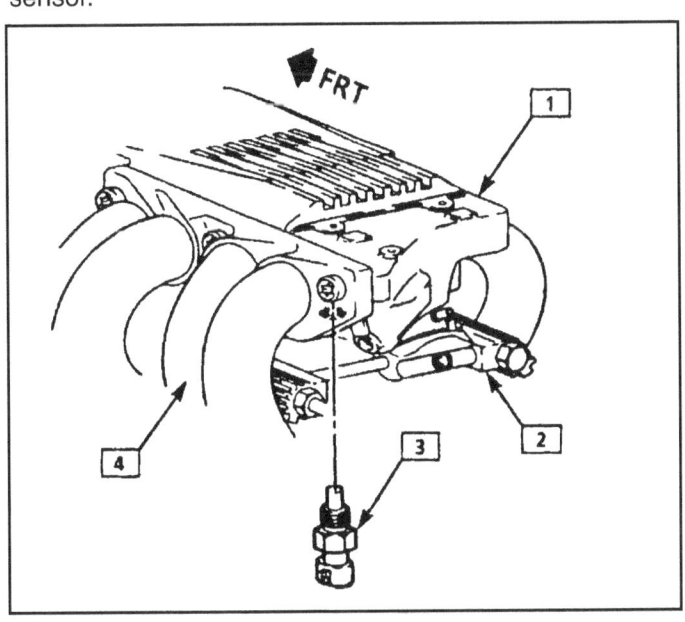

Chevy TPI Swapper's Guide

"NON-SCAN" DIAGNOSTICS

CODE 23
MANIFOLD AIR TEMPERATURE (MAT) SENSOR CIRCUIT
(LOW TEMPERATURE INDICATED)

1
- DISCONNECT MAT SENSOR.
- IGNITION "ON", ENGINE STOPPED.
- CHECK VOLTAGE BETWEEN MAT SENSOR HARNESS TERMINALS USING A DIGITAL VOLTMETER (J-34029-A) OR EQUIVALENT.

4 VOLTS OR OVER

2
- CHECK RESISTANCE ACROSS MAT SENSOR TERMINALS. SHOULD BE LESS THAN 25,000 OHMS, SEE TABLE FOR APPROXIMATE TEMPERATURE TO RESISTANCE VALUES.

OK
CHECK FOR SIGNAL CIRCUIT BEING SHORTED TO VOLTAGE. IF NOT, CODE 23 IS INTERMITTENT. IF ADDITIONAL CODES WERE STORED, SEE APPLICABLE CHARTS.

NOT OK
REPLACE SENSOR.

BELOW 4 VOLTS
- CHECK VOLTAGE BETWEEN HARNESS CONNECTOR SIGNAL CIRCUIT AND GROUND.

4 VOLTS OR OVER
FAULTY SENSOR GROUND CIRCUIT, FAULTY CONNECTION(S) OR FAULTY ECM.

BELOW 4 VOLTS
OPEN SIGNAL CIRCUIT, FAULTY CONNECTION OR FAULTY ECM.

DIAGNOSTIC AID

ENGINE COOLANT TEMPERATURE SENSOR		
TEMPERATURE VS. RESISTANCE VALUES (APPROXIMATE)		
°C	°F	OHMS
100	212	177
90	194	241
80	176	332
70	158	467
60	140	667
50	122	973
45	113	1188
40	104	1459
35	95	1802
30	86	2238
25	77	2796
20	68	3520
15	59	4450
10	50	5670
5	41	7280
0	32	9420
-5	23	12300
-10	14	16180
-15	5	21450
-20	-4	28680
-30	-22	52700
-40	-40	100700

Used with permission of General Motors

"AFTER REPAIRS," REFER TO DTC CRITERIA ON FACING PAGE AND CONFIRM DTC DOES NOT RESET.

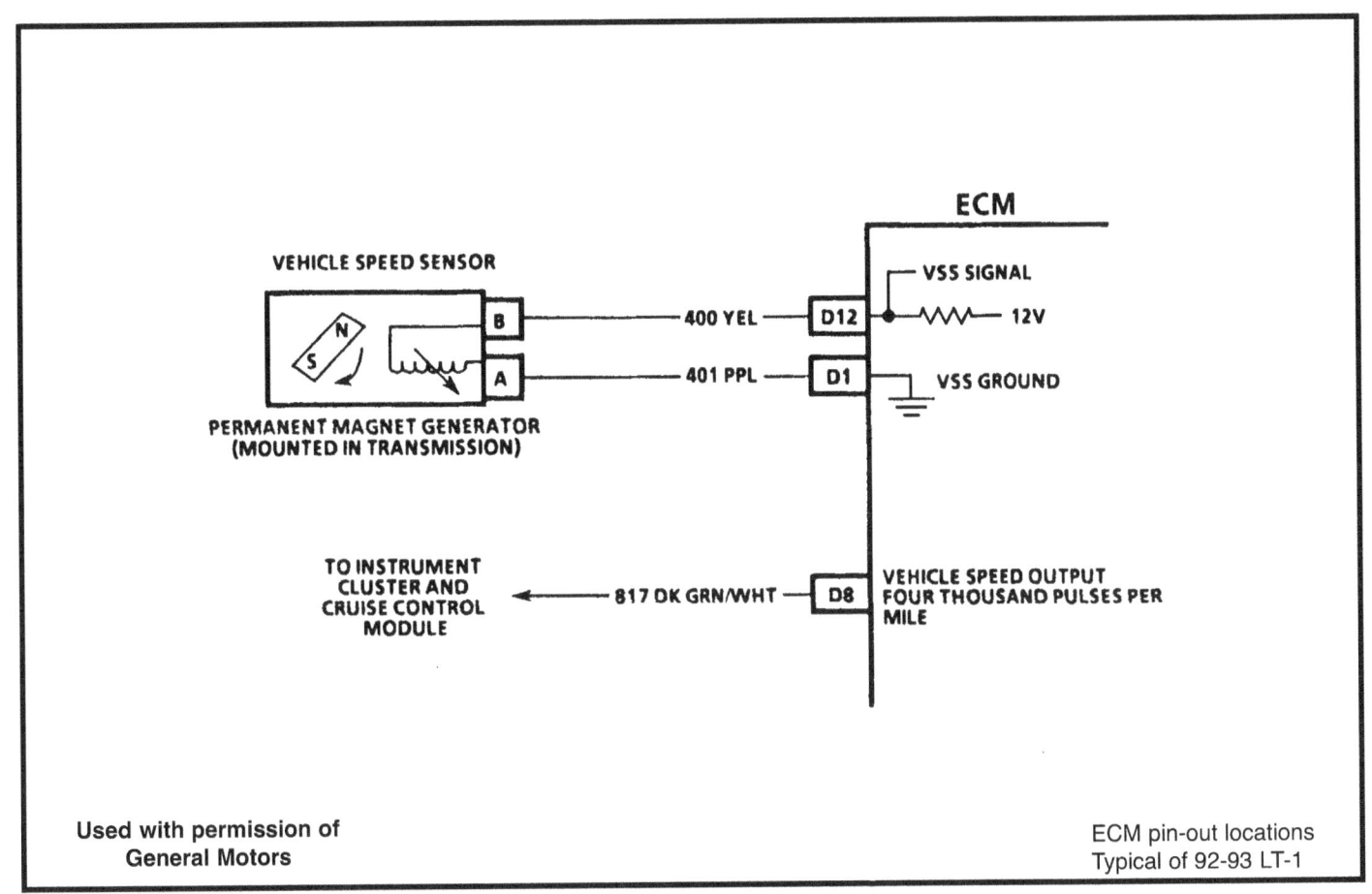

Used with permission of General Motors

ECM pin-out locations
Typical of 92-93 LT-1

DTC 24
VEHICLE SPEED SENSOR (VSS) CIRCUIT
TYPICAL OF 90-96 TPI & LT-1

Circuit Description:

Vehicle speed information is provided to the ECM by the vehicle speed sensor, which is a Permanent Magnet (PM) generator located in the transmission. The PM generator produces a pulsing voltage. The AC voltage level and the number of pulses increases as the speed of the vehicle increases. The ECM then converts the pulsing voltage to vehicle speed which is used for calculations. The vehicle speed can be displayed with a Tech 1.

The ECM supplies a signal, on CKT 817, to operate the speedometer and the odometer. The VSS signal is also sent to the cruise control module.

Test Description:

Numbers below refer to circled numbers on the diagnostic chart.

1. DTC 24 will set if vehicle speed is less than 5 km/h (3 mph) when:

   Engine speed is between 1250 and 3000 RPM.
   TP sensor is less than 2%.
   Low load conditions.
   MAP less than 22 kPa.
   Above conditions met for 4 seconds.

These conditions are met during a road load deceleration.
2. DTC 24 is being caused by a faulty ECM, faulty PROM or an incorrect PROM.

Diagnostic Aids:

Check CKTs 400 and 401 for proper connections to be sure they are clean and tight and the harness is routed correctly.

Chevy TPI Swapper's Guide

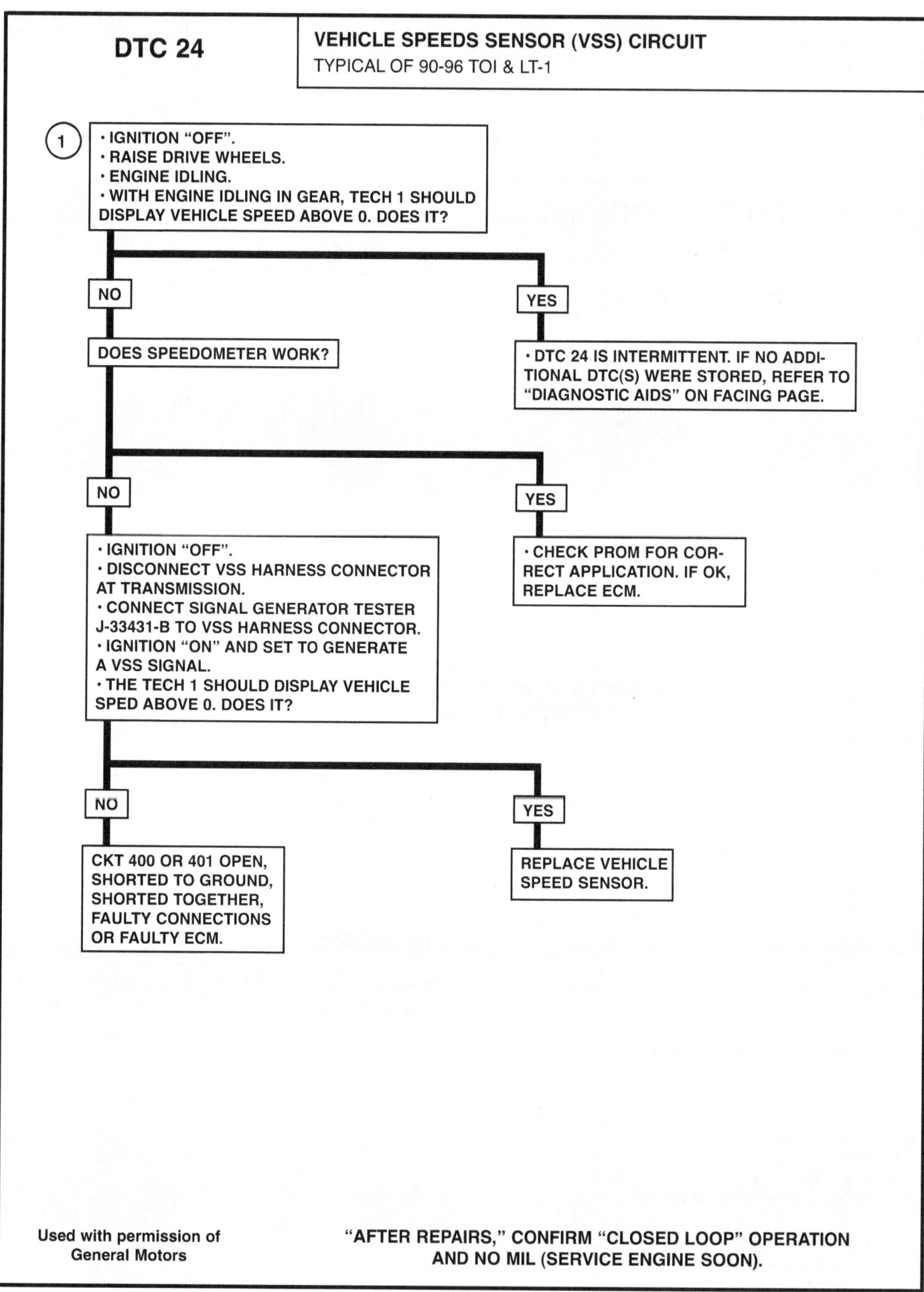

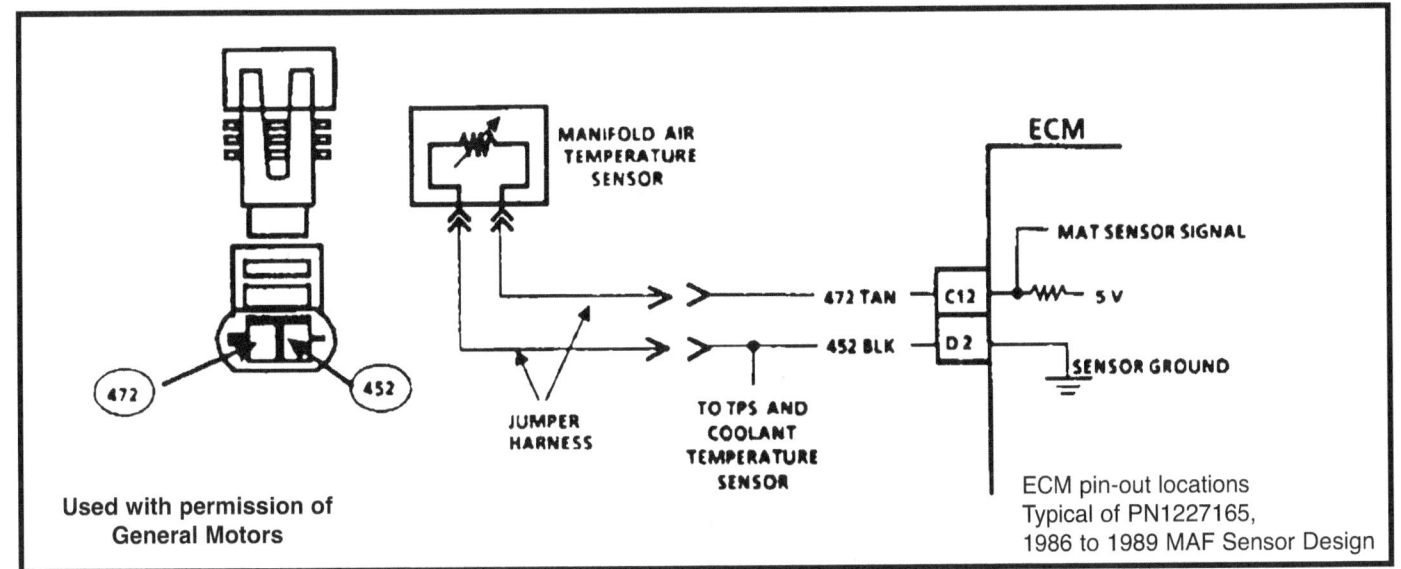

CODE 25
MANIFOLD AIR TEMPERATURE (MAT) SENSOR CIRCUIT
(HIGH TEMPERATURE INDICATED)

Circuit Description:

The manifold air temperature (MAT) sensor uses a thermistor to control the signal voltage to the ECM. The ECM applies a voltage (4-6) on CKT 472 to the sensor. When the manifold air is cold, the sensor (thermistor) resistance is high, therefore the ECM will see a high signal voltage. As the air warms, the sensor resistance becomes less, and the voltage drops.

Test Description:

Numbers below refer to circled numbers on the diagnostic chart.

1. CODE 25 will set if:

   Signal voltage indicates a manifold air temperature greater than 150°C (302°F) for 2 seconds.

   Time since engine start is 1 minute or longer.

   A vehicle speed is present.

2. If the resistance is greater than 100 ohms, replace the sensor.

"NON-SCAN" DIAGNOSTICS

CODE 25 — MANIFOLD AIR TEMPERATURE (MAT) SENSOR CIRCUIT
(HIGH TEMPERATURE INDICATED)

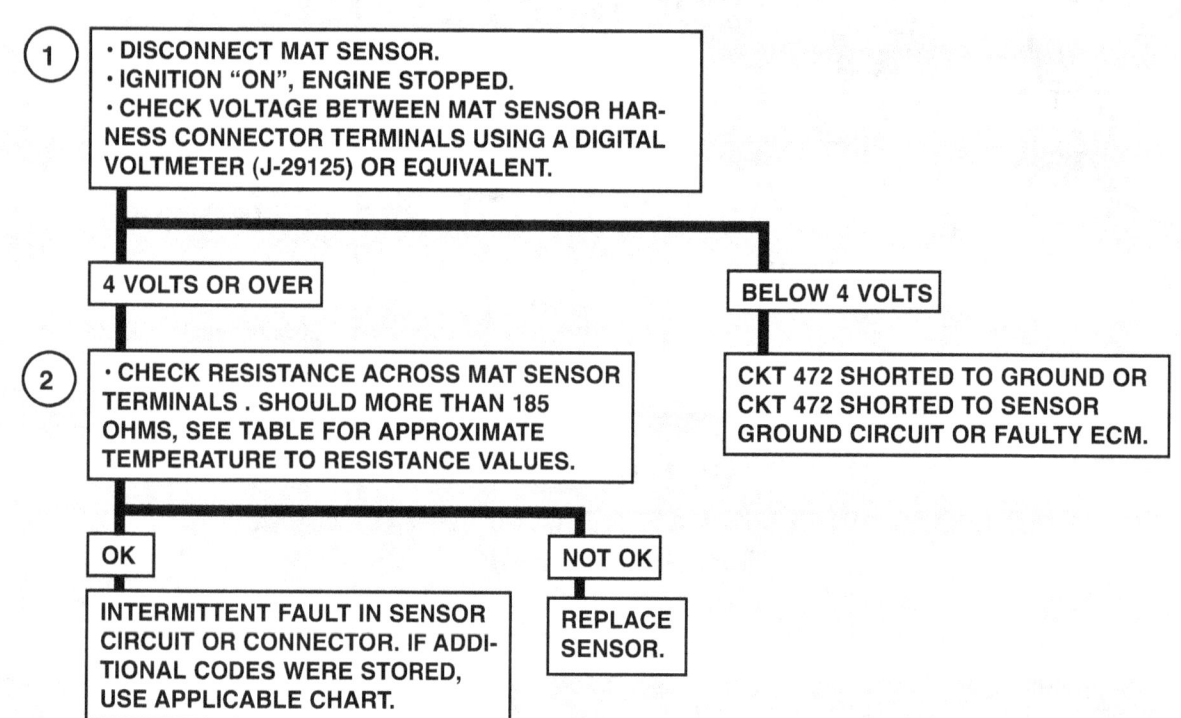

(1)
- DISCONNECT MAT SENSOR.
- IGNITION "ON", ENGINE STOPPED.
- CHECK VOLTAGE BETWEEN MAT SENSOR HARNESS CONNECTOR TERMINALS USING A DIGITAL VOLTMETER (J-29125) OR EQUIVALENT.

4 VOLTS OR OVER

(2)
- CHECK RESISTANCE ACROSS MAT SENSOR TERMINALS. SHOULD MORE THAN 185 OHMS, SEE TABLE FOR APPROXIMATE TEMPERATURE TO RESISTANCE VALUES.

OK — INTERMITTENT FAULT IN SENSOR CIRCUIT OR CONNECTOR. IF ADDITIONAL CODES WERE STORED, USE APPLICABLE CHART.

NOT OK — REPLACE SENSOR.

BELOW 4 VOLTS

CKT 472 SHORTED TO GROUND OR CKT 472 SHORTED TO SENSOR GROUND CIRCUIT OR FAULTY ECM.

MAT SENSOR		
TEMPERATURE VS. RESISTANCE VALUES (APPROXIMATE)		
°C	°F	OHMS
210	100	185
160	70	450
100	38	1600
70	20	3400
40	4	7500
20	-7	13500
0	-18	25000
-40	-40	100700

Used with permission of General Motors

CLEAR CODES AND CONFIRM "CLOSED LOOP" OPERATION AND NO "SERVICE ENGINE SOON" LIGHT.

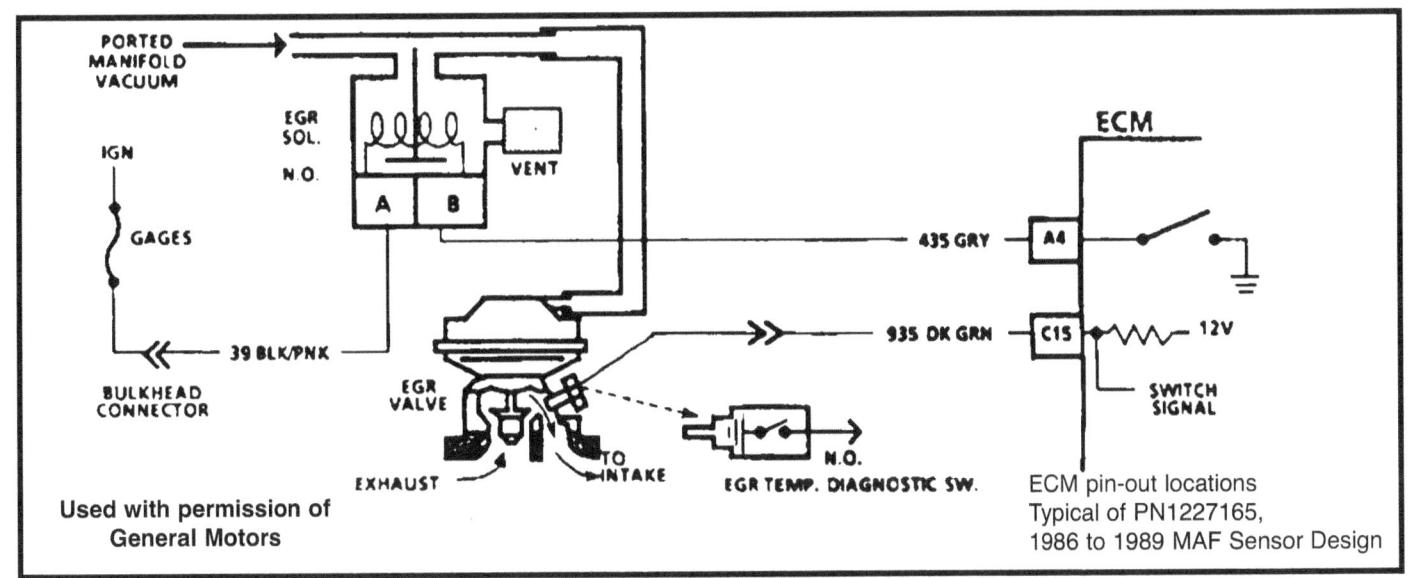

Used with permission of General Motors

ECM pin-out locations Typical of PN1227165, 1986 to 1989 MAF Sensor Design

CODE 32
EXHAUST GAS RECIRCULATION (EGR) CIRCUIT

Circuit Description:

THE EGR valve vacuum is controlled by an ECM controlled solenoid. The ECM will turn the EGR "ON" and "OFF" (duty cycle) by grounding CKT 435. The duty cycle is calculated by the ECM based on information from the coolant and mass air flow sensor and engine rpms. There should be (NO EGR) when in park or neutral when TPS input is below a specified value or when TPS is indicating wide open throttle (WOT).

With the ignition "ON", engine stopped, the EGR solenoid is de-energized and, by grounding the diagnostic terminal, the solenoid is energized. Diagnostic switch will close when the EGR valve opens and exhaust gas is present at the switch.

Test Description:

Numbers below refer to circled numbers on the diagnostic chart.

Code 32 means that the EGR diagnostic switch was closed during start-up or that the switch was not detected closed under the following conditions:

Coolant temperature greater than 80°C (176°F).

EGR duty cycle commanded by the ECM is greater than 48%.

TPS less than wide open throttle (WOT), but not at idle.

Codes 21, 22, 33, 34 not present.

If the switch is detected closed during start-up, or if the switch is detected open when the above conditions are met, the "Service Engine Soon" light will remain "ON" unless the switch changes state.

1. This test will determine if the ECM set the code due to CKT 935 being grounded on start-up.

2. This test checks if there is any faulty switch or ECM.

3. This test will check for a possible open in CKT 935.

4. By grounding the diagnostic terminal, the EGR solenoid should close and allow vacuum to be applied and the vacuum should hold.

5. This test will determine if the electrical control part of the system is at fault or if the connector or solenoid are at fault.

6. By plugging the EGR valve side and ungrounding the diagnostic terminal, the solenoid valve should open and allow vacuum to bleed off through the vent.

7. With the engine running and vacuum applied to the valve, the valve should move to the fully open position.

8. Due to this engine using a negative back pressure valve, the valve should close when the engine is cranked over.

Chevy TPI Swapper's Guide **83**

"NON-SCAN" DIAGNOSTICS

CODE 32 — EXHAUST GAS RECIRCULATION (EGR) CIRCUIT

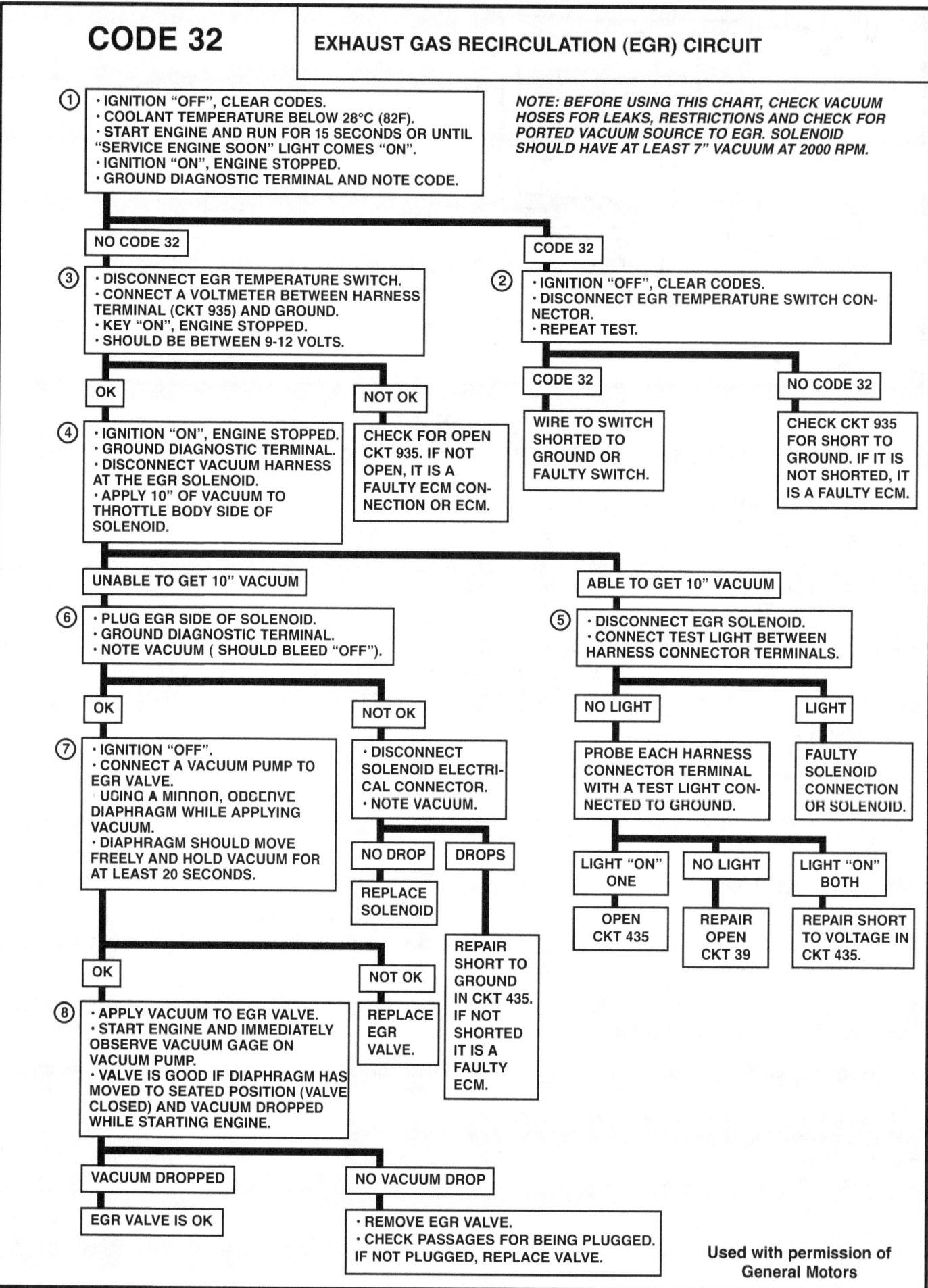

Used with permission of General Motors

Chevy TPI Swapper's Guide

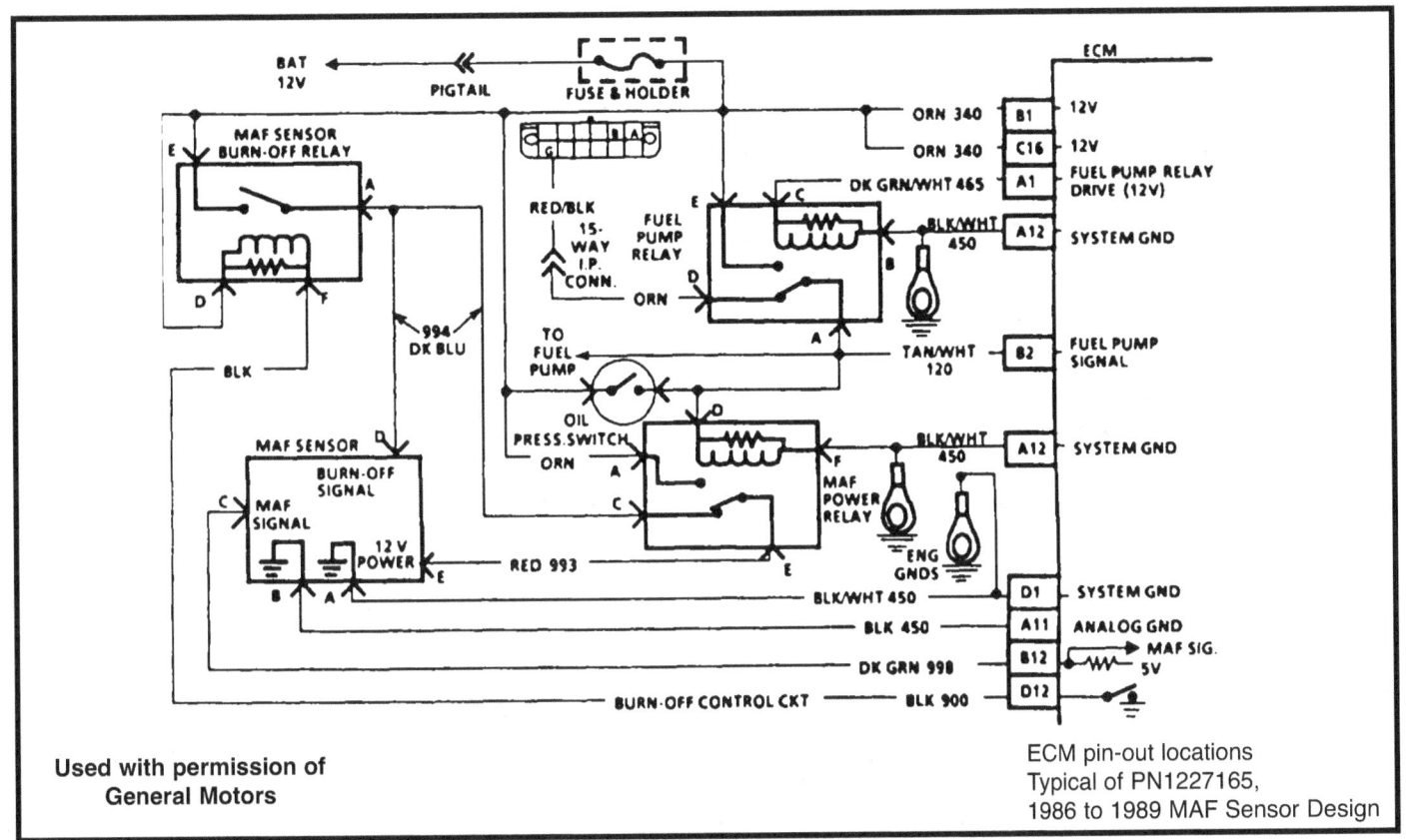

Used with permission of General Motors

ECM pin-out locations Typical of PN1227165, 1986 to 1989 MAF Sensor Design

CODE 33
MASS AIR FLOW (MAF) SENSOR CIRCUIT
(GM/SEC HIGH)

Circuit Description:

The mass air flow (MAF) sensor measures the amount of air which passes through it. The ECM uses this information to determine the operating condition of the engine and control fuel delivery.

The oil pressure switch or the ECM, through control of the fuel pump relay, will provide 12 volts for the MAF power relay which provides the 12 volts needed by the MAF sensor.

The ECM provides a current limiting 5V on the signal line (CKT 998). The MAF sensor then changes the signal by dropping the voltage so that with low air flow the ECM sees a low voltage and a high air flow will cause the ECM to see near the 5 volt supply.

Test Description:

Numbers below refer to circled numbers on the diagnostic chart.

Code 33 indicates: ECM has seen flow in excess of 45 grams per second (above 2.2 volts) for one second when:

Engine is first started

OR

TPS is less than 1/4 throttle.
RPM is less than 2000.

Due to the 5 volt pull-up resistor in the ECM if CKT 998 becomes open, the ECM will see a high voltage signal and set a Code 33.

1. This test will determine if the conditions to set the code still exist.

2. With the ALDL terminal "G" jumpered to 12 volts, there should be 12 volts at the sensor. If no voltage is present, make sure that the fuel pump is running. If not, repair fuel pump circuit.

3. If a burn off signal is present at the MAF sensor with the engine running, a Code 33 will set. Be sure no voltage is present on CKT 994 for the first 2 seconds after the ignition is turned "ON" or after the 2 second period.

4. The ECM sources a voltage (4-6 volts) to the MAF sensor on CKT 998. This test checks for that voltage.

"NON-SCAN" DIAGNOSTICS

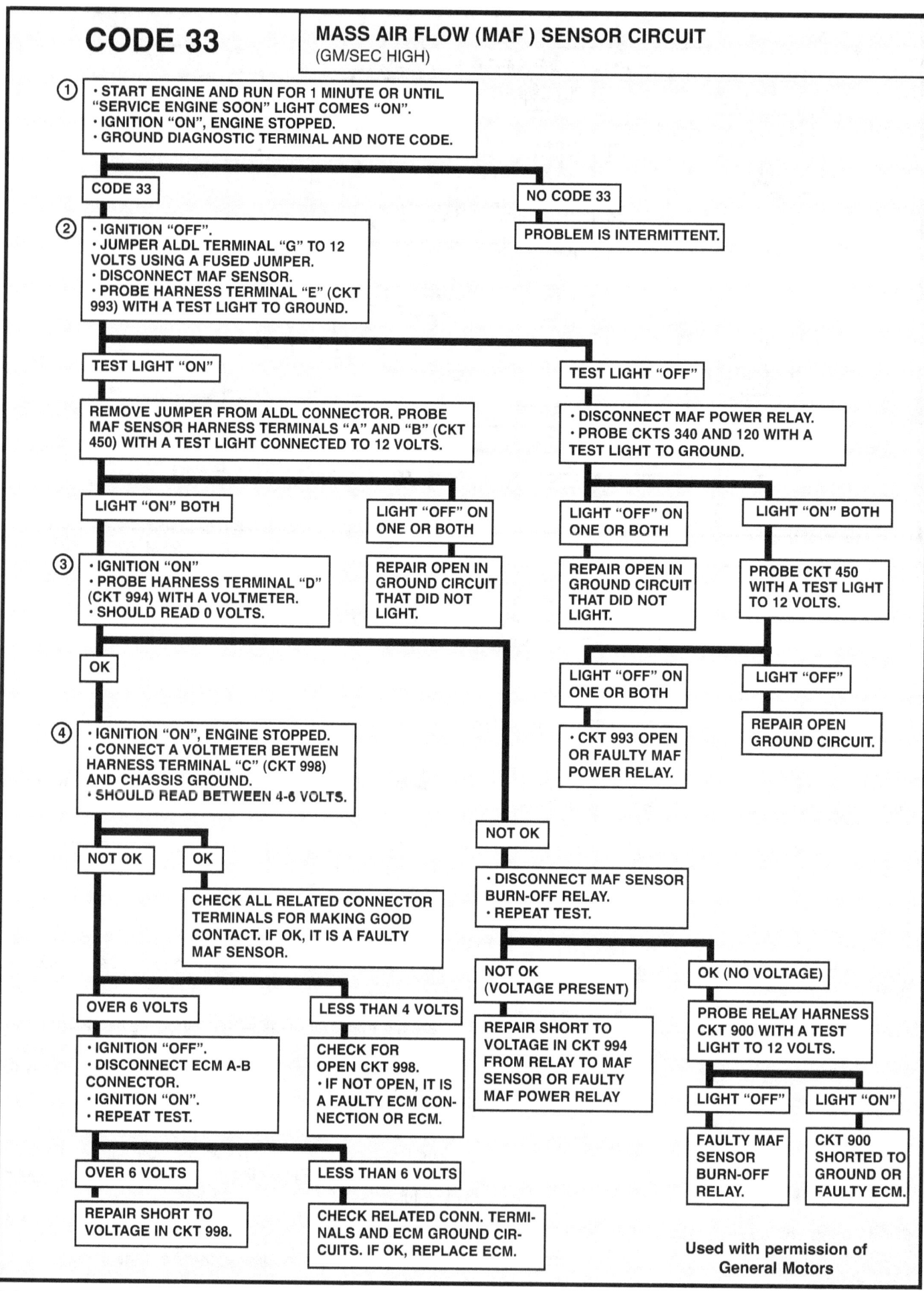

Used with permission of General Motors

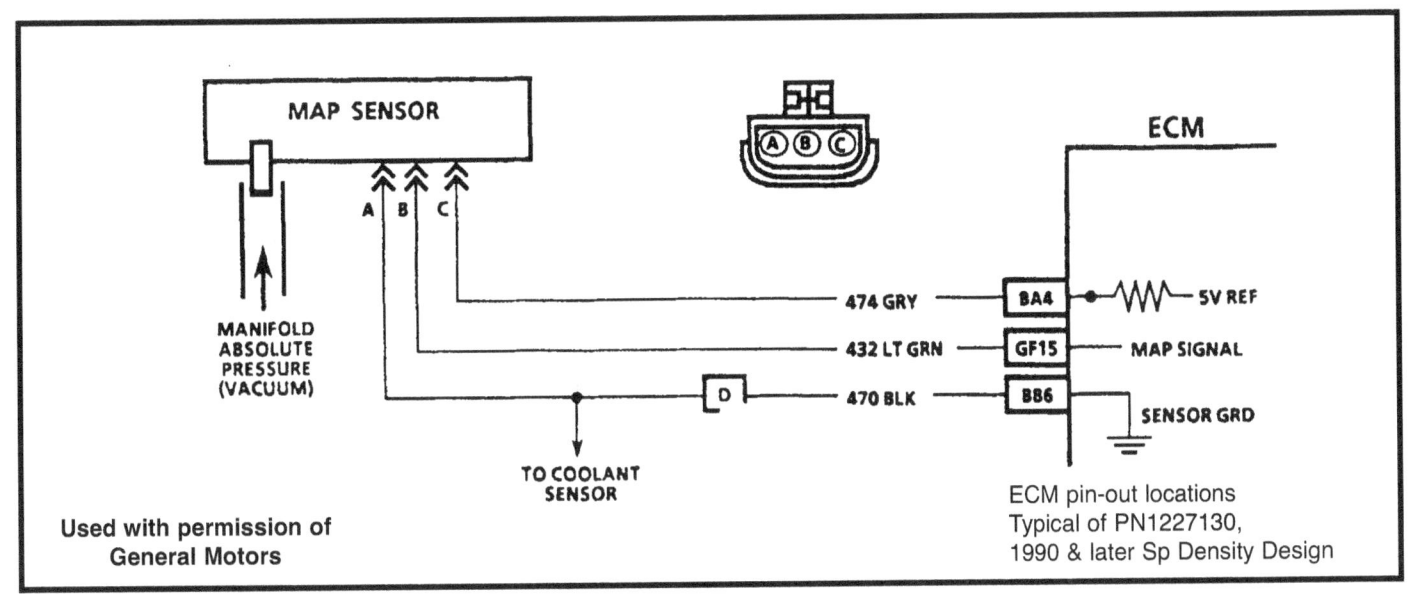

CODE 33
MANIFOLD ABSOLUTE PRESSURE (MAP) SENSOR CIRCUIT
(SIGNAL VOLTAGE HIGH-LOW VACUUM)

Circuit Description:

The Manifold Absolute Pressure (MAP) sensor responds to changes in manifold pressure (vacuum). The ECM receives this information as a signal voltage that will vary from about 1-1.5 volts at idle to 4-4.5 volts at wide open throttle.

A :Scan" tool displays manifold pressure in volts. Low pressure (high vacuum) reads a low voltage while a high pressure (low vacuum) reads a high voltage.

If the MAP sensor fails the ECM will substitute a fixed MAP value and use the Throttle Position Sensor (TPS) to control fuel delivery.

Test Description:

Numbers below refer to circled numbers on the diagnostic chart.

1. Code 33 will set when:

   Signal is too high (kPa greater than 68 kPa or greater than 9" HG) for a time greater than 6 seconds.

   Throttle position less than 4%.

Engine misfire or low unstable idle may set Code 33. Disconnect MAP sensor and system will go into backup mode. I f the misfire or idle condition remains.

2.If the ECM recognizes the low MAP signal, the ECM and wiring are OK.

Diagnostic Aids:

An open in CKT 470 will result in a Code 33.

With the ignition "ON" and the engine stopped, the manifold pressure is equal to atmospheric pressure and signal voltage will be high. This information is used by the ECM as an indication of vehicle altitude and is referred to as BARO. Comparison of this BARO reading with a known good vehicle with the same sensor Is a good way to check accuracy of a "suspect" sensor. Reading should be the same, ±.4 volt.

"NON-SCAN" DIAGNOSTICS

CODE 33 — MANIFOLD ABSOLUTE PRESSURE (MAP) SENSOR CIRCUIT
(SIGNAL VOLTAGE HIGH - LOW VACUUM)

1. IF ENGINE IDLE IS ROUGH, UNSTABLE OR INCORRECT, CORRECT CONDITION BEFORE USING CHART.

- **YES →**
  2.
  - ENGINE "OFF".
  - DISCONNECT MAP SENSOR ELECTRICAL CONNECTOR.
  - IGNITION "ON".
  - "SCAN" TOOL SHOULD READ A VOLTAGE OF 1 VOLT OR LESS. DOES IT?

- **NO →** CODE 33 IS INTERMITTENT. IF NO ADDITIONAL CODES WERE STORED, REFER TO "DIAGNOSTIC AIDS" ON FACING PAGE.

From step 2:

- **YES →**
  - PROBE SENSOR GROUND CIRCUIT WITH A TEST LIGHT TO BATTERY VOLTAGE.
  - TEST LIGHT SHOULD LIGHT. DOES IT?

- **NO →** CKT 432 SHORTED TO VOLTAGE, SHORTED TO CKT 474, OR FAULTY ECM.

From ground circuit test:

- **YES →** PLUGGED OR LEAKING SENSOR VACUUM HOSE OR FAULTY MAP SENSOR.
- **NO →** OPEN SENSOR GROUND CIRCUIT.

MAT SENSOR VOLTAGE VS. ALTITUDE
WITH IGNITION "ON" AND ENGINE "OFF"

ALTITUDE		VOLTAGE RANGE
METERS	FEET	
Below 305	Below 1000	3.8-5.5V
305-610	1000-2000	3.6-5.3V
610-914	2000-3000	3.5-5.1V
914-1219	3000-4000	3.3-5.0V
1219-1524	4000-5000	3.2-4.8V
1524-1829	5000-6000	3.0-4.6V
1829-2133	6000-7000	2.9-4.5V
2133-2438	7000-8000	2.8-4.3V
2438-2743	8000-9000	2.6-4.2V
2743-3048	9000-10000	2.5-4.0V

LOW ALTITUDE = HIGH PRESSURE = HIGH VOLTAGE

Used with permission of General Motors

CLEAR CODES AND CONFIRM "CLOSED LOOP" OPERATION AND NO "SERVICE ENGINE SOON" LIGHT.

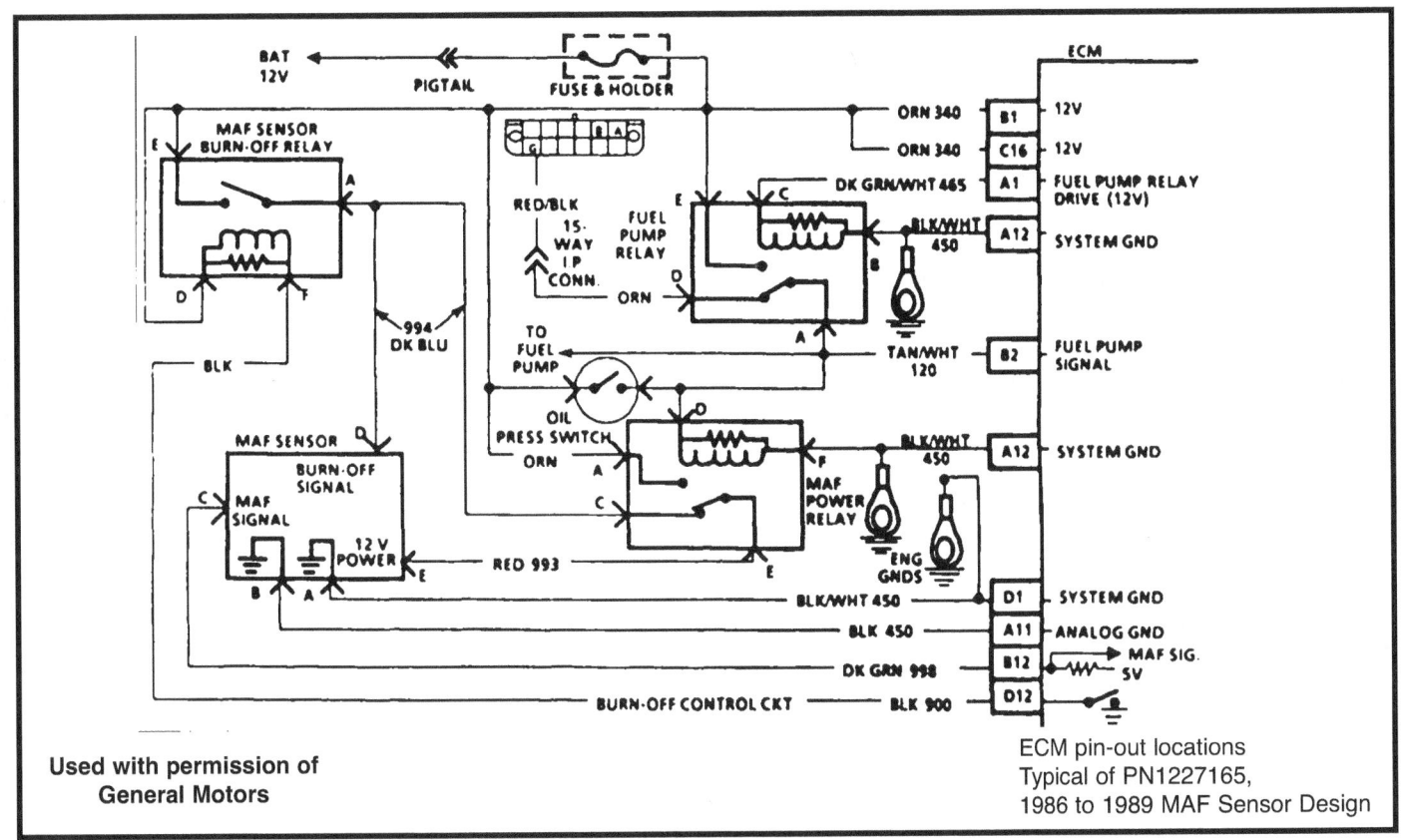

Used with permission of General Motors

ECM pin-out locations
Typical of PN1227165,
1986 to 1989 MAF Sensor Design

CODE 34
MASS AIR FLOW (MAF) SENSOR CIRCUIT
(GM/SEC LOW)

Circuit Description:

The mass air flow (MAF) sensor measures the amount of air which passes through it. The ECM uses this information to determine the operating condition of the engine and control fuel delivery. For a detailed description of the MAF sensor operation, refer to Section "C".

The oil pressure switch or the ECM, through control of the fuel pump relay, will provide 12 volts for the MAF power relay which provides the 12 volts needed by the MAF sensor.

The ECM provides a current limiting 5V on the signal line (CKT 998). The MAF sensor then changes the signal by dropping the voltage so that with low air flow the ECM sees a low voltage and a high air flow will cause the ECM to see near the 5 volt supply.

Test Description:

Numbers below refer to circled numbers on the diagnostic chart.

Code 34 indicates: ECM has seen low air flow less than 2.5 grams per second (low voltage) for one second when:

Engine is first started

OR

RPM is above 600.
TPS is above 6%. To obtain 6%, the engine has to be running at about 2300 rpm in neutral.

1. A Code 34 may be caused by an engine that exhibits a low, rough, unstable or incorrect idle problem. If this condition exists, disconnect the MAF sensor. If the unstable idle still exists, see Symptoms in Section "B" (Rough, Unstable, Incorrect Idle or Stalling.) If the idle improved with the sensor disconnected, replace it.

2. This test will determine if the conditions still exist to set a code or if the problem is intermittent.

3. With the MAF sensor disconnected, the ECM should see a high signal voltage and set a Code 33. If a Code 34 resets then the wiring or the ECM is at fault.

Chevy TPI Swapper's Guide

"NON-SCAN" DIAGNOSTICS

CODE 34
MASS AIR FLOW (MAF) SENSOR
(GM/SEC LOW)

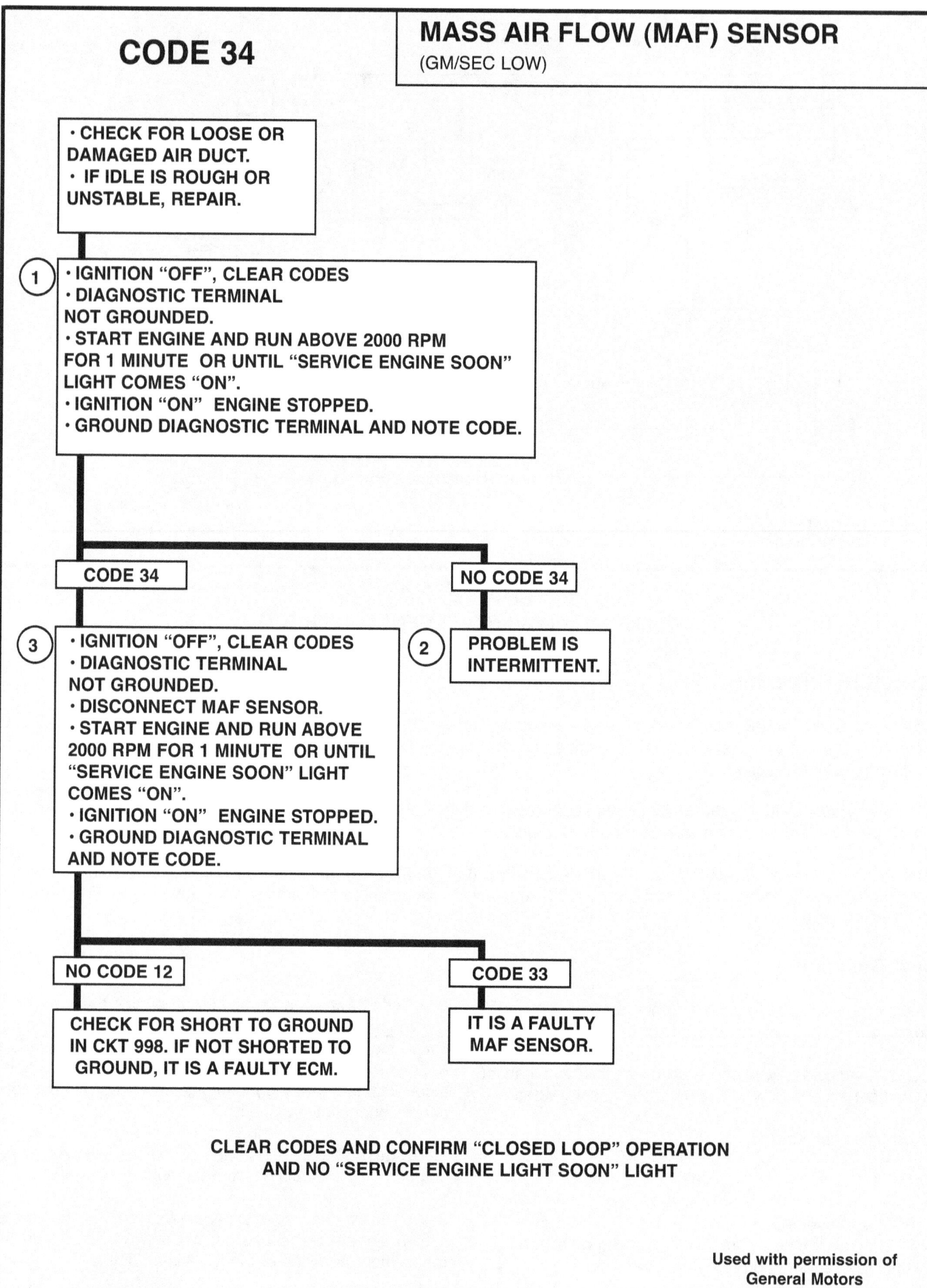

- CHECK FOR LOOSE OR DAMAGED AIR DUCT.
- IF IDLE IS ROUGH OR UNSTABLE, REPAIR.

(1)
- IGNITION "OFF", CLEAR CODES
- DIAGNOSTIC TERMINAL NOT GROUNDED.
- START ENGINE AND RUN ABOVE 2000 RPM FOR 1 MINUTE OR UNTIL "SERVICE ENGINE SOON" LIGHT COMES "ON".
- IGNITION "ON" ENGINE STOPPED.
- GROUND DIAGNOSTIC TERMINAL AND NOTE CODE.

CODE 34 → **(3)**
- IGNITION "OFF", CLEAR CODES
- DIAGNOSTIC TERMINAL NOT GROUNDED.
- DISCONNECT MAF SENSOR.
- START ENGINE AND RUN ABOVE 2000 RPM FOR 1 MINUTE OR UNTIL "SERVICE ENGINE SOON" LIGHT COMES "ON".
- IGNITION "ON" ENGINE STOPPED.
- GROUND DIAGNOSTIC TERMINAL AND NOTE CODE.

NO CODE 34 → **(2) PROBLEM IS INTERMITTENT.**

NO CODE 12: CHECK FOR SHORT TO GROUND IN CKT 998. IF NOT SHORTED TO GROUND, IT IS A FAULTY ECM.

CODE 33: IT IS A FAULTY MAF SENSOR.

CLEAR CODES AND CONFIRM "CLOSED LOOP" OPERATION AND NO "SERVICE ENGINE LIGHT SOON" LIGHT

Used with permission of General Motors

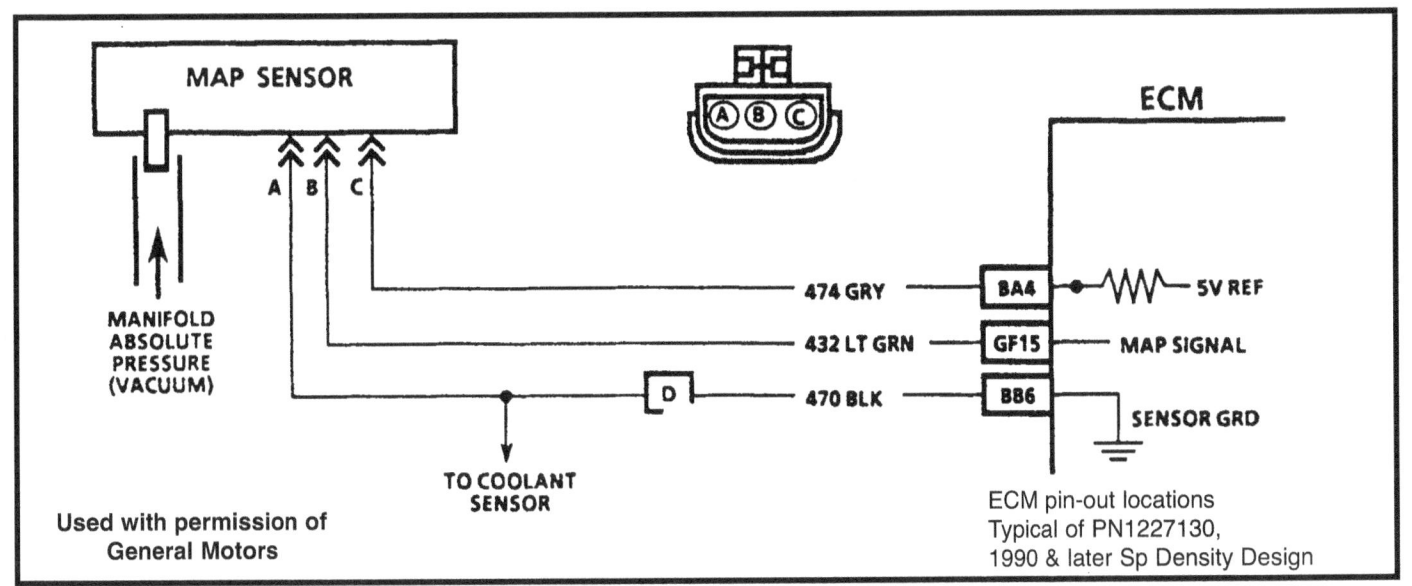

CODE 34
MANIFOLD ABSOLUTE PRESSURE (MAP) SENSOR CIRCUIT
(SIGNAL VOLTAGE LOW-HIGH VACUUM)

Circuit Description:

The Manifold Absolute Pressure (MAP) sensor responds to changes in manifold pressure (vacuum). The ECM receives this information as a signal voltage that will vary from about 1-1.5 volts at idle to 4-4.5 volts at wide open throttle.

A :Scan" tool displays manifold pressure in volts. Low pressure (high vacuum) reads a low voltage while a high pressure (low vacuum) reads a high voltage.

If the MAP sensor fails the ECM will substitute a fixed MAP value and use the Throttle Position Sensor (TPS) to control fuel delivery.

Test Description:

Numbers below refer to circled numbers on the diagnostic chart.

1. Code 34 will set when:

   Signal is too low (less than 14 kPa or greater than 28" HG) and engine running less than 1200 rpm.

   OR

   Engine running greater than 1200 rpm.

   Throttle position greater than 21% (over 1.5 volts)

2. If the ECM recognizes the high MAP signal, the ECM and wiring are OK.

3. The "Scan" tool may not display 12 volts. The important thing is that the ECM recognizes the voltage as more than 4 volts, indicating that the ECM and CKT 432 are OK.

Diagnostic Aids:

An intermittent open in CKT 432 or 474 will result in a Code 34.

With the ignition "ON" and the engine stopped, the manifold pressure is equal to atmospheric pressure and signal voltage will be high. This information is used by the ECM as an indication of vehicle altitude and is referred to as BARO. Comparison of this BARO reading with a known good vehicle with the same sensor is a good way to check accuracy of a "suspect" sensor. Reading should be the same, ±.4 volt.

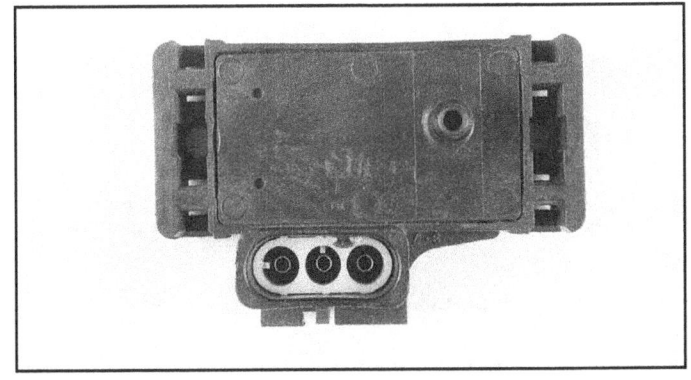

"NON-SCAN" DIAGNOSTICS

CODE 34 — MANIFOLD ABSOLUTE PRESSURE (MAP) SENSOR CIRCUIT
(SIGNAL VOLTAGE LOW - HIGH VACUUM)

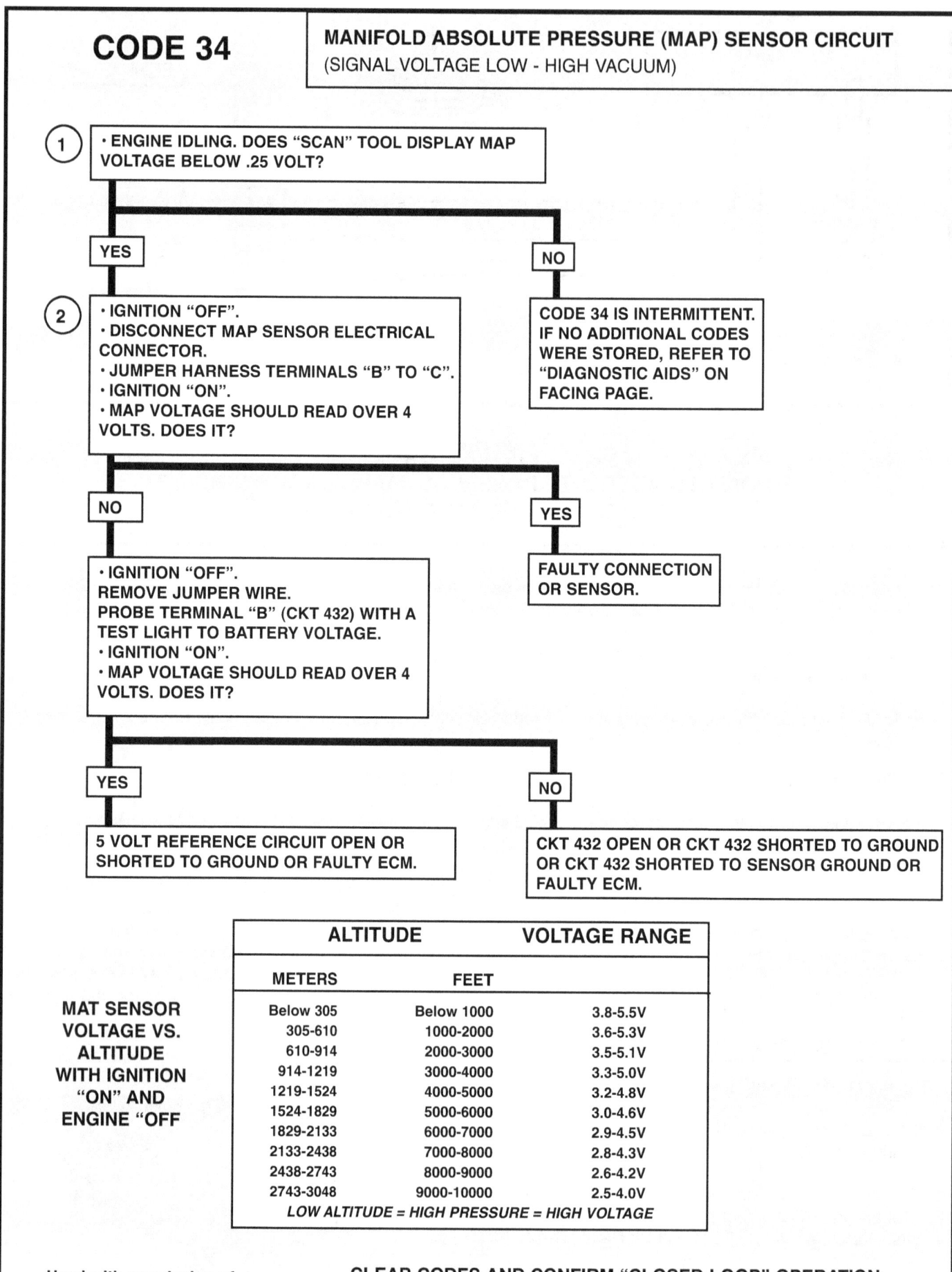

1. ENGINE IDLING. DOES "SCAN" TOOL DISPLAY MAP VOLTAGE BELOW .25 VOLT?

- **NO:** CODE 34 IS INTERMITTENT. IF NO ADDITIONAL CODES WERE STORED, REFER TO "DIAGNOSTIC AIDS" ON FACING PAGE.

- **YES:**

2.
- IGNITION "OFF".
- DISCONNECT MAP SENSOR ELECTRICAL CONNECTOR.
- JUMPER HARNESS TERMINALS "B" TO "C".
- IGNITION "ON".
- MAP VOLTAGE SHOULD READ OVER 4 VOLTS. DOES IT?

- **YES:** FAULTY CONNECTION OR SENSOR.

- **NO:**
  - IGNITION "OFF".
  - REMOVE JUMPER WIRE.
  - PROBE TERMINAL "B" (CKT 432) WITH A TEST LIGHT TO BATTERY VOLTAGE.
  - IGNITION "ON".
  - MAP VOLTAGE SHOULD READ OVER 4 VOLTS. DOES IT?

  - **YES:** 5 VOLT REFERENCE CIRCUIT OPEN OR SHORTED TO GROUND OR FAULTY ECM.

  - **NO:** CKT 432 OPEN OR CKT 432 SHORTED TO GROUND OR CKT 432 SHORTED TO SENSOR GROUND OR FAULTY ECM.

MAT SENSOR VOLTAGE VS. ALTITUDE WITH IGNITION "ON" AND ENGINE "OFF"

ALTITUDE		VOLTAGE RANGE
METERS	FEET	
Below 305	Below 1000	3.8-5.5V
305-610	1000-2000	3.6-5.3V
610-914	2000-3000	3.5-5.1V
914-1219	3000-4000	3.3-5.0V
1219-1524	4000-5000	3.2-4.8V
1524-1829	5000-6000	3.0-4.6V
1829-2133	6000-7000	2.9-4.5V
2133-2438	7000-8000	2.8-4.3V
2438-2743	8000-9000	2.6-4.2V
2743-3048	9000-10000	2.5-4.0V

LOW ALTITUDE = HIGH PRESSURE = HIGH VOLTAGE

Used with permission of General Motors

CLEAR CODES AND CONFIRM "CLOSED LOOP" OPERATION AND NO "SERVICE ENGINE SOON" LIGHT.

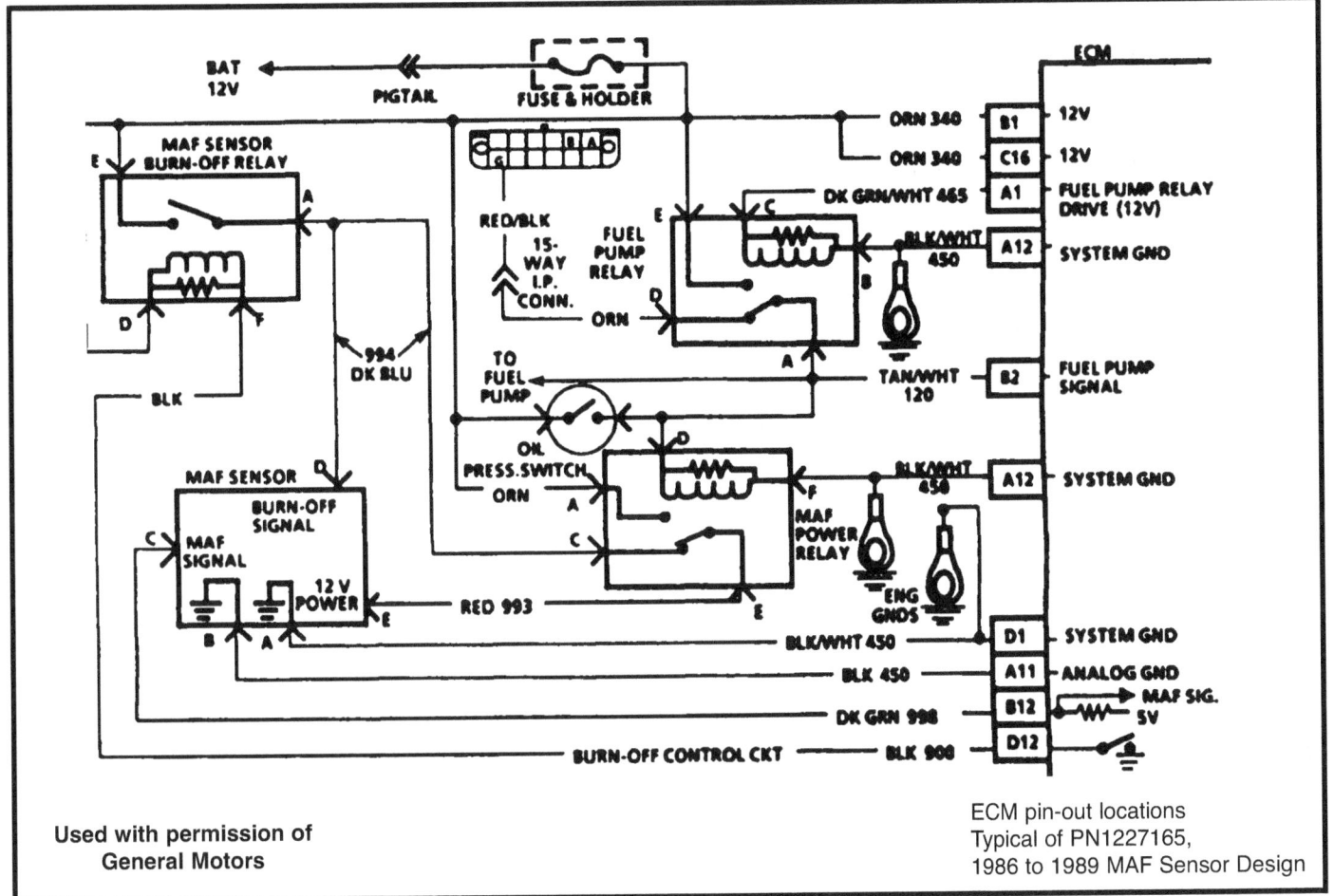

ECM pin-out locations
Typical of PN1227165,
1986 to 1989 MAF Sensor Design

Used with permission of
General Motors

CODE 36
MASS AIR FLOW (MAF) BURN OFF CIRCUIT

Circuit Description:

The mass air flow (MAF) sensor measures the amount of air which passes through it. The ECM uses this information to determine the operating condition of the engine and control fuel delivery. For a detailed description of the MAF sensor operation, refer to Section "C".

Contaminates in the atmosphere will result in a residue build up on the MAF sensor sensing wire. To maintain an accurate reading from the sensor, a "burn-off" cycle will occur when the ignition is turned "OFF" after the engine has been warmed up and running a specified amount of time. The burn-off function is enabled when the ECM grounds CKT 900 which energizes the MAF sensor burn-off relay. With the MAF sensor burn-off relay energized, voltage will be supplied to the MAF sensor terminal "D". Voltage will also be supplied through the normally closed set of contacts in the MAF power relay which will supply 12 volts to terminal "E" of the MAF sensor.

Test Description:

Numbers below refer to circled numbers on the diagnostic chart.

1. This test will determine if the burn-off function is operative or if the code was set due to intermittent condition.

2. Check for continuous 12 volt supply to burn-off relay.

3. Grounding CKT 900 should energize the relay and close the contacts. CKT 900 should be grounded by using a jumper wire at ECM connector "D12". If the test light is dim, check for corroded or faulty connections. If OK, replace relay.

4. With the burn-off relay energized there should be 12 volts supplied to the MAF sensor on terminal "D" and "E" (CKTs 993 and 994). If the test light is dim, check for corroded or faulty connections. If OK, replace relay.

Chevy TPI Swapper's Guide   93

"NON-SCAN" DIAGNOSTICS

CODE 36 — MASS AIRFLOW (MAF) BURN-OFF CIRCUIT

(1)
- IGNITION "OFF", CLEAR CODES.
- DIAGNOSTIC TERMINAL GROUNDED.
- START ENGINE AND WAIT FOR "SERVICE ENGINE SOON" LIGHT TO INDICATE "CLOSED LOOP".
- UNGROUND DIAGNOSTIC TEST TERMINAL.
- TURN IGNITION "OFF" AND WAIT 20 SECONDS.
- RESTART ENGINE AND RUN 20 SECONDS OR UNTIL "SERVICE ENGINE SOON" LIGHT COMES "ON".
- IGNITION "ON", ENGINE STOPPED.
- GROUND DIAGNOSTIC TERMINAL AND NOTE CODE.

CODE 36:

(2)
- DISCONNECT MAF SENSOR BURN-OFF RELAY.
- PROBE BOTH 340 CKTS WITH A TEST LIGHT TO GROUND.

NO CODE 36: PROBLEM IS INTERMITTENT.

LIGHT "ON" BOTH:

(3)
- RECONNECT RELAY.
- DISCONNECT MAF SENSOR.
- GROUND BURN-OFF RELAY CKT 900.
- PROBE MAF SENSOR HARNESS TERMINAL "D" WITH A TEST LIGHT TO GROUND.

LIGHT "OFF" ON ONE OR BOTH: REPAIR OPEN IN CIRCUIT THAT DID NOT LIGHT.

LIGHT "ON":
- CKT 900 STILL GROUNDED.
- PROBE TERMINAL "E" (CKT 993) WITH A TEST LIGHT TO GROUND.

LIGHT "OFF": CKT 900 OPEN, CKT 994 OPEN OR SHORTED TO GROUND, OR FAULTY CONNECTION OR FAULTY RELAY.

LIGHT "ON":
- DISCONNECT BURN-OFF RELAY.
- IGNITION "ON".
- PROBE CKT 900 WITH A TEST LIGHT T TO

LIGHT "OFF":
- OPEN CKT 993, OPEN CIRCUIT BETWEEN MAF SENSOR RELAY AND THE BURN-OFF RELAY, FAULTY CONNECTION, OR FAULTY MAF SENSOR POWER RELAY.

LIGHT "ON": REPAIR SHORT TO VOLTAGE IN CKT 900.

LIGHT "OFF": FAULTY ECM CONNECTION OR ECM. CODE 36 CAN SET DUE TO A POOR CONNECTION AT ANY OF THE RELAYS OR THE MAF SENSOR, OR BY HIGH RESISTANCE IN THE RELAY CONTACTS OR CONNECTIONS. BE SURE THAT THESES CONNECTIONS ARE AND TERMINALS ARE OK BEFORE REPLACING ECM.

Used with permission of General Motors

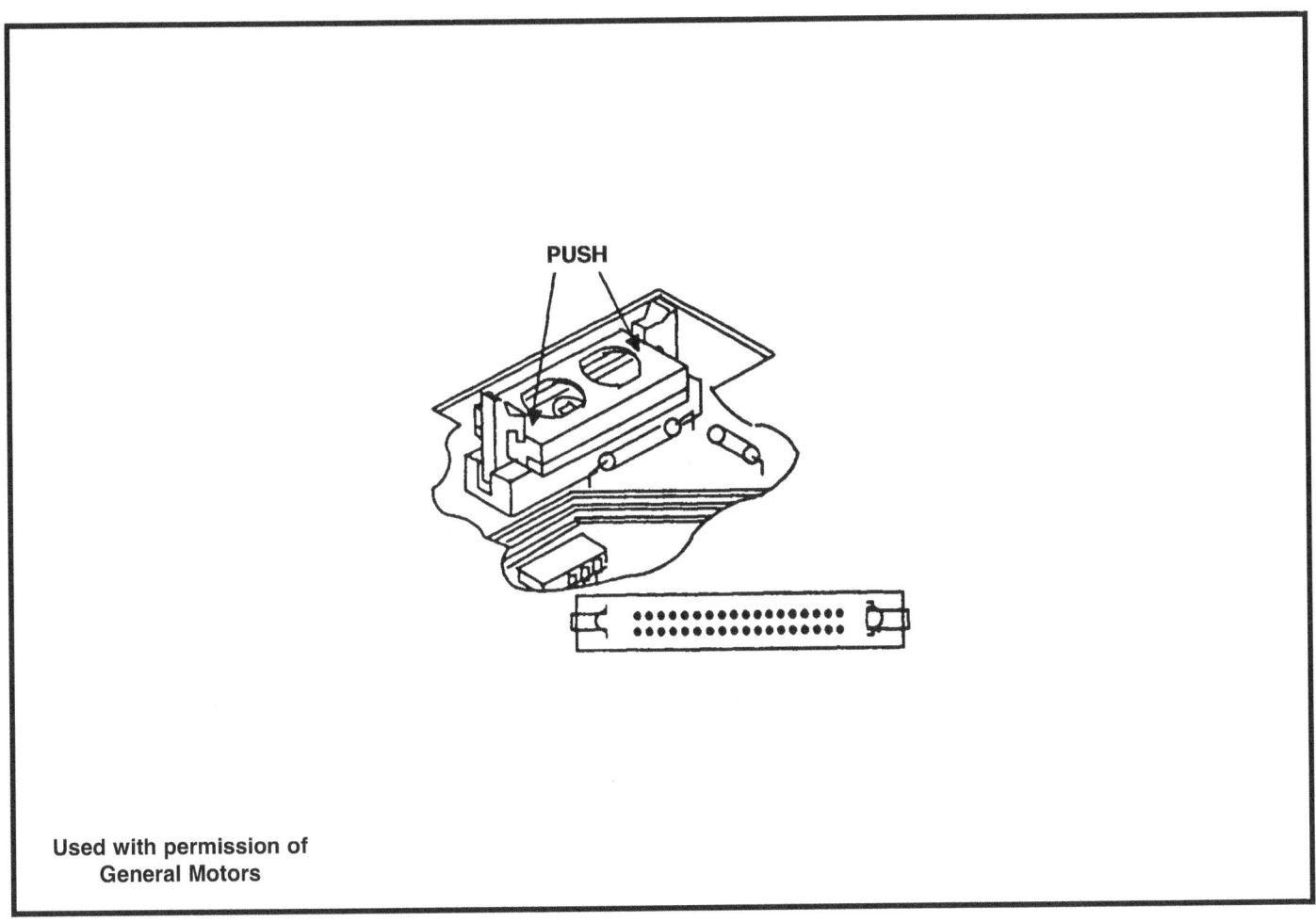

Used with permission of General Motors

CODE 41
CYLINDER SELECT ERROR - TPI
(FAULTY OR INCORRECT MEM-CAL)

Test Description:

Numbers below refer to circled numbers on the diagnostic chart.

1. The ECM used for this engine can also be used for other engines, and the difference is in the Mem-Cal. If a Code 41 sets, the incorrect Mem-Cal has been installed, may not be installed properly, or it is faulty and it must be replaced.

Diagnostic Aids:

Check Mem-Cal to be sure locking tabs are secure.

Also check the pins on both the Mem-Cal and ECM to assure they are making proper contact. Check the Mem-Cal part number to assure it is the correct part. If the Mem-Cal is faulty, it must be replaced. It is also possible that the ECM is faulty, however, it should not be replaced until all of the above have been checked.

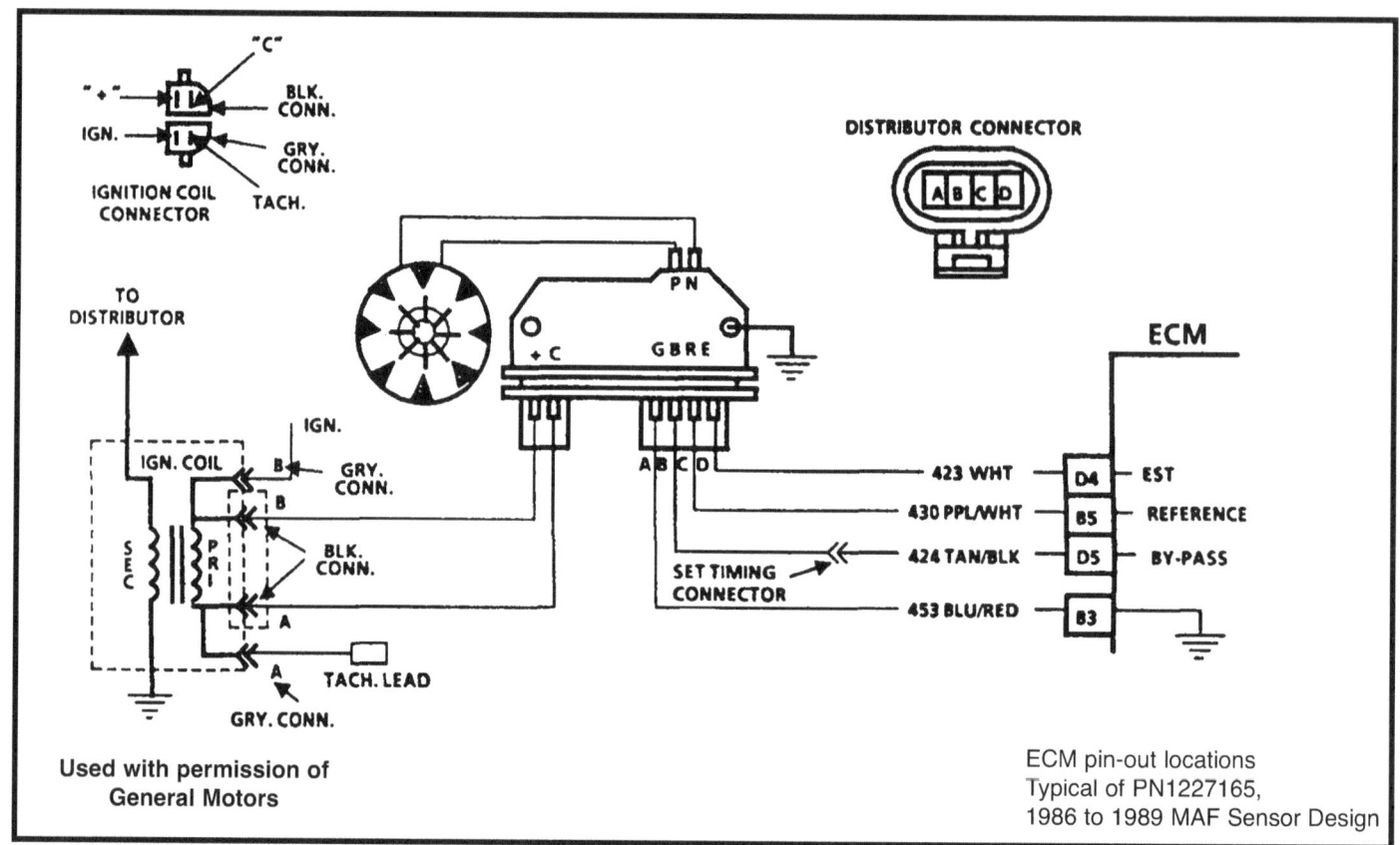

ECM pin-out locations
Typical of PN1227165,
1986 to 1989 MAF Sensor Design

CODE 42
ELECTRONIC SPARK TIMING (EST) CIRCUIT

Circuit Description:

When the system is running on the ignition module, that is, no voltage on the bypass line, the ignition module grounds the EST signal. The ECM expects to see no voltage on the EST during this condition. If it sees a voltage, it sets Code 42 and will not go into EST mode.

When the rpm for EST is reached (about 400 rpm) and bypass voltage applied, the EST should no longer be grounded in the ignition module, so the EST voltage should be varying.

If the bypass line is open or grounded, the ignition module will not switch to EST mode so the EST voltage will be low and Code 42 will be set.

If the EST line is grounded, the ignition module will switch to EST but, because the line is grounded, there will be no EST signal. A Code 42 will be set.

Test Description:

Numbers below refer to circled numbers on the diagnostic chart.

1. Code 42 means the ECM has seen an open or short to ground in the EST or bypass circuits. This test confirms Code 42 and that the fault causing the code is present.

2. Checks for a normal EST ground path through the ignition module. An EST CKT 423 shorted to ground will also read less than 500 ohms, however, this will be checked later.

3. As the test light voltage touches CKT 424 the module should switch, causing the ohmmeter to "overrange" if the meter is in the 1000-2000 ohms position. Selecting the 10-20,000 ohms position will indicate above 5000 ohms. The important thing is that the module "switched".

4. The module did not switch and this step checks for:
   EST CKT 423 shorted to ground.
   Bypass CKT 424 open.
   Faulty ignition module connection or module.

5. Confirms that Code 42 is a faulty ECM and not an intermittent in CKTs 423 or 424.

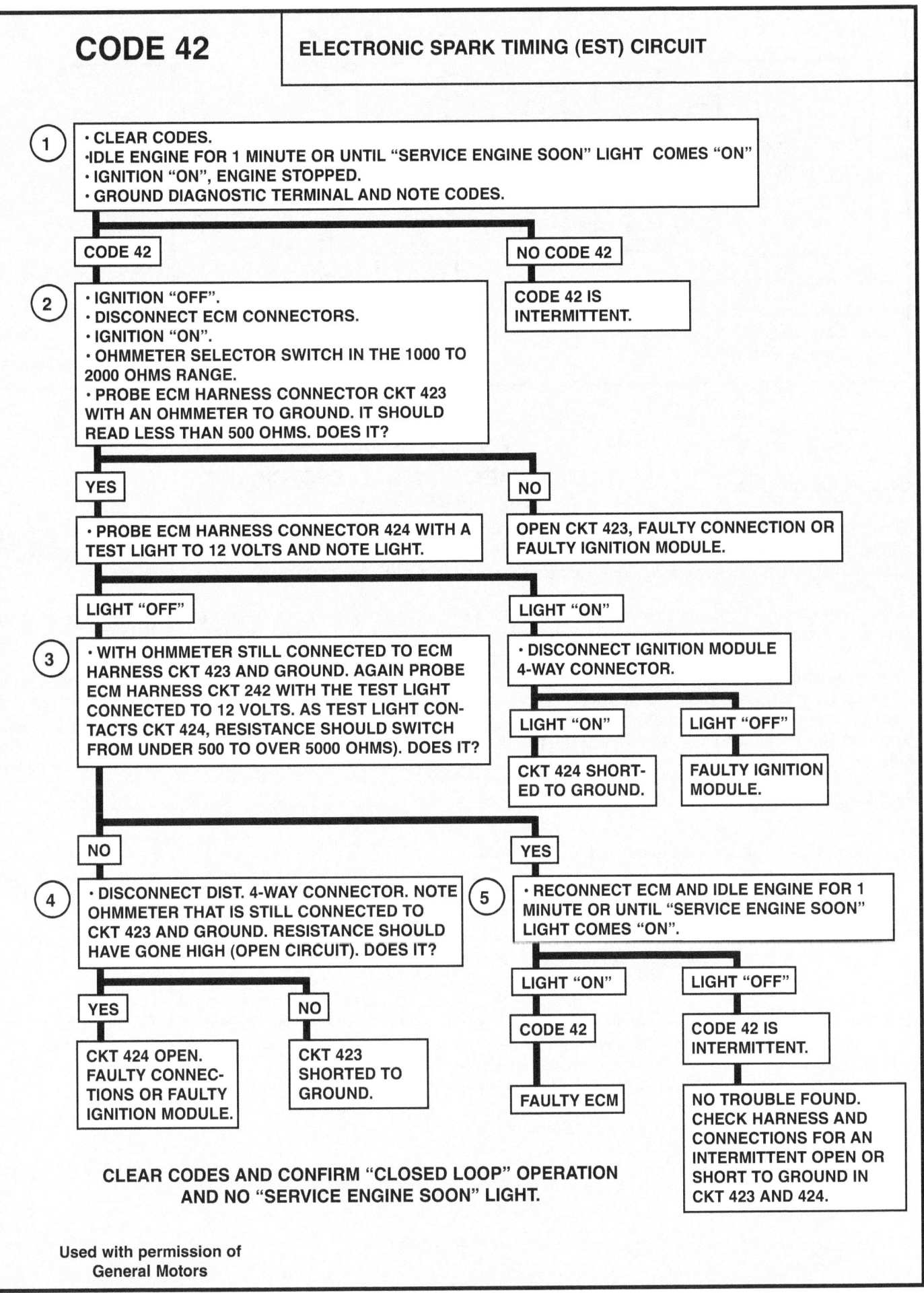

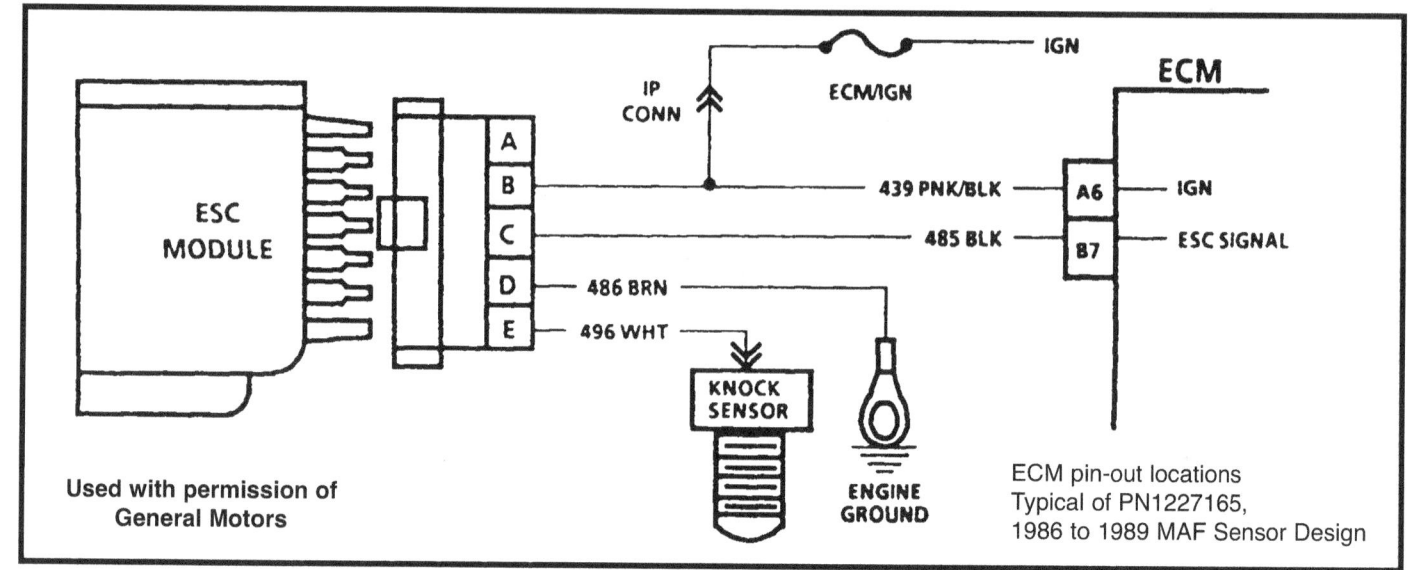

ECM pin-out locations
Typical of PN1227165,
1986 to 1989 MAF Sensor Design

CODE 43

Circuit Description:
ELECTRONIC SPARK CONTROL (ESC) CIRCUIT
1985-89 TPI ONLY

Electronic spark control is accomplished with a module that sends a voltage signal to the ECM. When the knock sensor detects engine knock, the voltage from the ESC module to the ECM drops and this signals the ECM to retard timing. The ECM will retard the timing when knock is detected and rpm is above about 900 rpm.

Code 43 means the ECM has been low voltage at CKT 485 terminal "B7" for longer than 5 seconds, with the engine running or the system has failed the functional check.

This system performs a functional check once per start-up to check the ESC system. To perform this test the ECM will advance the spark when coolant is above 95°C and at a high load condition (near WOT). The ECM then checks the signal at "B7" to see if a knock is detected. The functional check is performed once per start-up and if a knock is detected when coolant is below 95°C (194°F) the test has passed and the functional check will not be run. If the function check fails, the "Service Engine Soon" light will remain "ON" until ignition is turned "OFF", or until a knock signal is detected.

Test Description:

Numbers below refer to circled numbers on the diagnostic chart.

1. If the conditions for a Code 43 are present, the "Scan" will always display "yes". There should not be a knock at idle unless an internal engine problem or a system problem exists.

2. This test will determine if the system is functioning at this time. Usually a knock signal can be generated by tapping on the right exhaust manifold. If no knock signal is generated, try tapping on the block close to the area of the sensor.

3. Because Code 43 sets when the signal voltage on CKT 485 remains low, this test should cause the signal on CKT 485 to go high. The 12 volts signal should be seen by the ECM as "no knock" if the ECM and wiring are OK.

4. This test will determine if the knock signal is being detected on CKT 496 or if the ESC module is at fault.

5. If CKT 496 is routed close to secondary ignition wires, the ESC module may see the interference as a knock signal.

6. This checks the ground circuit to the module. An open ground will cause the voltage on CKT 485 to be about 12 volts, which would cause the Code 43 functional test to fail.

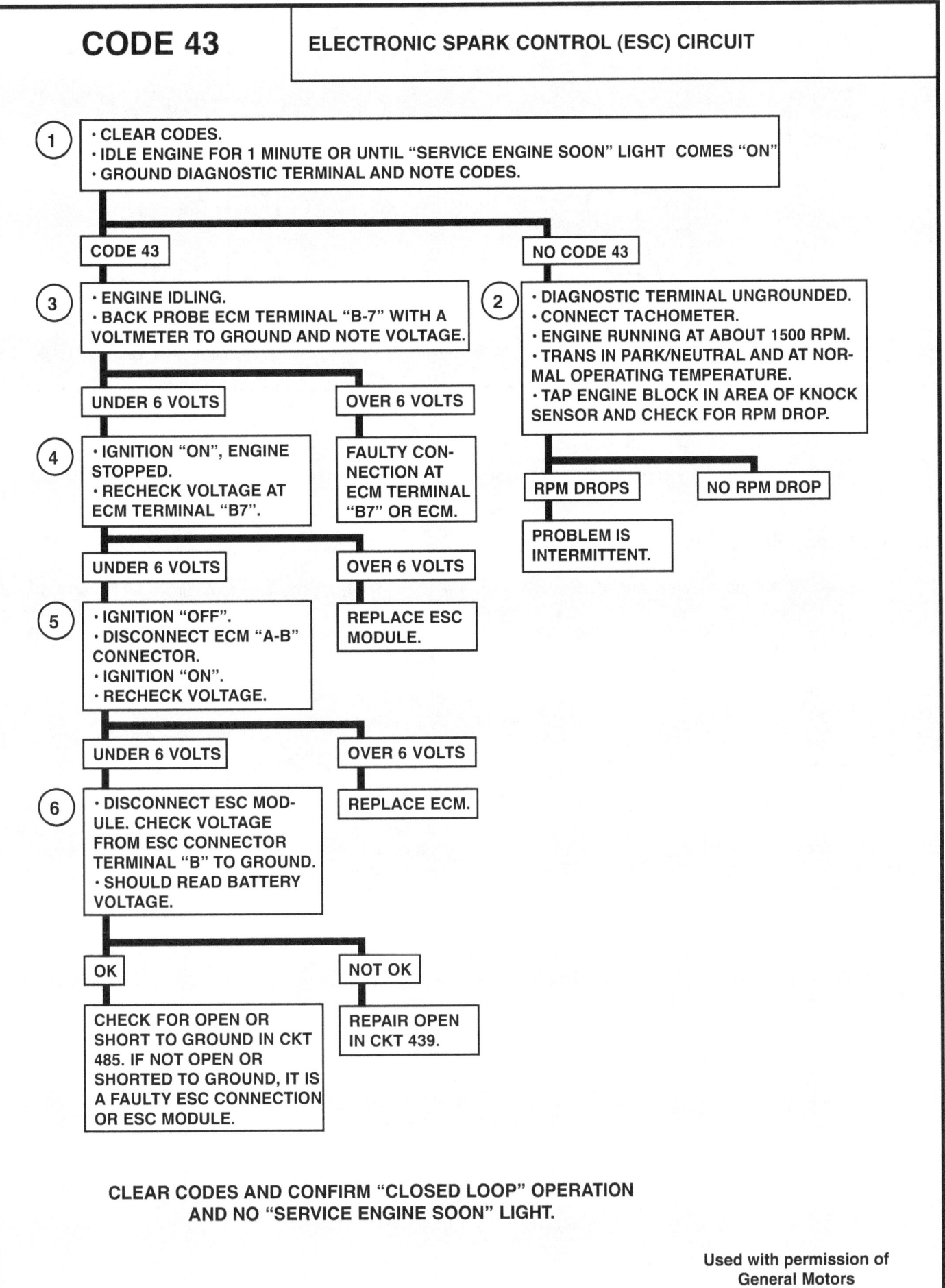

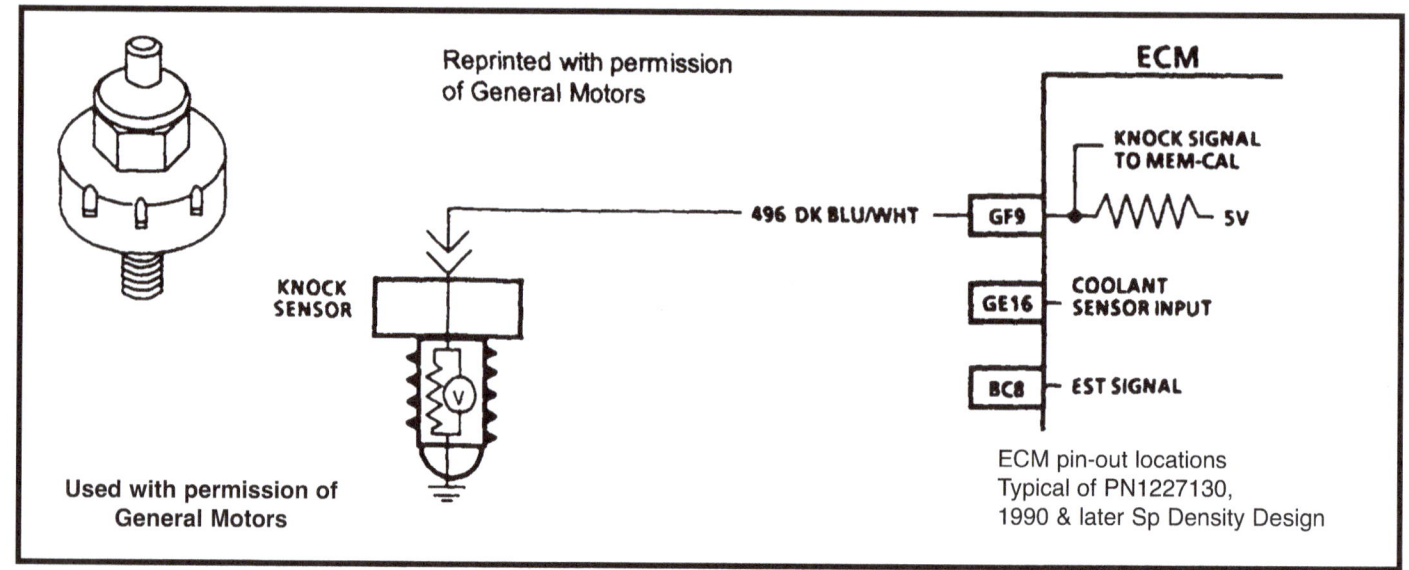

CODE 43
ELECTRONIC SPARK CONTROL (ESC) CIRCUIT
1990-96 TPI AND LT-1

Circuit Description:

The knock sensor is used to detect engine detonation and the ECM will retard the electronic spark timing based on the signal being received. The circuitry within the knock sensor causes the ECM 5 volts to be pulled down so that, under a no knock condition, CKT 496 would measure about 2.5 volts. The knock sensor produces an AC signal which rides on the 2.5 volts DC voltage. The amplitude and signal frequency is dependent on the knock level.

If CKT 496 becomes open or shorted to ground, the voltage will either go above 3.5 volts or below 1.5 volts. If either of these conditions are met for about 1/2 second, a Code 43 will be stored.

Test Description:

Numbers below refer to circled numbers on the diagnostic chart.

1. This step determines if conditions for Code 43 still exhaust (voltage on CKT 496 above 3.5 volts or below 1.5 volts). The system is designed to retard the spark 15 ° if either condition exists.

2. The ECM has a 5 volt pull up resistor, which applies 5 volts to CKT 496. The 5 volt signal should be present at the knock sensor terminal during these test conditions.

3. This step determines if the knock sensor resistance is 3300 to 4500 ohms the sensor is OK.

Diagnostic Aids:

If CKT 496 is not open or shorted to ground and the voltage reading is below 4 volts, the most likely cause is an open circuit in the ECM. It is possible that a faulty Mem-Cal could be drawing the 5 volt signal down and it should be replaced if a replacement ECM did not correct the problem.

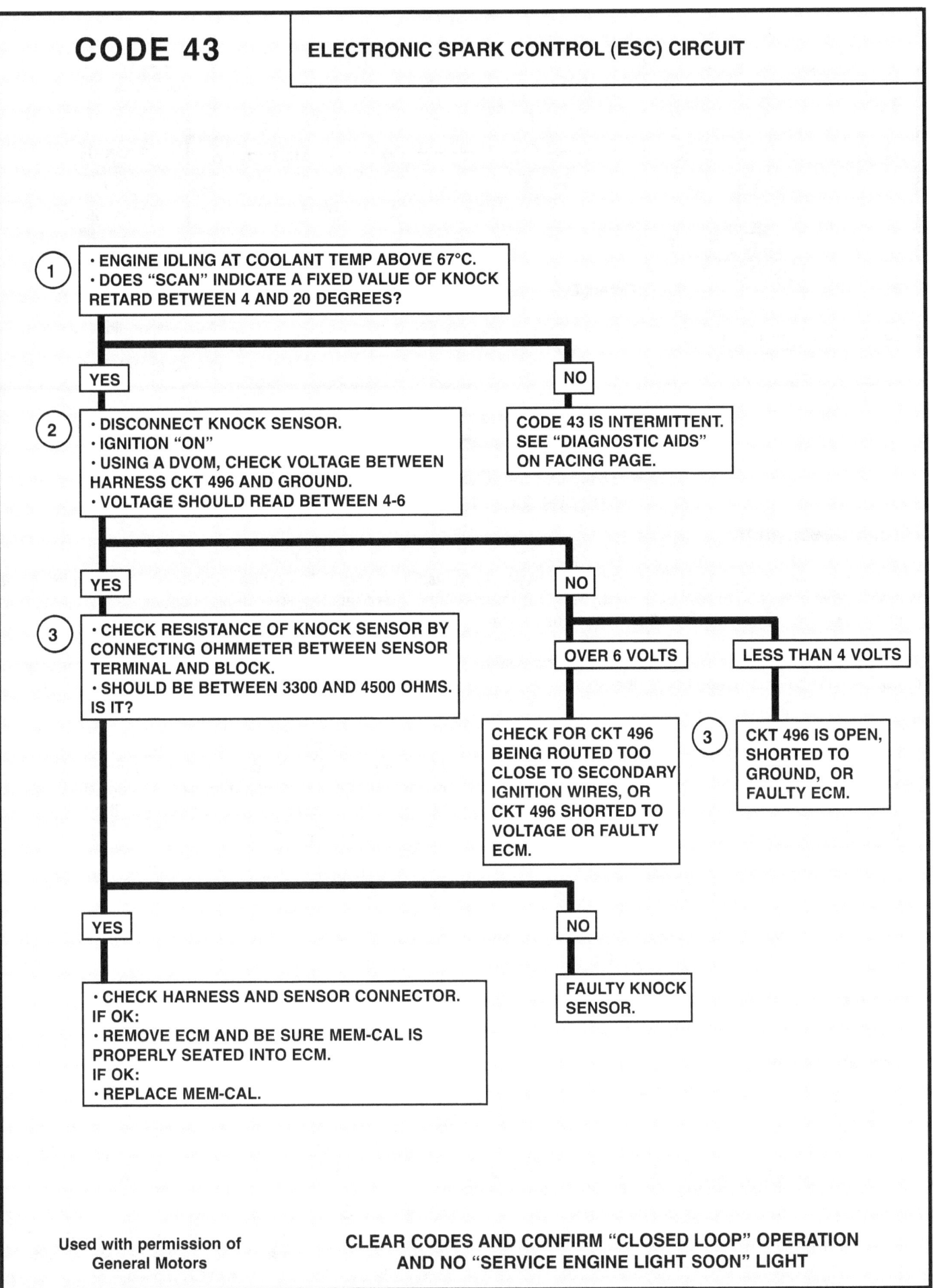

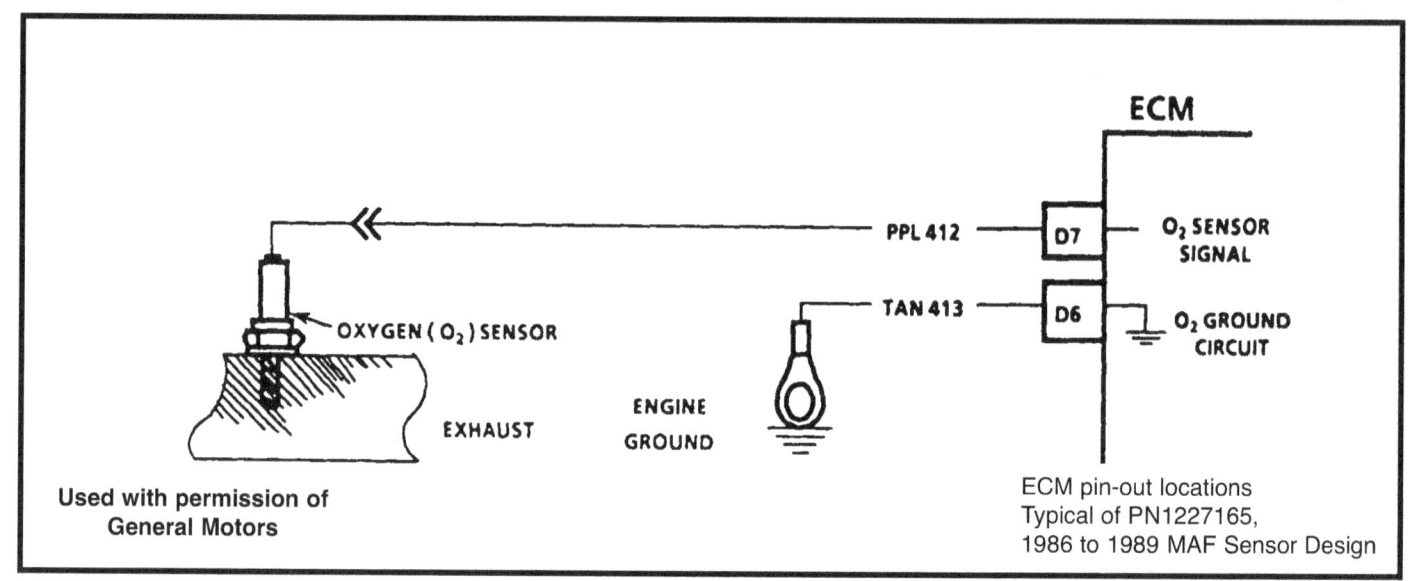

ECM pin-out locations
Typical of PN1227165,
1986 to 1989 MAF Sensor Design

CODE 44
OXYGEN SENSOR CIRCUIT - TPI & LT-1 LEFT BANK
(LEAN EXHAUST INDICATED)

Circuit Description:

The ECM supplies a voltage of about .45 volt between terminals "D6" and :D7". (If measured with a 10 megohm digital voltmeter, this may read as low as .32 volt.) The O-2 sensor varies the voltage within a range of about 1 volt if the exhaust is rich, down through about .10 volt if the exhaust is lean.

The sensor is like an open circuit and produces no voltage when it is below about 360°C (600°F). An open sensor circuit or cold sensor causes "Open Loop" operation.

Test Description:

Numbers below refer to circled numbers on the diagnostic chart.

1. Code 44 is set when the O-2 sensor signal voltage on CKT 412:
   Remains below .2 volt for 50 seconds.
   The system is operating in "Closed Loop".

2. A light out, or "Open Loop", indicates the fault is present. Disconnecting the)-2 sensor will raise the signal voltage above .2 volt. If the ECM and wiring are OK, the ECM should recognize the higher voltage, .35 to .55, and flash "Open Loop" when the engine is started.

Diagnostic Aids:

The Code 44 or lean exhaust is most likely caused by one of the following:

<u>O-2 Sensor Wire</u> Sensor pigtail may be mispositioned and contacting the exhaust manifold. Check for intermittent ground in wire between connector and sensor.

<u>MAF Sensor</u> A mass air flow (MAF) sensor output that causes the ECM to sense a lower than normal air flow will cause the system to go lean. Disconnect the MAF sensor and, if the lean condition is gone, replace the MAF sensor.

<u>CKT 413</u> If CKT 413 is open the CKT 412 voltage will be over 1 volt.

<u>Fuel Contamination</u> Water, even in small amounts, near the in-tank fuel pump inlet can be delivered to the injectors. The water causes a lean exhaust and can set a Code 44.

<u>Fuel Pressure</u> System will be lean if pressure is too low. It may be necessary to monitor fuel pressure while driving the car at various road speeds and/or loads to confirm. Refer to "Fuel System Diagnosis", CHART A-7.

<u>Exhaust Leaks</u> If there is an exhaust leak, outside air will be pulled into the exhaust and past the sensor. Vacuum or crankcase leaks can cause a lean condition.

<u>Air System</u> Be sure air is not being directed to the exhaust ports while in "Closed Loop". I f the block learn value goes down while squeezing air hose to left side exhaust ports, air divert is faulty. If the above are OK, it is a faulty oxygen sensor.

"NON-SCAN" DIAGNOSTICS

CODE 44
OXYGEN SENSOR CIRCUIT
(LEAN EXHAUST INDICATED)

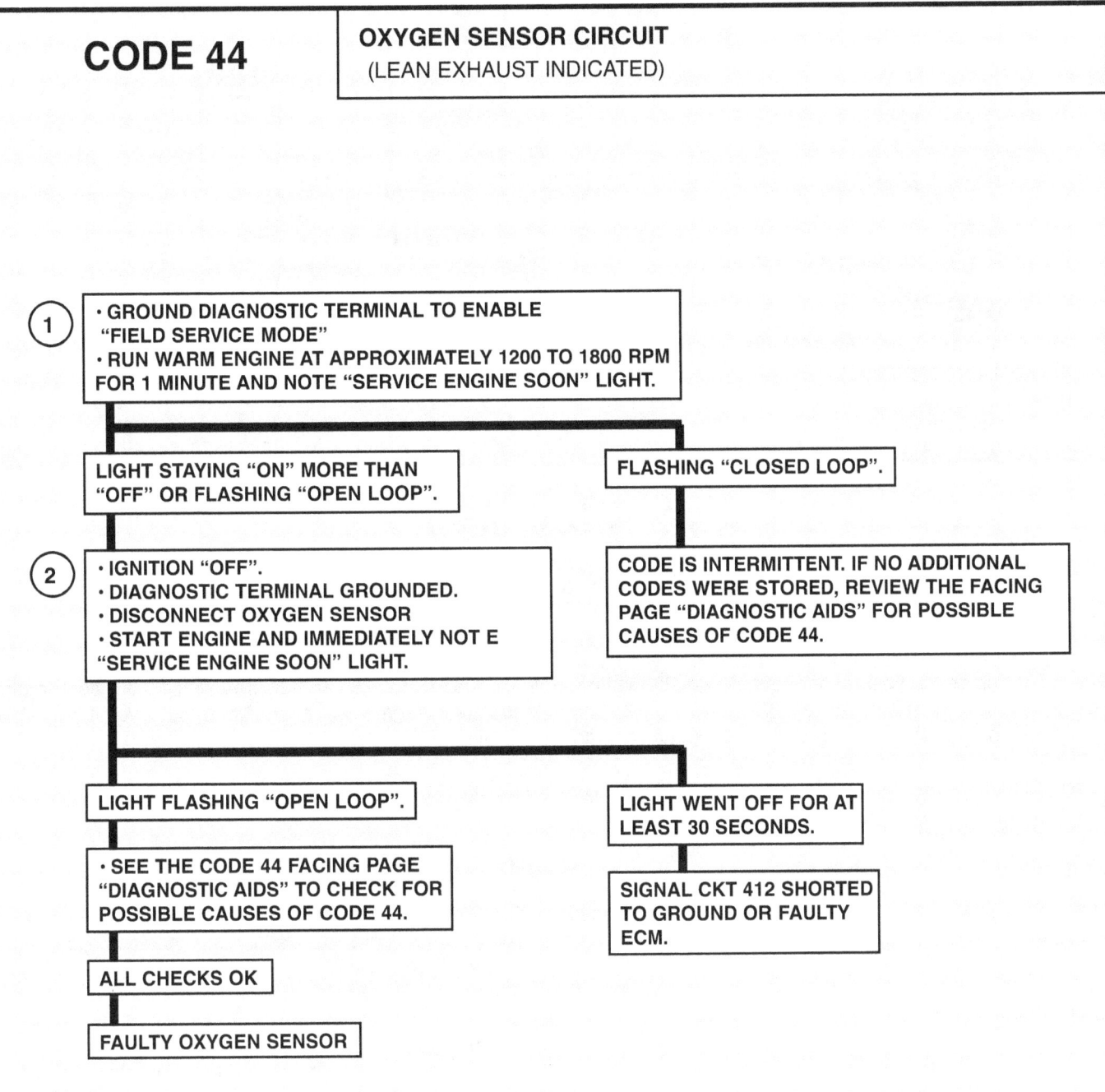

FIELD SERVICE MODE:
- ENGINE RUNNING, DIAGNOSTIC TERMINAL GROUNDED.
- "OPEN LOOP", "SERVICE ENGINE SOON" LIGHT FLASHES AT A RATE OF 2.5 TIMES PER SECOND.
- "CLOSED LOOP, "SERVICE ENGINE SOON" LIGHT FLASHES AT A RATE OF 1 TIME PER SECOND.

Used with permission of General Motors

CLEAR CODES AND CONFIRM "CLOSED LOOP" OPERATION AND NO "SERVICE ENGINE LIGHT SOON" LIGHT

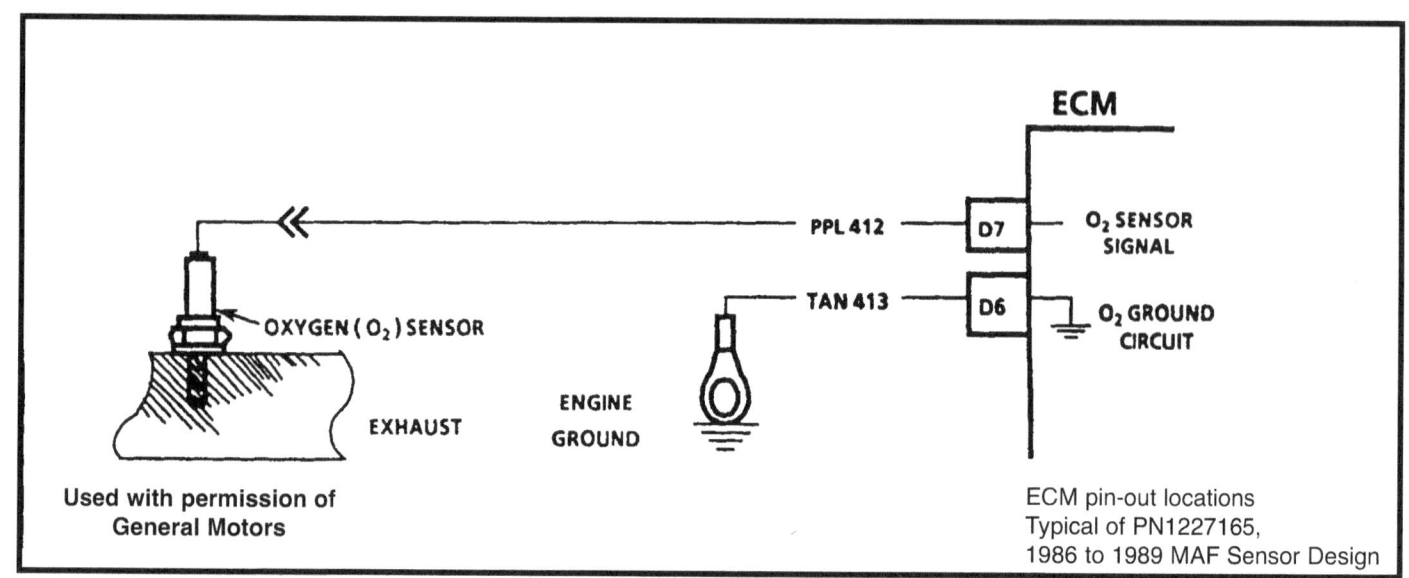

ECM pin-out locations
Typical of PN1227165,
1986 to 1989 MAF Sensor Design

CODE 45
OXYGEN SENSOR CIRCUIT - TPI & LT-1 LEFT BANK
(RICH EXHAUST INDICATED)

Circuit Description:

The ECM supplies a voltage of about .45 volt between terminals "D6" and :D7". (If measured with a 10 megohm digital voltmeter, this may read as low as .32 volt.) The O-2 sensor varies the voltage within a range of about 1 volt if the exhaust is rich, down through about .10 volt if the exhaust is lean.

The sensor is like an open circuit and produces no voltage when it is below about 360°C (600°F). An open sensor circuit or cold sensor causes "Open Loop" operation.

Test Description:

Numbers below refer to circled numbers on the diagnostic chart.

1. Code 45 is set when the O-2 sensor signal voltage on CKT 412:

    Remains above .7 volt for 50 seconds;
    and in "Closed Loop".

    Engine time after start is 1 minute or more.

    Throttle angle greater than 2% (about .2 volt above idle voltage.

2. A steady light or "Open Loop" indicates the fault is present. Grounding CKT 412 causes a low O-2 signal voltage. If the ECM and wiring are OK, the ECM should recognize the low voltage and confirm the lean signal by turning "OFF" the "Service Engine Soon" light for at least 15 seconds.

Diagnostic Aids:

<u>Fuel Pressure</u> System will go rich if pressure is too high. The ECM can compensate for some increase. However, if it gets too high, a Code 45 may be set. Use the "Fuel System Diagnosis", CHART A-7. Check for fuel contaminated oil.

<u>HEI Shielding</u> An open ground CKT 453)ignition system reflow) may result in EMI, or induced electrical "noise". The ECM looks at this "noise" as reference pulses. The additional pulses result in a higher than actual engine speed, which can help in diagnosing this problem.

<u>Canister Purge</u> Check for fuel saturation. If full of fuel, check canister control and hoses.

<u>MAF Sensor</u> An output that causes the ECM to sense a higher than normal airflow can the system to go rich. Disconnecting the MAF sensor will allow the ECM to set a fixed value for the sensor. Substitute a different MAF sensor if the ruch condition is gone while the sensor is disconnected. Check for leaking fuel pressure regulator diaphragm by checking vacuum line to regulator for fuel.

<u>TPS</u> An intermittent TPS output will cause the system to go rich, due to a false indication of the engine accelerating.

"NON-SCAN" DIAGNOSTICS

CODE 45 — OXYGEN SENSOR CIRCUIT (RICH EXHAUST INDICATED)

(1)
- GROUND DIAGNOSTIC TERMINAL TO ENABLE "FIELD SERVICE MODE"
- RUN WARM ENGINE AT APPROXIMATELY 1200 TO 1800 RPM FOR 1 MINUTE AND NOTE "SERVICE ENGINE SOON" LIGHT.

LIGHT STAYING "ON" MORE THAN "OFF" OR FLASHING "OPEN LOOP".

FLASHING "CLOSED LOOP".
- CODE IS INTERMITTENT. IF NO ADDITIONAL CODES WERE STORED, REVIEW THE FACING PAGE "DIAGNOSTIC AIDS" FOR POSSIBLE CAUSES OF CODE 45.

(2)
- IGNITION "OFF".
- DIAGNOSTIC TERMINAL GROUNDED.
- DISCONNECT OXYGEN SENSOR CONNECTOR AND JUMPER HARNESS CONNECTOR SIGNAL CKT 412 TO GROUND.
- START ENGINE AND IMMEDIATELY NOT E "SERVICE ENGINE SOON" LIGHT.

"SERVICE ENGINE SOON" LIGHT WENT OFF FOR AT LEAST 30 SECONDS.

STEADY LIGHT

SYSTEM RICH

IT IS A FAULTY ECM.

SEE "DIAGNOSTIC AIDS" INFORMATION ON FACING PAGE OF CODE 45.

FIELD SERVICE MODE:
- ENGINE RUNNING, DIAGNOSTIC TERMINAL GROUNDED.
- "OPEN LOOP", "SERVICE ENGINE SOON" LIGHT FLASHES AT A RATE OF 2.5 TIMES PER SECOND.
- "CLOSED LOOP, "SERVICE ENGINE SOON" LIGHT FLASHES AT A RATE OF 1 TIME PER SECOND.

Used with permission of General Motors

CLEAR CODES AND CONFIRM "CLOSED LOOP" OPERATION AND NO "SERVICE ENGINE LIGHT SOON" LIGHT

CODE 46
VEHICLE ANTI-THEFT SYSTEM (VATS) CIRCUIT

Circuit Description:

The VATS system was designed for production TPI and LT-1 Corvette, Camaro, Trans-AM and 55 Impala vehicles to disable operation if the incorrect key or starting procedure is used. In production cars a VATS decoder module in the instrument panel sends a signal to the ECM if the correct key is being used. If the proper signal does not reach the ECM, the ECM will not pulse the injectors, and thus not allow the vehicle to be started.

A DTC Code 46 will usually be stored in the ECM memory if you try to start an engine that has a production Mem-Cal, or production 94-96 LT-1 Ecm. 94-96 LT-1s will actually run for a few seconds and then shut off.

To test for non-pulsing injectors, connect a 6 or 12 volt test light across the terminals on any injector connector (after it has been removed from the injector) and crank the engine. If the light does not flash while cranking, the ECM most likely has a VATS program or Mem-Cal in it. (NOTE: This test will also show if you are not getting a distributor reference signal.)

In a production vehicle with this problem, you will want to get the correct ignition key, or repair the VATS system to retain its anti-theft properties. In the case of a late model engine transplanted into another vehicle, Howell Engine Developments can supply a suitable Mem-Cal or in the case of 94-96 LT-1s, a reprogrammed ECM that have the VATS provision defeated.

CODE 51
CODE 52
CODE 53

CODE 51

MEM-CAL ERROR

(FAULTY OR INCORRECT MEM-CAL)

CHECK THAT ALL PINS ARE FULLY INSERTED IN THE SOCKET AND THAT MEM-CAL IS PROPERLY LATCHED. IF OK, REPLACE MEM-CAL, CLEAR MEMORY, AND RECHECK. IF CODE 51 REAPPEARS, REPLACE ECM.

CLEAR CODES AND CONFIRM "CLOSED LOOP" OPERATION AND NO "SERVICE ENGINE SOON" LIGHT.

CODE 52

CALPAK ERROR

(FAULTY OR INCORRECT CALPAK)

CHECK THAT THE MEM-CAL IS FULLY SEATED AND LATCHED INTO THE MEM-CAL SOCKET. IF OK, REPLACE MEM-CA, CLEAR MEMORY, AND RECHECK. IF CODE 52 REAPPEARS, REPLACE ECM

CLEAR CODES AND CONFIRM "CLOSED LOOP" OPERATION AND NO "SERVICE ENGINE SOON" LIGHT.

CODE 53

SYSTEM OVER VOLTAGE

THIS CODE INDICATES THERE IS A BASIC GENERATOR PROBLEM.
- CODE 53 WILL SET IF VOLTAGE AT ECM IGNITION INPUT PIN IS GREATER THAN 17.1 VOLTS FOR 2 SECONDS.
- CHECK AND REPAIR CHARGING SYSTEM. REFER TO SECTION "6D".

CLEAR CODES AND CONFIRM "CLOSED LOOP" OPERATION AND NO "SERVICE ENGINE SOON" LIGHT.

Used with permission of General Motors

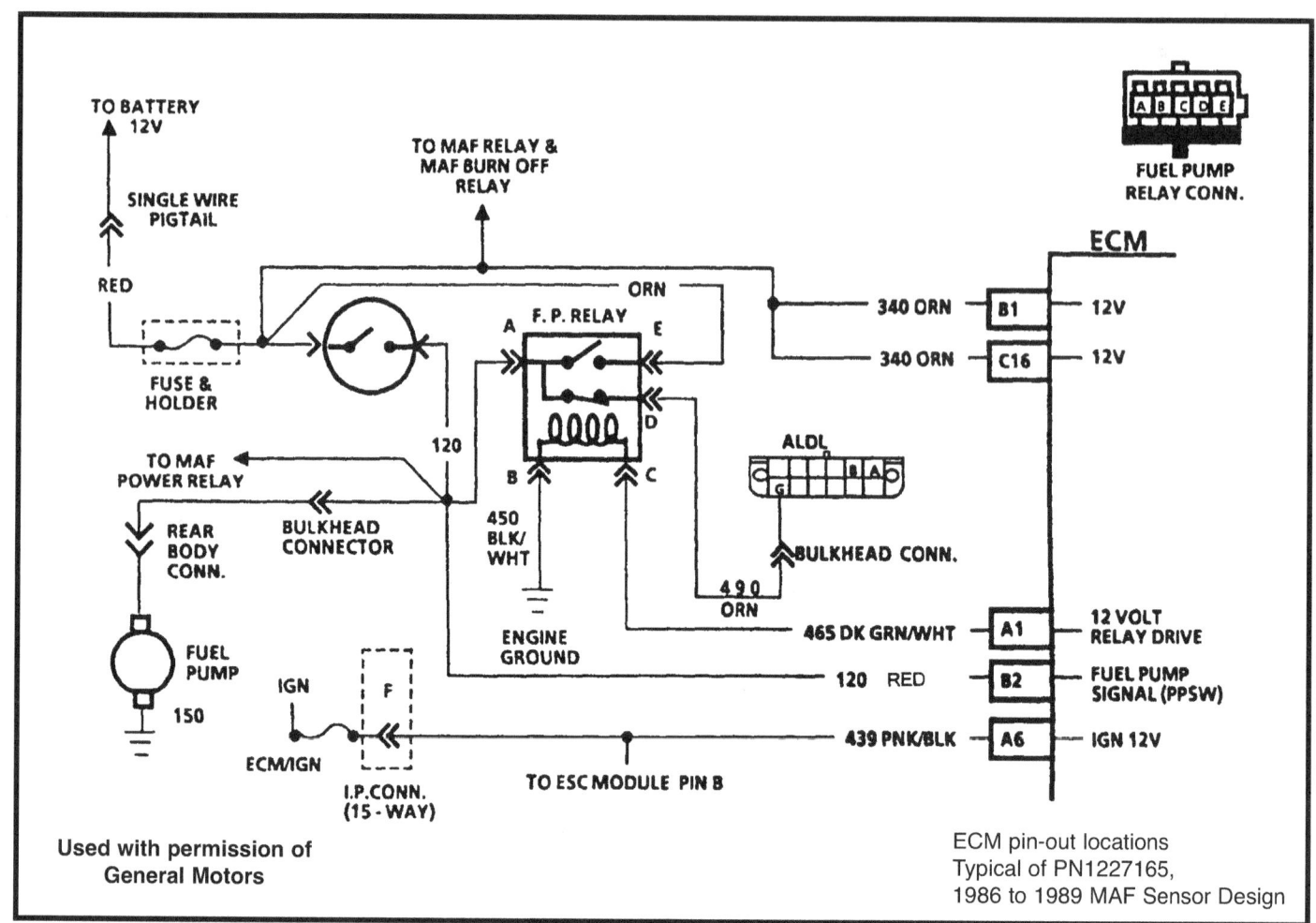

CODE 54
FUEL PUMP CIRCUIT - TPI
(LOW VOLTAGE)

Circuit Description:

The status of the fuel pump CKT 120 (PPSW) is monitored by the ECM at terminal "B2" and is used to compensate fuel delivery based on system voltage. This signal is also used to store a trouble code if the fuel pump relay is defective or fuel pump voltage is lost while the engine is running. There should be about 12 volts on CKT 120 for 2 seconds after the ignition is turned "ON", or any time reference pulses are being received by the ECM.

Code 54 will set if the voltage at terminal "B2" is less than 2 volts for 1.5 seconds since the last reference pulse was received. This code is designed to detect a faulty relay, causing extended crank time, and the code will help the diagnosis of an engine that "CRANKS BUT WILL NOT RUN".

If a fault is detected during start-up, the "Service Engine Soon" light will stay on until the ignition is cycled "OFF". However, if the voltage is detected below 2 volts, with the engine running, the light will remain "ON" while the condition exists.

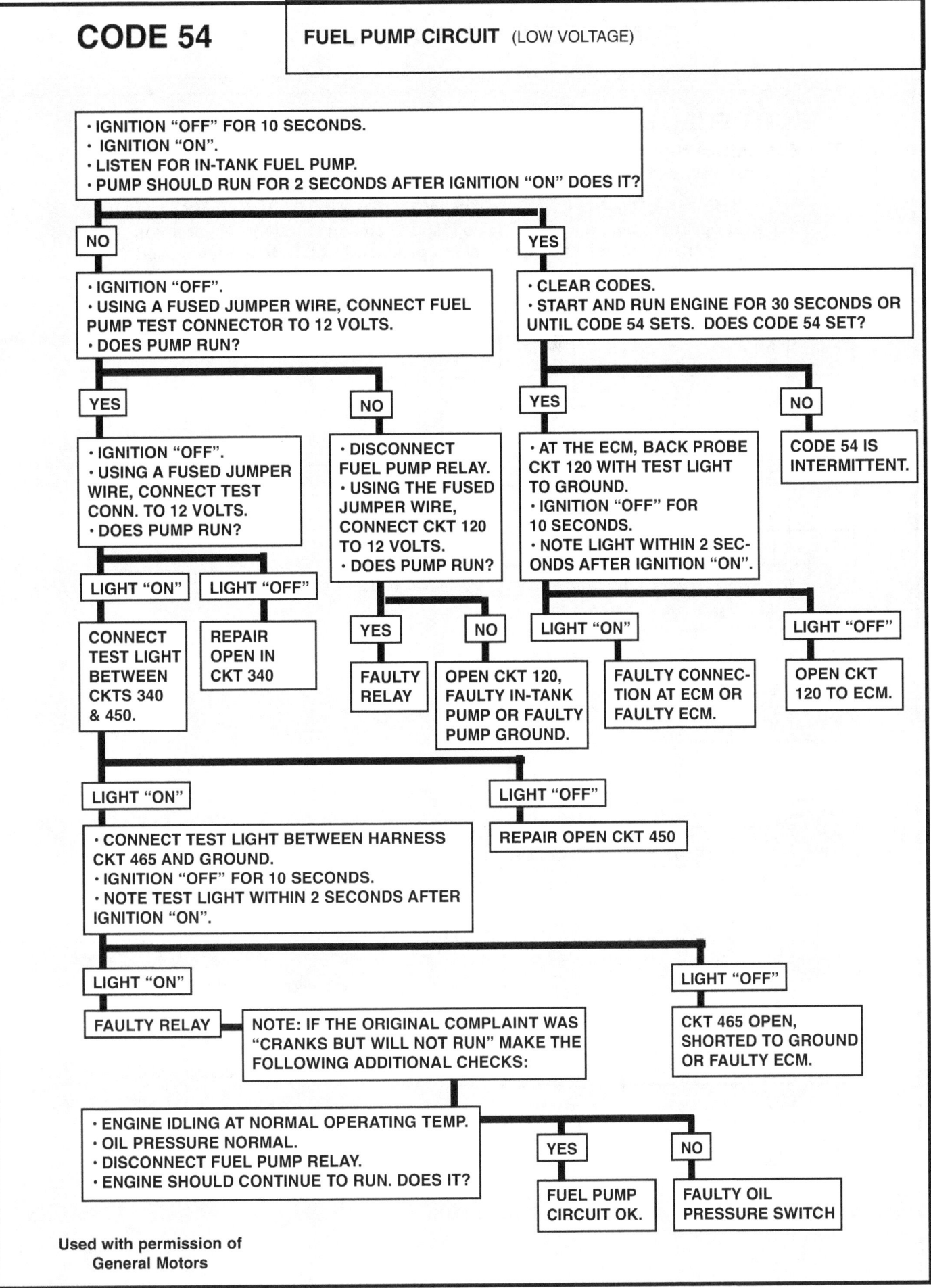

ECM PIN-OUTS TYPICAL OF 1227730 ECM 90-92 TPI

PORT FUEL INJECTION ECM CONNECTOR IDENTIFICATION

This ECM voltage chart is for use with a digital voltmeter to further aid in diagnosis. The voltages you get may vary due to low battery charge or other reasons, but they should be very close.

THE FOLLOWING CONDITIONS MUST BE MET BEFORE TESTING:
• Engine at operating temperature • engine idling in closed loop (For "Engine Run" column) in park or neutral • Test terminal not grounded • ALDL tool not installed

VOLTAGE					
KEY "ON"	ENG. RUN	CIRCUIT	PIN	WIRE COLOR	CKT NO.
			BA1		
5	5	+5V REFERENCE (MAP)	BA4	GRY	474
5	5	+5V REFERENCE (TPS)	BA5	GRY	416
B+	B+	IGNITION FEED	BA6	PNK/BLK	439
4.8	4.8	SERIAL DATA	BA8	ORN	461
0*	B+	FUEL PUMP RELAY DRIVE	BA11	DK GRN/WHT	465
0*	0*	ECM GROUND	BA12	BLK/WHT	450

VOLTAGE					
KEY "ON"	ENG. RUN	CIRCUIT	PIN	WIRE COLOR	CKT NO.
B+	B+	BATTERY	BB1	ORN	340
0*	0*	TPS MAT SENSOR GROUND	BB5	BLK	452
0*	0*	TPS MAT SENSOR GROUND	BB6	BLK	470
0*	①	VSS (LOW)	BB9	PPL	401
0*	①	VSS (HIGH)	BB10	YEL	400
B+	B+	VSS TO I.P. 4000 P/MI	BB11	BRN	437
			BB12		

▽ Less than 1 volt
· Less than .5 volt
1. Varies from .60 volt to Battery Voltage depending on position of drivewheels
2. Varies
3. Varies with temperature
4. Battery Voltage for first two seconds
5. Battery Voltage when fuel pump is running
6. Reads battery voltage when in gear

Used with permission of General Motors

Chevy TPI Swapper's Guide

ECM PIN-OUTS TYPICAL OF 1227730 ECM 90-92 TPI

VOLTAGE					
KEY "ON"	ENG. RUN	CIRCUIT	PIN	WIRE COLOR	CKT NO.
①		VEHICLE SPEED SIGNAL	BC1	RED	381
0*	5	BYPASS	BC7	TAN/BLK	424
0*	1.3	EST	BC8	WHITE	423
B+ / 0*	B+ / 0*	WITH A/C "ON" A/C REQUEST	BC9	DK.GRN	59
B+	B+	INJECTOR 1, 3, 5, 7	BC11	BLK/PINK	467
B+	B+	INJECTOR 2, 4, 6, 8	BC12	BLK/GRN	458
B+	B+	BATTERY	BC16	ORN	340

VOLTAGE					
KEY "ON"	ENG. RUN	CIRCUIT	PIN	WIRE COLOR	CKT NO.
0*	0*	ECM GROUND	BD1	BLK/WHT	450
0▲	0▲	INJ DRIVE LOW	BD6	BLK/WHT	450
0*	0*	INJ DRIVE LOW	BD7	BLK/WHT	450
0*	2.3	REFERENCE	BD8	PPL/WHT	430
0*	0*	REFERENCE LOW	BD9	BLK/RED	453
		A/C PRESS FAN SW	BD12	GRA	731
0*	0*	TCC 4TH GEAR SWITCH	BD14	LT. BLUE	446
0*	0*	P/N SWITCH	BD16	ORN/BLK	434

▽ Less than 1 volt

· Less than .5 volt

1. Varies from .60 volt to Battery Voltage depending on position of drivewheels
2. Varies
3. Varies with temperature
4. Battery Voltage for first two seconds
5. Battery Voltage when fuel pump is running
6. Reads battery voltage when in gear

Used with permission of General Motors

ECM PIN-OUTS TYPICAL OF 1227730 ECM 90-92 TPI

VOLTAGE					
KEY "ON"	ENG. RUN	CIRCUIT	PIN	WIRE COLOR	CKT NO.
			GE1		
NOT USEABLE		IAC-"A"HI	GE3	LT. BLUE/WHITE	441
NOT USEABLE		IAC-"A"LO	GE4	LT. BLUE/BLACK	442
NOT USEABLE		IAC-"B"HI	GE5	LT. GRN/WHITE	443
NOT USEABLE		IAC-"B"LO	GE6	LT. GRN/BLACK	444
0*	B+	"SERVICE ENGINE SOON" LIGHT	GE7	BROWN/WHITE	419
0* B+	0* B+	"ON" FAN RELAY "OFF" CONTROL	GE8	DK.GRN/WHITE	335
B+	1▽	ERG SOLENOID CONTROL	GE9	GRA	435
5	5	DIAG. TERMINAL	GE12	WHT/BLK	451
④	B+	FUEL PUMP SIGNAL	GE13	GRA	120
② .35-.55	.1-.9	O₂ SIGNAL	GE14	PPL	412
0*	0*	O₂ GROUND	GE15	TAN	413
⑤	⑤	COOLANT TEMP.	GE16	YEL	410

VOLTAGE					
KEY "ON"	ENG. RUN	CIRCUIT	PIN	WIRE COLOR	CKT NO.
0* B+	0* B+	M/T SHIFT LIGHT CONTROL	GF1	TAN/BLK	456
B+	B+	PORT (SWITCH) SOLENOID	GF2	BROWN	436
B+	1▽	CONVERTER (DIVERT) SOLENOID	GF4	BLK/PINK	429
0* B+	0* B+	TCC CONTROL A/T	GF6	TAN/BLK	422
B+	B+	CANISTER PURGE SOL. CONTROL	GF7	DK.GRN/YEL	428
9.2	9.3	ESC SIGNAL	GF9	DK BLUE	496
2.5	2.5	VATS MODULE	GF10	DK BLUE	229
.65	.65	TPS SIGNAL	GF13	DK BLUE	417
4.57	2	MAP SIGNAL	GF15	LT. GRN	432
③	③	MAT SIGNAL	GF16	TAN	472

▽ Less than 1 volt

· Less than .5 volt

1. Varies from .60 volt to Battery Voltage
2. Varies
3. Varies with temperature
4. Battery Voltage for first two seconds
5. Battery Voltage when fuel pump is running
6. Reads battery voltage when in gear

Used with permission of General Motors

Chevy TPI Swapper's Guide

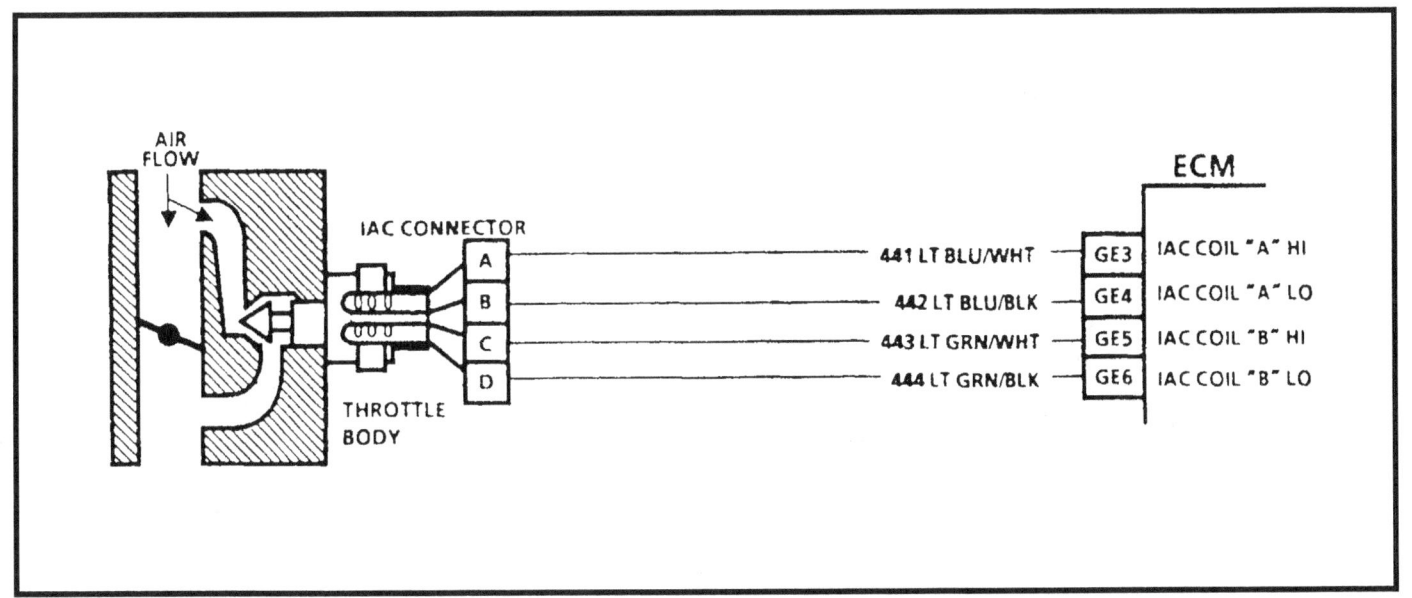

CHART C-2C
IDLE AIR CONTROL (IAC) SYSTEM CHECK

Circuit Description:
The ECM controls idle rpm with the IAC valve. To increase idle rpm, the ECM moves the IAC valve out, allowing more air to bypass the throttle plate. To decrease rpm, it moves the IAC valve in, reducing airflow bypassing the throttle plate. A "Scan" tool will read the ECM commands to the IAC valve in counts. The higher the counts, the more air allowed (higher idle). The lower the counts, the less air allowed (lower idle).

Function Test: Using the following procedure, you can test the IAC for proper function.
1. With a warmed up engine, determine the idle speed in neutral with a tachometer.
2. Jumper the "A" and "B" terminals in the diagnostic connector with a paper clip or suitable jumper.
3. Turn on the ignition, but do not start vehicle.
4. There should be an audible buzzing or clicking noise from the idle Air Control motor This is caused by the IAC seating itself repeatedly and closing the idle air passage.
5. Unplug the 4 pin IAC connector and remove the diagnostic connector jumper.
6. Restart the engine and observe the idle speed If the IAC is working properly, the idle speed should now be somewhat lower than before. With correctly adjusted throttle stop screw, the idle speed with IAC closed should be about 100 rpm below the ECM controlled idle speed.

A diagnostic scanner will read out the position of the IAC motor, and the pre-programmed desired idle speed. Correctly adjusted throttle blades should give IAC counts between 10 and 60 with engine warmed up and idling in neutral. See the following diagnostic aids if idle speed is slow, fast, or unstable.

Diagnostic Aids:
A slow, unstable, or fast idle may be caused by a non-IAC system problem that cannot be overcome by the IAC valve. of control range IAC "Scan" tool counts will be above 60 if idle is too low, and zero counts if idle is too high. The following checks should be made to repair a non-IAC system problem.

Vacuum leak (High Idle)
If idle is too high, stop the engine. Fully extend or close the IAC. Start engine. If idle speed is above 800 rpm, locate and correct vacuum leak including PCV system. Also check for binding of throttle blade or linkage.

System too lean (High Air/fuel Ratio)
Idle speed may be too high or too low. Engine speed may vary up and down and disconnecting IAC does not help. Code 44 may be set. Scan O2 voltage will be less than 300 mV (.3 volts). Check for low regulated fuel pressure, water in the fuel or a restricted injector.

System too rich (Low Air/Fuel Ratio).
The idle speed will be too low. Scan O2 voltage will be fixed above 800mV (.8 volt). Check for high fuel pressure, leaking or sticking injector. Silicone contaminated O2 sensor will scan an O2 voltage slow to respond.

Throttle body
Remove IAC and inspect bore for foreign material.

PCV Valve
An incorrect or faulty PCv valve may result in an incorrect idle speed.
Refer to rough, unstable, incorrect idle or stalling in "Symptoms", Section B, Page 48.
If intermittent poor drivability or idle symptoms are resolved by disconnecting the IAC, carefully recheck connections, valve terminal resistance, or replace IAC.

Chevy TPI Swapper's Guide

CHEVY TPI Fuel Injection Swapper's Guide
Modifying TPI Systems

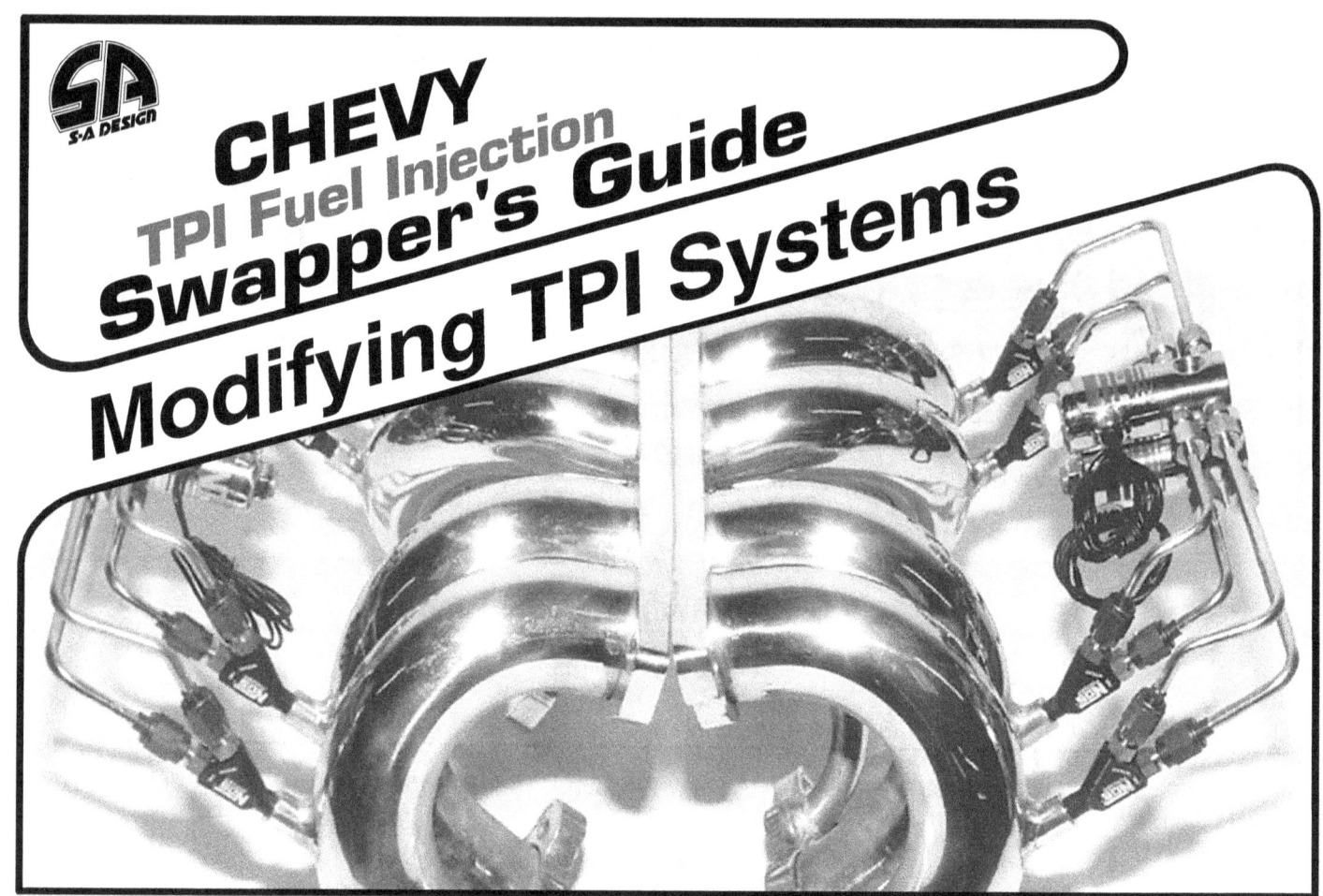

One of the most difficult aspects of modifying a car equipped with electronic fuel injection is understanding which modifications can be made while still using the original computer and PROM, and knowing how far you can go. Most tuners will make modifications to improve their car's performance within the operable parameters of the stock ECM (Electronic Control Module); however, many people feel the need for speed in excess of what the factory computer can manage. What then?

In order to understand how performance modifications affect the ECM, it is important to understand how the ECM is originally set up. The factory calls this process calibration. Car companies spend millions of dollars developing programming for their computers and they don't pass this information out freely to the public. Recalibrating a factory computer is left to those people who have access to factory information or aftermarket chip manufacturers who write their own programs.

This leads many people to assume that modifying an EFI car is not possible. However, savvy aftermarket manufacturers have provided the tools to build EFI engines that can push street drivers into the 9's and beyond. Generally, factory ECMs can handle basic modifications that still provide good vacuum at idle, but anything extensive, such as a 500hp small block will require recalibration. ACCEL, Crane, Electromotive, Haltech, and N.O.S. all manufacture ECMs or ECM products that allow you to calibrate for your particular engine combination.

WHAT IS CALIBRATION?

Calibration is simply matching fuel delivery and spark timing to the specific requirements of the engine. Jetting a carburetor and adjusting the distributor advance are the traditional equivalents of calibrating a non-computer car.

Changing carburetor jets or springs in a mechanical advance distributor is something that most car people can do. Unfortunately, EFI systems do not have jets or mechanical weights in the distributor. Factory EFI systems are not adjustable. The information that controls the injection and the spark curves is stored in a memory device called the PROM (programmable read only memory). This information, called the calibration, represents the jets and weights of a modern EFI system.

BASIC PROM PROGRAMMING SCHEME

PROMs are programmed in binary which uses ones and zeros. Compare the decimal numbers below to their binary counterparts.

Decimal Base 10	Hexadecimal Base 16	Binary Base 2
1	1	1
2	2	10
3	3	11
4	4	100
5	5	101
6	6	110
7	7	111
8	8	1000
9	9	1001
10	a	1010
11	b	1011
12	c	1100
13	d	1101
14	e	1110
15	f	1111
16	10	10000

AIR/FUEL RATIO LIMITS

Basic Air/Fuel ratio limits for internal combustion engines.

6.0:1	Rich run limit
9.0:1	Black smoke, power loss
11.5:1	Rich best torque (RBT) at WOT
12.5:1	Safe best power at WOT
13.2:1	Lean best torque (LBT)
14.7:1	Chemically correct air/fuel ratio
15.5:1	Lean light load (part throttle)
16.2:1	Best fuel economy (part throttle)
18-22:1	Lean run limit

A PROM is simply a tiny bank of switches that are configured in either the on or off position. On is represented by the number zero, and off is represented by a one. All information in the PROM is represented by strings of ones and zeros, by electronically setting the switches in the appropriate positions. This numbering system is called base two (or binary) and each unit of information is called a bit. The computer processes all numbers in base two. Groups of switches are gathered together in one area called an address. The information in one address is reported in base 16 (or hexadecimal). All of the addresses are also numbered in hexadecimal. Table 1 on this page compares binary, decimal, and hexadecimal numbers. Table 2 shows some of the output of a PROM.

PROMs come in many different configurations and sizes, but most store 32K, 128K, or 256K of information (one "K" equals 1000 "bits"). PROMs are erased by exposing the integrated circuit to strong ultraviolet (UV) light, causing all the switches to be set in the on position. PROMs usually have a quartz window so that they can be erased, though it is typically covered by a decal to prevent damaging the data by accidental exposure. PROMs are programmed with a device that can identify the address in the PROM and set the switches to a position as specified by the program.

HOW THE FACTORY CALIBRATES FUEL SYSTEMS

The first step is to place the engine with all of the accessories including the catalytic converter and the entire exhaust system on a computer-controlled dynamometer. Sensors are connected to the engine to measure:

- Operating temperatures
- Pressures
- Airflow
- Fuel flow
- Air/Fuel ratio (A/F)
- Emission
- Horsepower/Torque

The engine is then run under every operating condition from idle to wide open throttle. All this information is compiled into a map of the engine's fuel and spark requirements, from which the initial calibration is programmed.

Of particular interest is how the calibration is performed for the wide-open throttle points. The wide-open curves are: leanest for best torque (LBT) for fuel and minimum timing for mean best torque (MBT) for spark.

The way these curves are identified is by holding the engine at one rpm and testing for the highest torque reading on the dynamometer. The LBT point is always approached from the rich side. The engine is held at rpm and leaned out until the torque reading starts to fall off or detonation occurs. The LBT point is the air/fuel ratio point where the high torque reading occurs. At the same rpm, spark advance is increased until torque drops off, which is the MBT point. In most cases timing can be advanced several degrees beyond MBT before torque drops off. If torque continues to climb while advance is increased and then detonation occurs, the engine is said to be knock limited.

This procedure is repeated approximately every 400 rpm to the maximum rpm. The MBT spark and LBT fuel curves define the performance of the engine. Most engines make best torque at an air/fuel ratio of

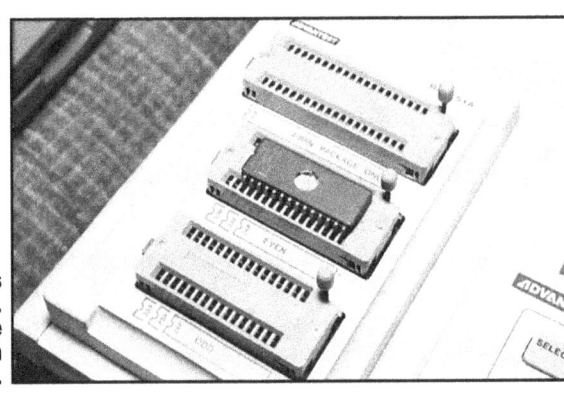

PROM "burner" accepts all different chip styles. Chips are loaded into the slots and the calibration is loaded to the chip.

approximately 12.5:1, for gasoline, though this will change significantly with changes in fuels. Most small block Chevys will produce the best torque with 34-38 degrees of total timing.

After the dynamometer testing is completed, the calibration engineer takes over. The engineer tunes the fuel system in the car and the calibration is refined to cover drivability, emission, and cold and hot starting. This process may take weeks or months as hardware and soft~ware changes are made to the vehicle.

MODIFYING TPI SYSTEMS

OEM fuel systems are adaptable to changes because of the closed-loop control system based on the 02 sensor and the ECM's memory. How far can you go before your modifications exceed the limit of the OEM computer? Most aftermarket parts manufacturers have experience with late-model cars and can advise you as to which parts will be tolerated by the car's ECM. The following outline provides a guide as to which parts are likely to be accepted without recalibrating the ECM. Mass flow fuel systems will accept basic modifications easily, while speed density systems require more careful selection of modifications. Generally modifications that still provide high intake manifold vacuum will be OK with stock computers.

WHAT REQUIRES RECALIBRATION?

Except as noted below, the engine parameters that will most likely require recalibration when changed are:

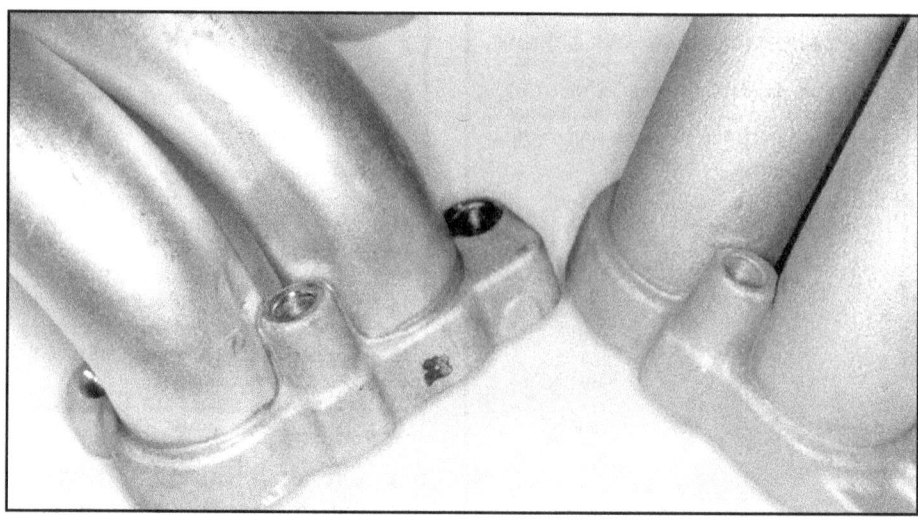

Stock tuned port runners are dimpled at the attachment point to provide easy access for fasteners. Some tuners like to take the dimple out by forcing the appropriate size steel ball through the runner to open it up.

- Intake manifold
- Camshaft
- Engine displacement

Air Filters—
Air filters are not a problem, NOTE: Some filters are coated with a silicone-based filter oil that can damage the 02 sensor.

Throttles—
Changing to a larger throttle body will not require recalibration, although the largest bodies may require more acceleration enrichment (pump shot).

Intake Manifolds—
Radical changes to the intake manifold may require recalibration, though mass flow systems are somewhat more tolerant of intake changes, GM TPI engines can handle runner and intake base changes without requiring recalibration. but changing to a box manifold will.

Camshafts—
The mildest cams, designed for computer-controlled engines may not need recalibration. but aggressive cams that reduce manifold vacuum most certainly will.

Cylinder Heads—
Porting usually will not require recalibration but increases in compression or changes to high-flow heads will.

Headers—
Generally headers with small primaries will be accepted without the need for recalibration.

Exhaust—
No need for recalibration if the catalyst is in place.

Changes in Displacement—
Changes in displacement that are greater than 10% will require recalibration.

FUEL CALIBRATION

An engine burns a combination of air and fuel. The mass or weight ratio of the air to fuel that an engine receives (air/fuel ratio) is the best description of this mixture. The chemically correct air/fuel ratio for gasoline is approximately 14.7 parts air to 1 part fuel. As additional air is added, the mixture is said to be lean, and if additional fuel is added, then the mixture is said to be rich. Table 2 reviews how air/fuel ratio affects engine operation.

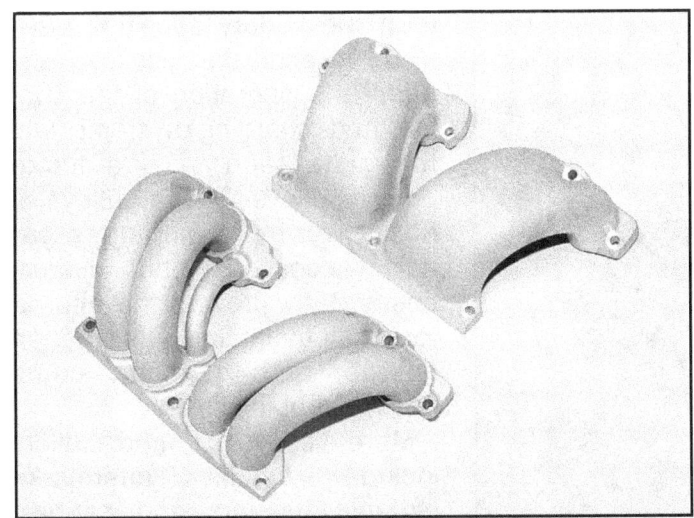 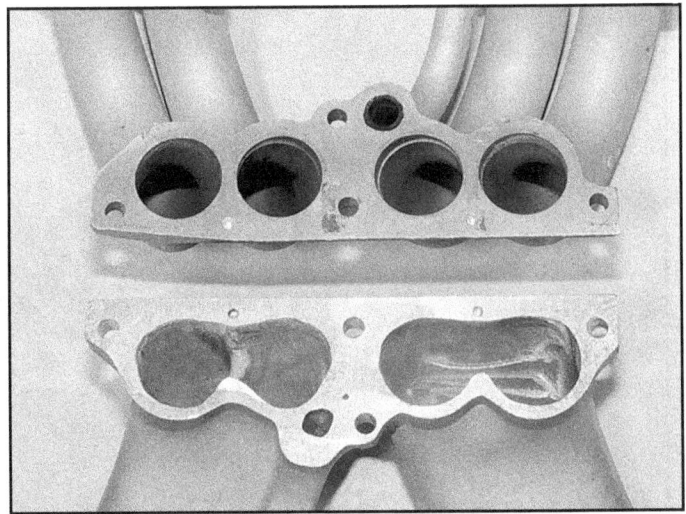

Increasing runner size, and or, siamesing the runners is a proven approach to increasing power in TPI equipped engines. Stock runners are shown here compared to a SLP Engineering runner that is siamesed with larger diameter passages and individual tuned lengths as shown in the photo on the right. These type of runners provide a significant gain when used with a modified lower intake, a larger throttle body and the correct camshaft and ECM calibration.

OTHER MIXTURE CONSIDERATIONS

Cold Operation—

Cold engine operation requires extra fuel since only a small portion of the fuel can vaporize at low temperatures. Cold starts at temperatures below freezing can require air/fuel ratios as rich as 6.0:1 or 7.0:1. The mixture must be leaned out as the engine warms up.

Idle—

At idle the engine is severely choked and is not operating efficiently. Generally the idle mixture may need to be slightly richer than the chemically correct AFR. As cam overlap increases, the mixture will need to be made richer yet. Very large cams may need to be at 12.5:1 air/fuel ratio at idle.

Off Idle and Light Load—

This is a high-vacuum condition similar to idle. Generally the air/fuel ratio can be set at 14.7:1. Larger cams will require more fuel than small ones. Long runner manifolds can use less fuel under these conditions.

Cruise and Light Acceleration—

Under mild acceleration an A/F of 14.7:1 will work for most applications. Best fuel economy will be at 16:1 to 16.5:1 with additional spark advance. Again large cams will want to be at least one A/F ratio richer. As load increases at part throttle, fuel will need to be added.

High-Load, Part Throttle—

High-Load— Part-throttle conditions will require an A/F approaching that of WOT, which is usually between 13.0:1 and 14.0:1.

Wide-Open Throttle—

The best place to be is between LBT and RBT. For most normally aspirated four-stroke engines this will be approximately 12.5:1.

Since air/fuel ratio is so critical to proper engine operation and power production, an air/fuel ratio analyzer makes fuel system calibration much easier. One of the finest A/F analyzers is sold by Horiba. This analyzer can measure air/fuel ratio very accurately under almost all conditions, but it is very expensive, on the order of ($8000 to $9000).

Edelbrock, MSD, Electromotive, Haltech, and many other companies sell air/fuel ratio indicators that read the output of an O2 sensor. These indicators are quite affordable but are not as critically accurate under rich conditions. Nevertheless, they can be helpful in calibrating a fuel system.

AFTERMARKET ECMS

If you want to build an EFI engine that goes beyond what an OEM calibration can support, ACCEL, Crane, Edelbrock, Electromotive, Haltech, N.O.S., and many other companies make ECMs or ECM products that will allow you to build an EFI system for your particular engine.

ACCEL's Power Processor and Cal-Map software allow you to program your TPI computer with a laptop computer. The Cal-Map software allows you to calibrate the ECM on the fly. It has a convenient, built-in air/fuel ratio indicator to help with part-throttle calibration. Cal-Map allows you to change injector pulse width or spark advance while you drive. Almost any aspect of the fuel system's

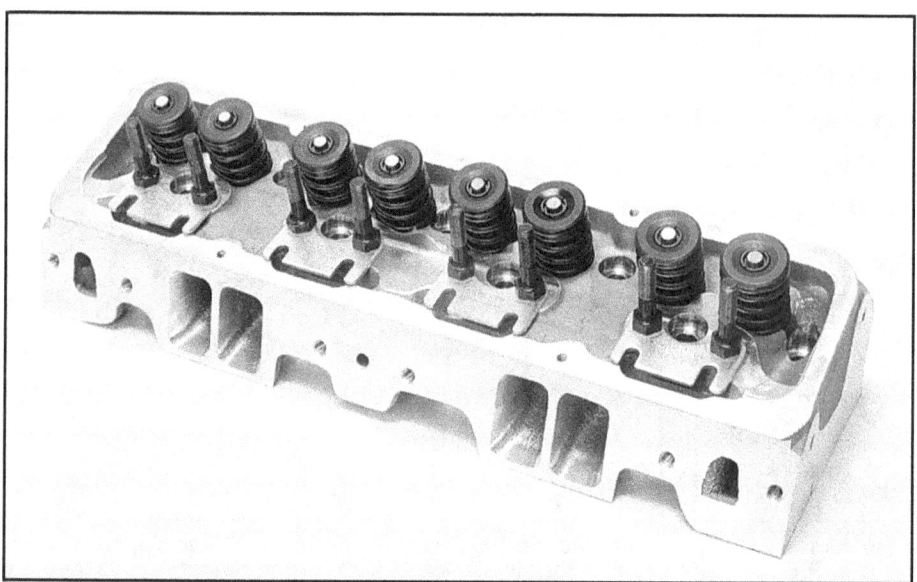

Air Flow Research's "smog legal" aluminum street cylinder heads are the ideal choice for modified TPI engines. These fully CNC ported heads feature stainless steel valves, bronze guides, 1.450-inch diameter high performance springs with 10° retainers and locks and ¾-inch thick decks. The 190cc intake ports are appropriately sized for most hot street engines in the 350 to 475 horsepower range.

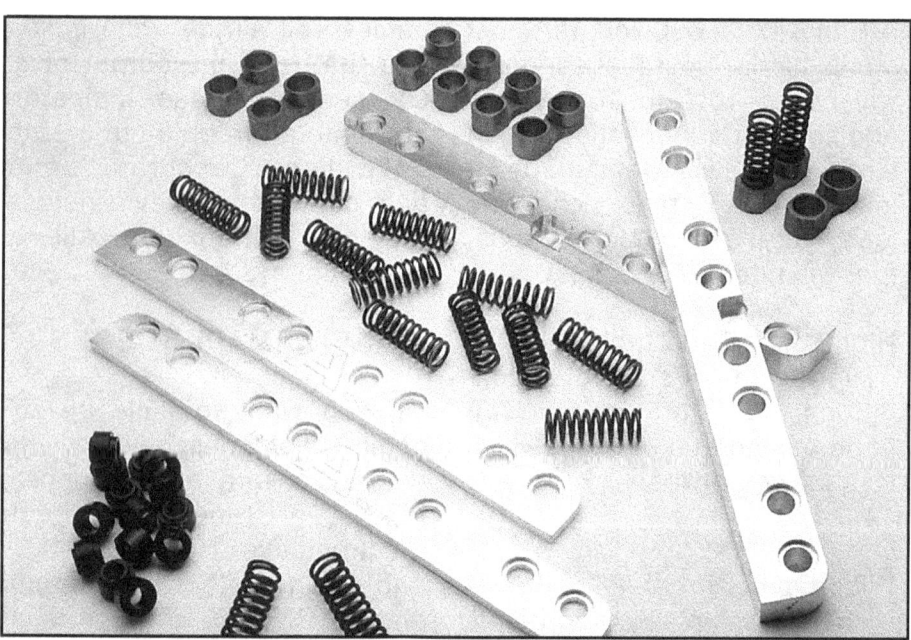

AFR's HydraREV system is the perfect complement to its high performance cylinder head. The HydraREV can add up to 1000 rpm to your engine's potential. It minimizes many of the typical problems associated with factory, and some aftermarket roller cams, including early valve float, hydraulic plunger collapse and excessive valve train wear. The AFR system distributes spring pressure without overloading the plunger mechanism, allowing a wider peak power band without damage to valve train components.

than the factory specified 220°. Keep in mind that you can also affect the operation of the cooling and charging systems with the installation of aftermarket power pulleys. These pulleys do add power by slowing down parasitic accessories, but in some cases, they prevent the alternator from maintaining full battery charge, and they may cause cooling problems.

More effective modifications include tubular aftermarket exhaust headers and cat-back exhaust systems available from Edelbrock, Hedman, SLP Engineering, Walker and Borla. On the intake side you can port or extrude-hone the intake manifold, plenum runners and even the cylinder head in search of power. Remember, the TPI's primary benefit is the superior torque provided by the long runners. Many of these modifications can extend the rev range and help the engine gain power upstairs without losing torque on the bottom end. This works up to a point. Generally a TPI equipped engine can be made to run hard up to 6000 rpm with the modifications discussed here. That's not to say that 6000 rpm is the absolute limit, rather it is the typical limit for most applications. Beyond 330 horsepower, the throttle body becomes restrictive and a larger unit is required to flow the necessary air. These are available from Arizona Speed and Marine, Accel, SLP, Lingenfelter Performance and other aftermarket sources. There are plenty of examples of engines making way over 400 horsepower with the basic tuned port configuration. This typically requires siamesed runners, good cylinder heads and camshaft, aftermarket exhaust, and appropriate ECM calibration, but it still delivers the strong low end punch that characterizes TPI engines.

operation can be programmed. Changes can be saved to the ECM or to a disk for later use.

OTHER CONSIDERATIONS

As with any high performance situations, there are a lot of things to consider when chasing every last horsepower. If you need to run a cooler thermostat, be sure not to go below 180°, or the system may never go into closed loop operation. Aftermarket PROMs can turn the cooling fans on at 180° if you prefer rather

Tuned Port Fuel Injection Tips & Tricks

TPI CAMSHAFT RECOMMENDATIONS

These Comp Cams grinds are specifically profiled for use with tuned port injection applications ranging from stock to fully modified with aftermarket intakes, plenums, runners, throttle bodies, computer chips, high stall converters and stiffer rear gears. The wide, stock-like lobe separation angles are used to maintain adequate engine vacuum for proper ECM operation. Specific profiles are available for both 5.0L and 5.7L engines, and for early flat tappet hydraulic cam equipped engines or later roller cam equipped engines.

Cam	Type	Duration @ .050 lift	Lift	Lobe Separation	Application
CS-260AH-12	Hydraulic	212°/212°	.444/.444	112°	Replacement cam for stock TPI engines
CS-260AH-14	Hydraulic	212°/218°	.444/.444	114°	For stock 350 TPI or 305 TPI with aftermarket computer chip
CS-268-AH-14	Hydraulic	222°/226°	.464/.464	114°	Modified 350 TPI with aftermarket chip
CS-262H-R12	Hyd. Roller	206°/210°	.450/.480	112°	Stock TPI with stock computer
CS-264H-R12	Hyd. Roller	210°/220°	.480/.480	112°	TPI with modified aftermarket chip
CS-266HR-14	Hyd. Roller	210°/220°	.500/.510	114°	TPI w/modified plenum, runners & chip
CS-276HR-14	Hyd. Roller	220°/230°	.510/.510	114°	Highly modified TPI with stock converter
CS-290HR-12	Hyd. Roller	230°/244°	.510/.540	112°	Highly modified TPI with 2500 rpm converter, 2000 to 6000 rpm.

Comp Cams 1.6:1 ratio Hi-Tech Stainless, Magnum or Pro Magnum roller rockers are an easy way to increase cam lift without adversely affecting the ECM calibration. These are recommended when using aftermarket cylinder heads, or pre-roller cam factory heads. If you are using the late Corvette aluminum cylinder head, use Comp's replacement "rail rockers" for consistent rocker ratios on each cylinder. Also be sure to match your camshaft selection to the appropriate valve springs and associated hardware to ensure that your cam will deliver maximum torque and power in its intended rpm range. Failure to provide adequate valve spring tension is the inevitable downfall of many high performance camshaft installations.

TUNED PORT Fuel Injection Tips & Tricks

USING NITROUS WITH TPI

One of the easiest ways to pump up the power in a tuned port injection system is the use of nitrous oxide injection. A basic plate system from NOS bolts between the throttle body and the plenum, and is capable of adding about 100 horsepower. This system is easy to hook up and remove. For more aggressive combinations, NOS offers a direct port injection system that is tied directly into the vehicle's on-board computer. This system uses modified calibration to alter the injector pulse width for increased fuel flow while the nitrous oxide is activated. The amount and duration of nitrous injection can be computer controlled to come on "progressively" for optimum power production without shocking the tires and breaking traction. NOS also offers smog legal nitrous oxide injection systems for tuned port engines.

It is important that nitrous use be carefully set up and controlled to avoid engine damage. Substantial power increases are available from relatively stock engines, but it is critical to keep nitrous use in perspective relative to the strength and durability of the components in the engine. It only takes a little too much nitrous to destroy an engine.

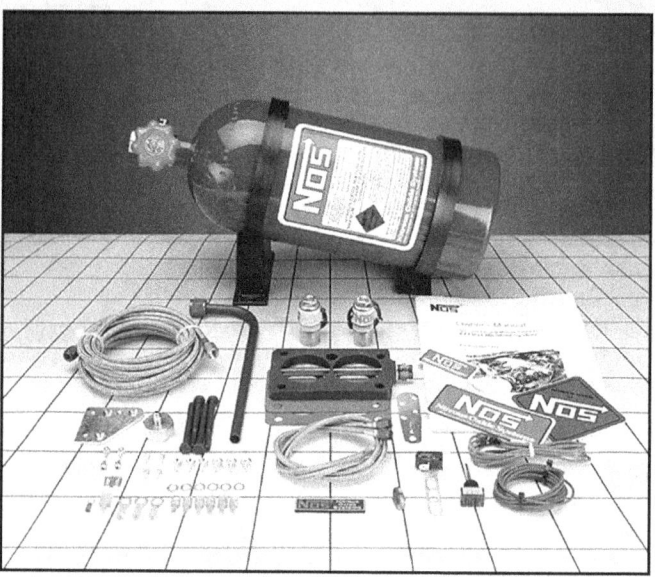

NOS tuned port nitrous system for 5.0L and 5.7L GM engines fits all TPI applications from 1985 to 1992. This easy to install spray bar plate system sandwiches between the throttle body and the plenum. It includes a throttle activated micro-switch and can be configured to deliver anywhere from 100 to 150 horsepower.

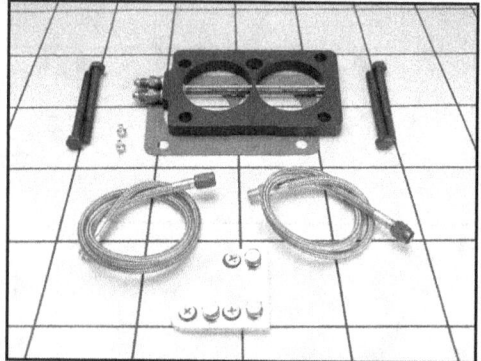

The spraybar arrangement uses dual spraybars that are sandwiched between the throttle body and the plenum on a common plate. One bar is for the nitrous while the other hooks directly to the existing fuel rail test port.

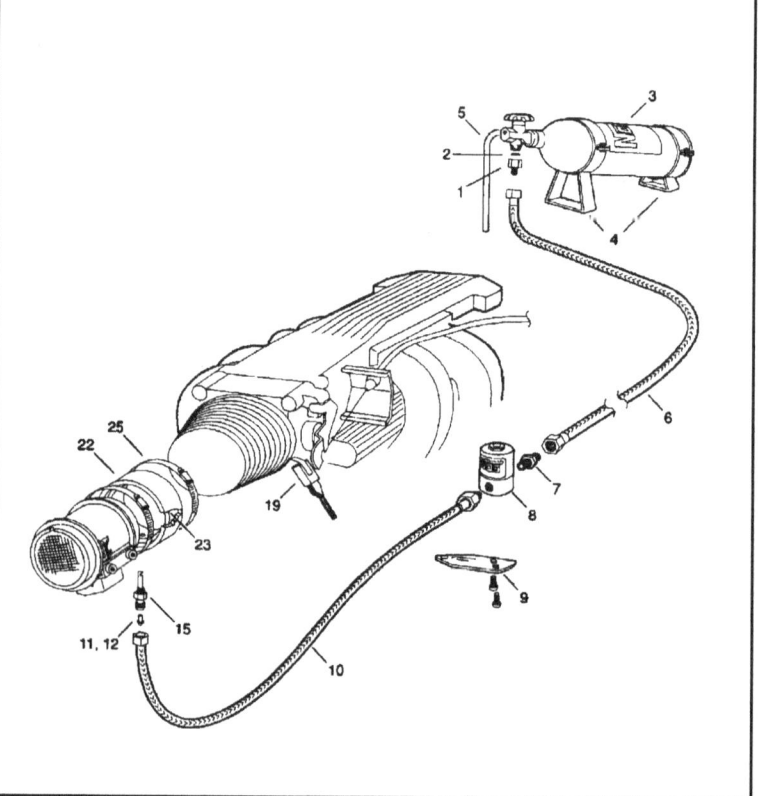

Illustration shows the basic layout of a NOS nitrous oxide injection system on a tuned port injection setup. In this setup, fuel enrichment is performed through the existing injectors via control from a modified ECM chip.

TUNED PORT Fuel Injection Tips & Tricks

TPI EXHAUST SYSTEMS

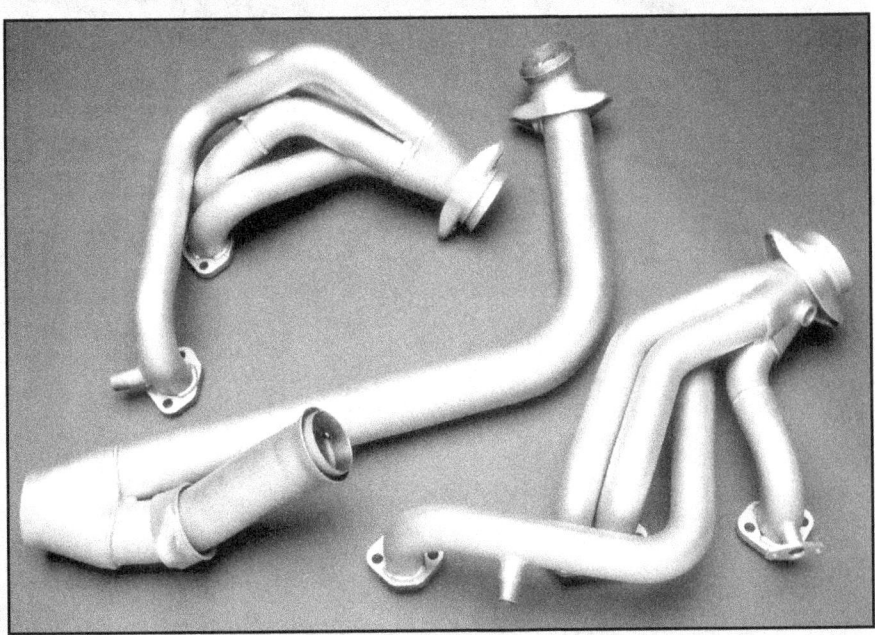

Exhaust systems for tuned port injection cars aren't particularly different from any other vehicle. You are still looking to minimize backpressure and ensure good flow characteristics. If you are upgrading an existing Corvette or F-body, excellent headers and cat-back exhaust systems are available from manufacturers such as SLP Engineering, Edelbrock, Tuned Port Induction Specialties, Arizona Speed & Marine and others.

Engine swaps are another story. In some cases you may be able to modify existing smog-style headers to suit your swap. Or, you may have performed a swap for which headers already exist. In this case you may be able to add the oxygen sensor fitting and sensor into the collector as close as possible to the exhaust ports to ensure quick sensor heating times for closed loop operation. A heated sensor can also be used if necessary. Depending on the state where you live, you will probably have to have the setup inspected and certified in order to obtain licensing.

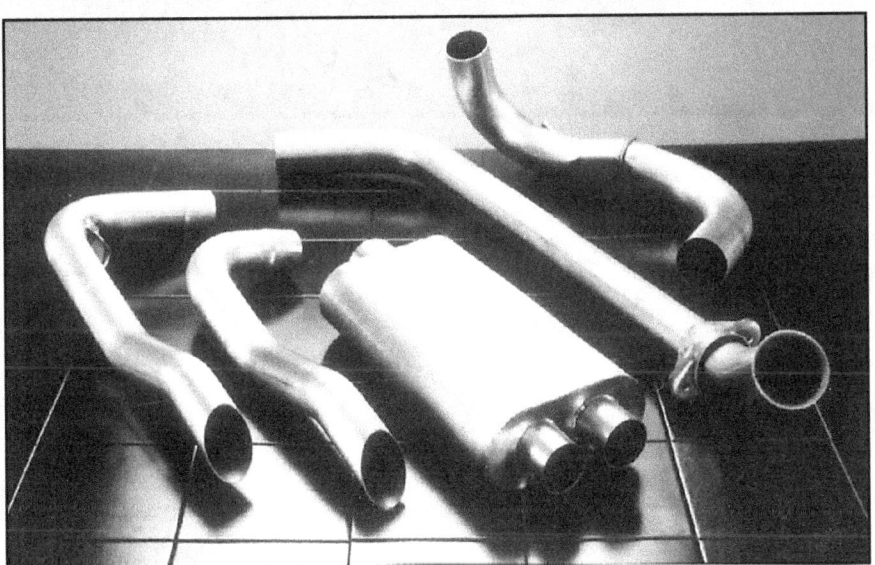

The exhaust system is a little easier since many cat-back systems are available for Camaros, Firebirds and Corvettes. In any other car, it will be typically pretty easy for a good exhaust technician to plumb a good high performance exhaust system on the car using the mufflers and tailpipe configuration of your choice. Be sure to use at least 2.25-inch diameter pipe or larger if room permits. As shown at the right, engine swaps that require factory cast iron exhaust manifolds should use those from factory tuned port equipped F-bodies because they have large 2.5-inch outlets.

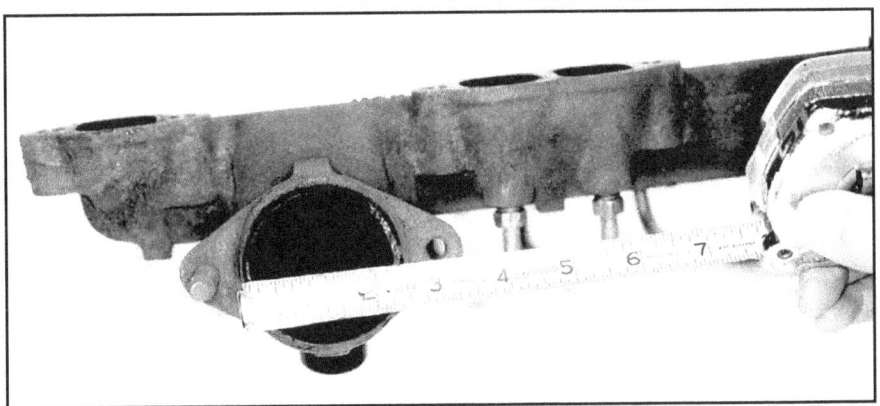

Chevy TPI Swapper's Guide **121**

S-A DESIGN

CHEVY TPI Fuel Injection Swapper's Guide

TPI Buyer's Guide

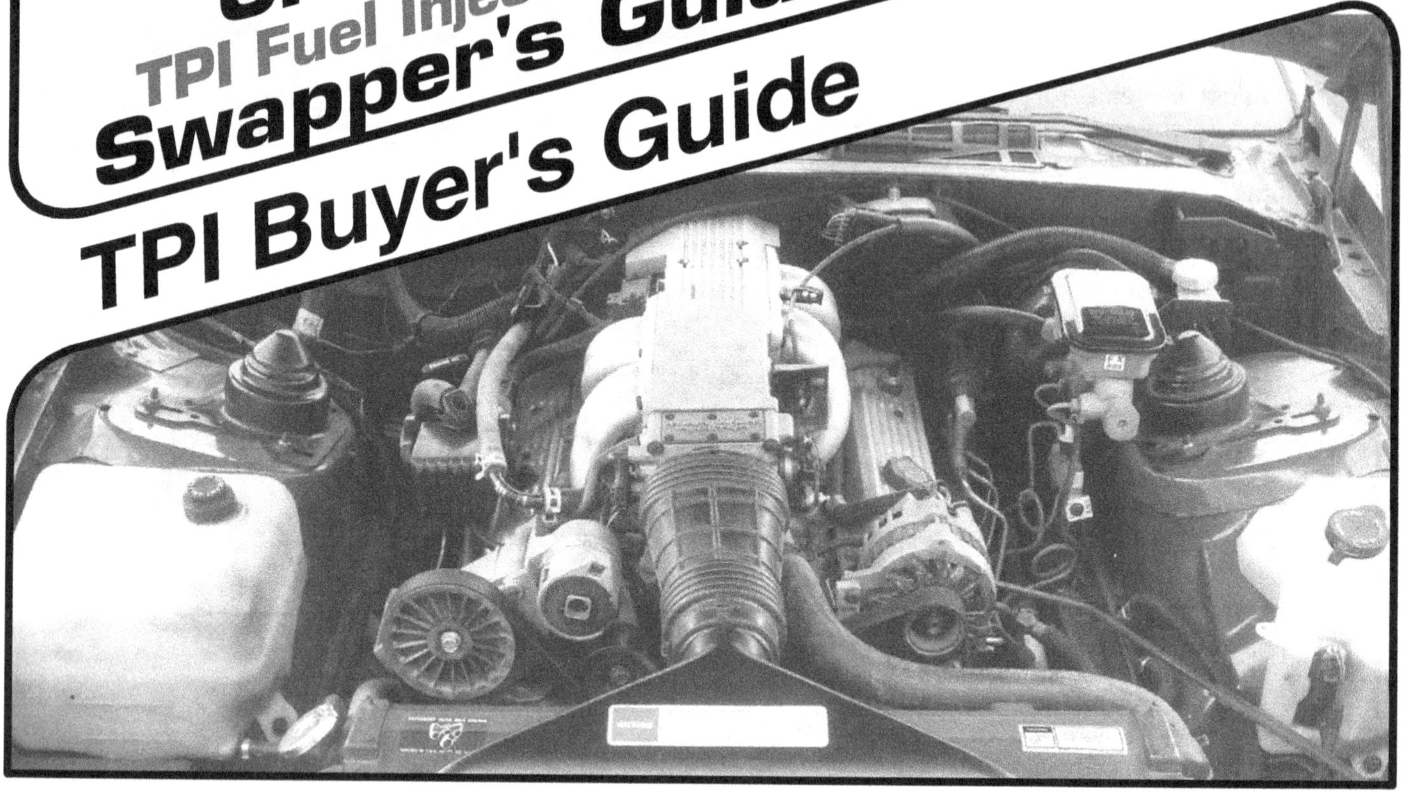

TUNED PORT Fuel Injection Buyer's Guide

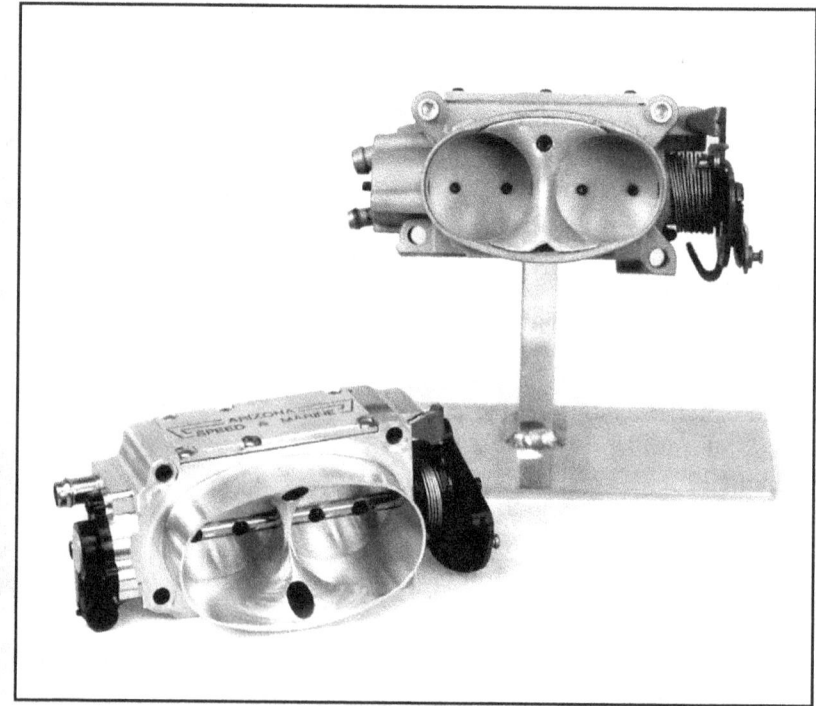

Most of the leading TPI suppliers listed in our sources section, make similar performance products for TPI engines. The 48mm and 52mm throttle bodies shown here are a good example. These are from Arizona Speed & Marine, but they are offered by most major tuned port suppliers.

TUNED PORT Fuel Injection Buyer's Guide

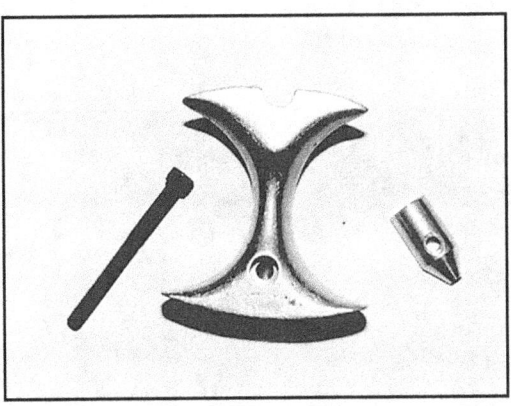

All of the tuned port injection suppliers offer the throttle body airfoil insert like this one from Tuned Port Induction Specialties. They are said to stabilize, straighten and increase inlet airflow.

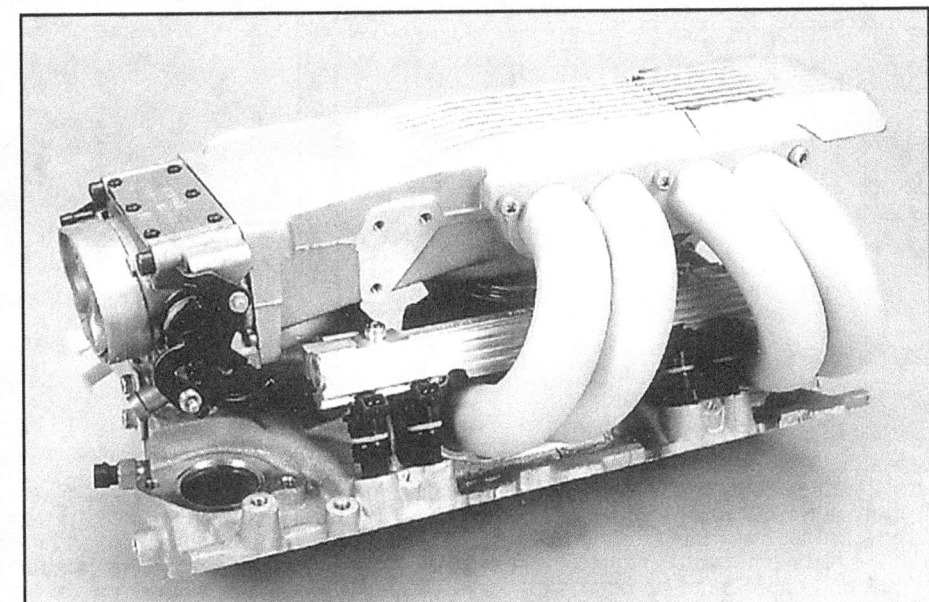

Arizona Speed & Marine offers these large tube intake setups for modified tuned port engines. They feature enlarged intake runners, a ported manifold base and plenum top and a high flow throttle body.

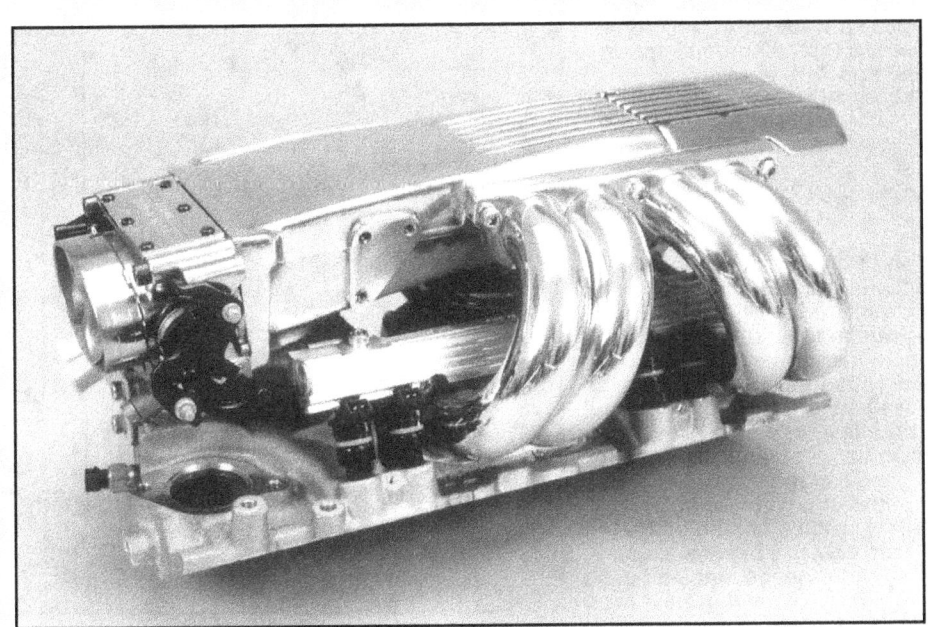

Arizona Speed & Marine also offers the large tube intake setups with polished runners. These are popular with street rodders and other custom car applications.

TUNED PORT Fuel Injection Buyer's Guide

Tuned Port Induction Specialties designed its "Big Mouth" replacement intake manifold for applications with high flow cylinder heads capable of making well over one horsepower per cubic inch. As shown above and at the top right, this manifold features substantially enlarged ports that must be used with the appropriate big tube runners or siamesed runners. It accepts all factory stock hardware and emissions components and provides up to 375 horsepower on a 350 and 440 horsepower on a 400 cubic inch engine.

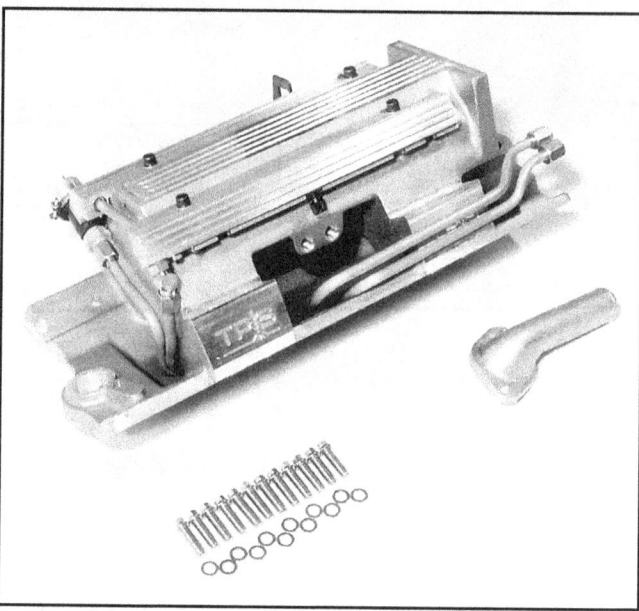

The Mini Ram II intake manifold from Tuned Port Induction Specialties offers gains of up to 125 horsepower on basic TPI combinations. Fully modified engines have delivered up to 460 horsepower from a 383, 550 horsepower from a 400 and 476 horsepower from a 406.

Tuned Port Induction Specialties backs up their TPI products with excellent literature to help TPI enthusiasts build their projects. The insider hints books provides numerous tips and references as well as official dyno tests and products specs. The L98 Update booklet describes all the latest development at TPIS, plus reprints of a wide range of technical articles on subjects such as exhaust oxygen sensors, cylinder heads, engine builds and project cars.

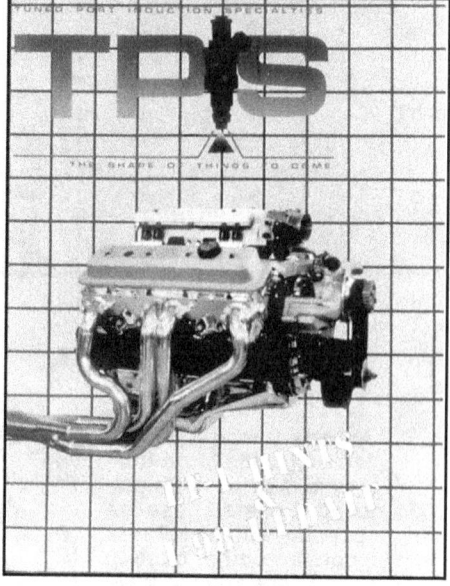

Tuned Port Fuel Injection Buyer's Guide

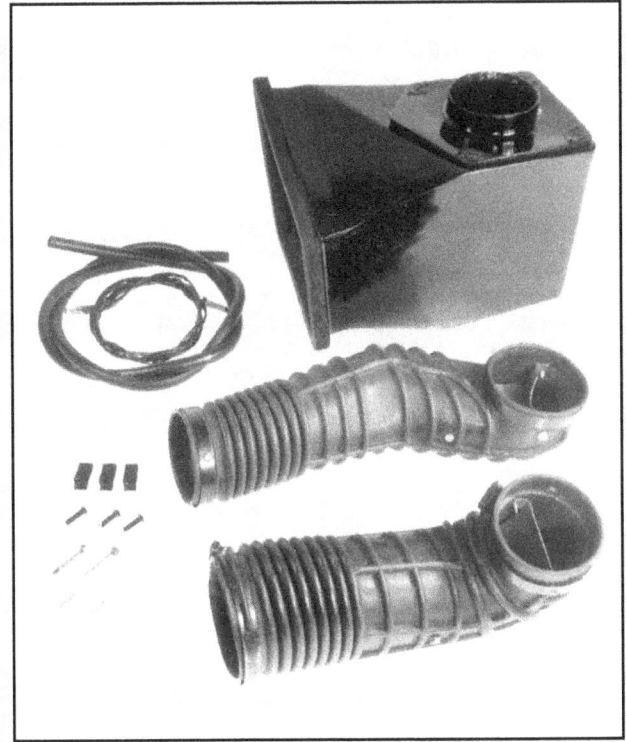

Many engine swap applications may be able to adapt existing Camaro/Firebird cold air induction packages such as these SLP Engineering pieces.

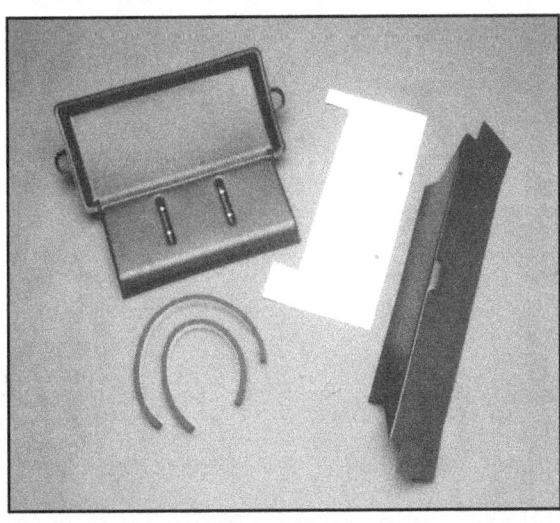

Some applications with low hood lines may find the Corvette cold air package from SLP Engineering useful. It offers a lot of filter area in a compact size that is easy to fit into cramped engine compartments.

Tuned Port Fuel Injection Buyer's Guide

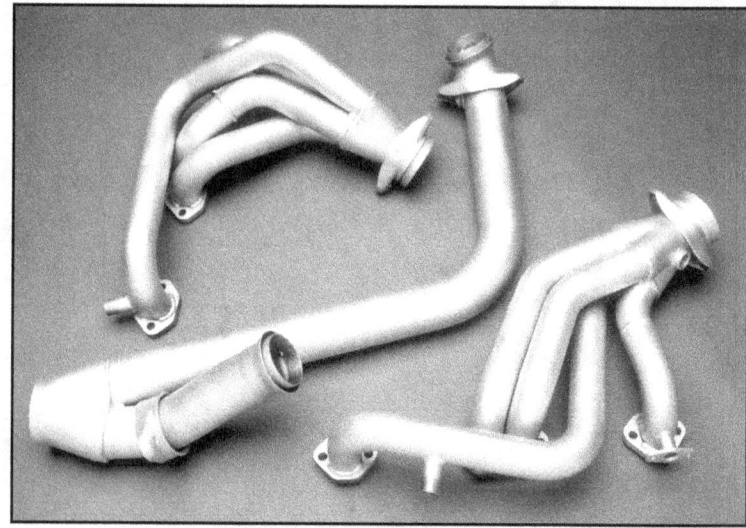

If you convert a non TPI Camaro/Firebird to TPI, aftermarket headers are a good power addition. SLP Engineering and other manufacturers offer smog legal headers that will provide a power boost, especially when teamed with a cat-back exhaust system.

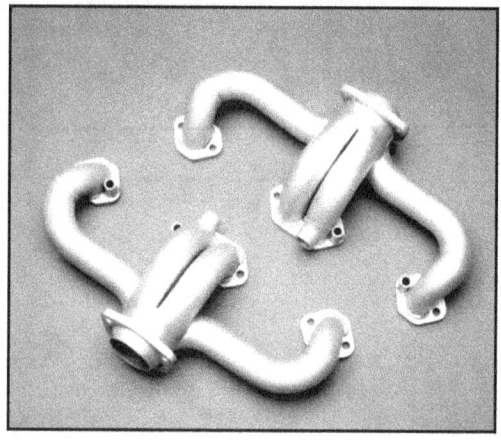

SLP Engineering also offers these Corvette headers for TPI engines. They can be useful in street rods and other engine swaps where clearance is tight.

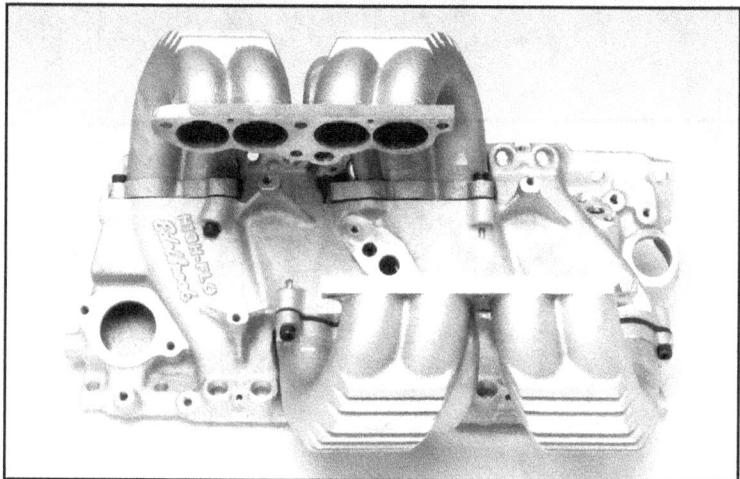

Edelbrock's High-Flo TPI baseplate and runners are setup to accept all factory components and require no calibration changes to improve performance. The runners are compatible with both stock and modified intake bases.

MSD Injectors are availalbe in all popular injector size ratings. These are precision manufactured injectors just like the factory units.

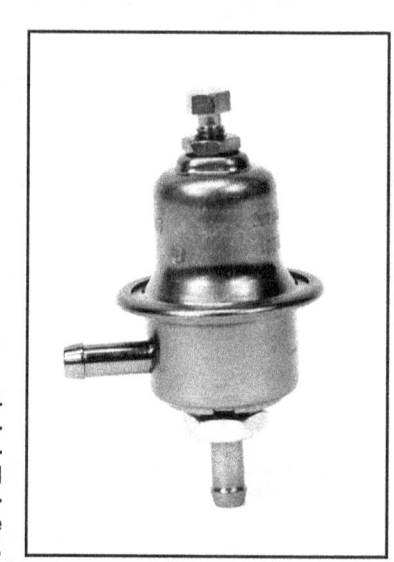

MSD fuel pressure regulator, like those available from other manufacturers, is designed to permit quick adjustment of fuel pressure for tuning purposes.

Chevy TPI Swapper's Guide

TUNED PORT Fuel Injection Buyer's Guide

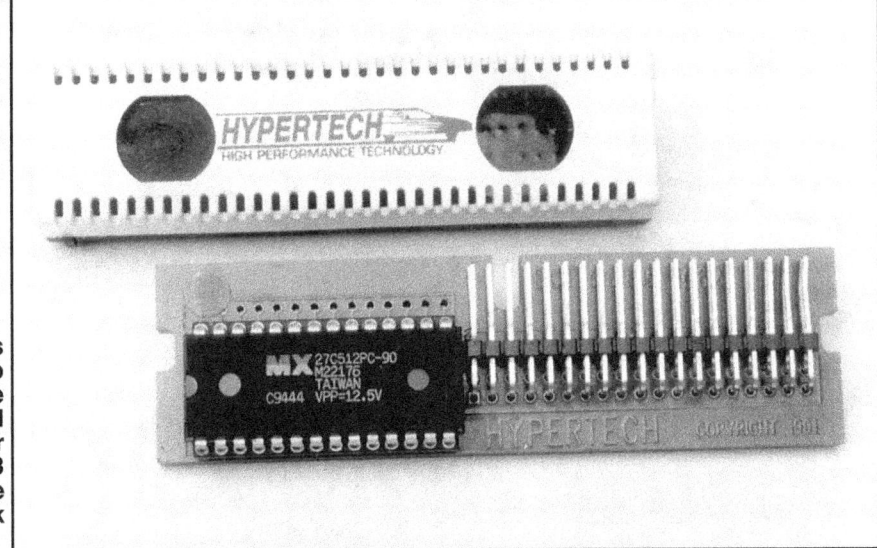

Street Runner Power Chips from Hypertech are designed to provide maximum performance calibration upgrades for TPI engines. They are approved for use in California under CARB E.O.#D-2603, and they are designed for use with a stock thermostat.

High performance pulleys available from Hypertech and other manufacturers reduce the power used to drive accessories. They reduce the speed of all driven accessories, thereby reducing the parasitic drag on the engine. These components definitely work, but in some cases they may not charge the battery sufficiently. If you convert to TPI and a serpentine belt drive system, these pulleys can add 5-10 horsepower to your package.

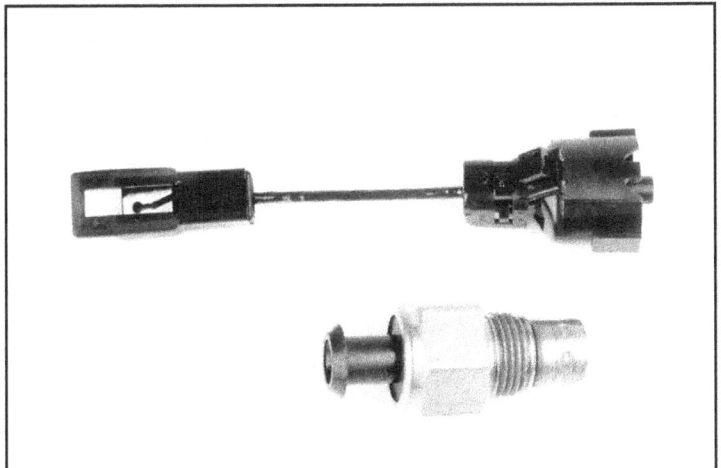

Hypertech also offers a Cool Fan switch to control TPI engine temperature. The switch turns the cooling fans on at a lower temperature: on at 176° and off at 166° for use with 160° thermostats, or on at 200° and off at 185° for use with 180° thermostat. They are designed to work in conjunction with Hypertech's Power Chip.

TPI engines using the HEI ignition with integral coil, can gain ignition performance with Hypertech's Power Coil. It delivers up to 53,000 volts to ensure optimum ignition performance. It is a direct bolt-on to enhance your TPI equipped engine's performance.

CHEVY TPI Fuel Injection Swapper's Guide Sources

Accel Engine Management Systems
37732 Hills Tech Drive
Farmington Hills, MI 48024
216/398-8300

Arizona Speed and Marine (ASM)
4834 S. 4th St
Phoenix, AZ 85040
602/437-2510

Bosch (Robert Bosch Company)
2800 South 25th Avenue
Broadview, IL 60153
708/865-5200

Comp Cams
3406 Democrat Rd.
Memphis, TN 38118
901/795-2400

Edelbrock Corporation
2700 California Street
Torrance, CA 90509
310/781-2222

Electromotive Inc.
9131 Centerville Rd.
Manassas, VA 22110
703/378-2444

Fel Pro Corp.
7450 N. McCormick Blvd.
Skokie, IL 60076
708/674-7700

Fuel Injection Specialties
2238 Encino Loop
San Antonio, TX 78259

GM Service Parts Operations
3031 West Grand Blvd.
Detroit, MI 48202

Horiba Instrument
17671 Armstrong Avenue
Irvine, CA 92714
800/446-7422

Howell
6201 Industrial Way
Marine City, MI 48039
810/765-5100

Hypertech
1910 Thomas Road
Memphis, TN 38134
901/382-8888

Lingenfelter Performance
Engineering
1557 Winchester Rd.
Decatur, IN 46733
219/724-2552

Lucas Aftermarket Operations
Lucas Industries Inc.
5600 Crooks Road, P.O. Box 7079
Troy, MI 48007-7079
810/280-8280

MSD (Autotronic Controls Corp.)
1490 Henry Brennan Drive
El Paso, TX 79936
915/857-5200

Nitrous Oxide Systems (NOS)
5930 Lakeshore Drive
Cypress, CA 90630
714/821-0580

SLP Engineering
1501 Industrial Way North
Toms River, NJ 08755
908/349-2109

Street and Performance
Rt 5. #1 Hot Rod Lane
Highway 375 S.
Mena, AR 71953
501/394-5711

TPI Specialties
4255 County Road 10 E.
Chaska, MN 55318
612/448-6021

Vortech Enginereing
5351 Bonsai Ave., Ste 1114
Moorpark, CA 93201
805/529-9330

Z-Industries, Inc. (custom chips)
10832 Lemon Drive,
Yorba Linda, CA 92886
714 779-6680

www.ingramcontent.com/pod-product-compliance
Lightning Source LLC
Chambersburg PA
CBHW081458070526
44586CB00019B/2418